COAL
AND
POLITICS
IN
LATE
IMPERIAL
RUSSIA

Aleksandr I. Fenin, 1866–1945

COAL
AND
POLITICS
IN LATE IMPERIAL
RUSSIA

Memoirs
of a
Russian
Mining Engineer

ALEKSANDR I.
FENIN

Translated by ALEXANDRE FEDIAEVSKY

Edited by SUSAN P. McCAFFRAY

Northern Illinois University Press / DeKalb 1990

© 1990 by Northern Illinois University Press
Published by the Northern Illinois University Press, DeKalb, Illinois 60115
∞ Manufactured in the United States of America using acid-free paper
Design by Julia Fauci

Library of Congress Cataloging-in-Publication Data
Fenin, Aleksandr I.
[Vospominaniia inzhenera. English]
Coal and politics in late Imperial Russia: memoirs of a Russian
mining engineer / Aleksandr I. Fenin; translated by Alexandre Fediaevsky;
edited by Susan P. McCaffray.
p.   cm.
Translation of: Vospominaniia inzhenera.
ISBN 0-87580-153-6
1. Fenin, Aleksandr I.   2. Mining engineers—Soviet Union—Biography.
3. Coal trade—Government policy—Soviet Union—History.
I. McCaffray, Susan Purves.   II. Title.
TN140.f445A3   1990
338.2'724'094709034—dc20   90-6824
CIP

Contents

Translation Notes

As readers of Russian history know, Russians used the old Julian calendar until 1918. Therefore, Russian dates in the nineteenth century were twelve days behind the Western, or Gregorian, calendar; in the twentieth century Russian dates were thirteen days behind. All of the notes, which we have supplied, render dates in the new style, that is, Gregorian, calendar system. Where Fenin himself gave a date in the old style, we have added the notation [O.S.] to make that clear.

Transliterating Russian words and names into the Latin alphabet also presents countless possibilities. Here we have employed the Library of Congress system throughout, inevitably with a few exceptions. The names of monarchs have been rendered in English (i.e., Catherine instead of Ekaterina, etc.). The names of a few other very famous people (Tolstoy, Tchaikovsky) have been spelled according to the now-accepted English usage.

Measurements

We have preserved Fenin's measurements in the text. The Russian measurements he uses and their American equivalents are as follows:

1 verst	=	3500 feet (.66 miles)
1 sazhen'	=	6.98 feet
1 desiatina	=	2.7 acres
1 pud	=	36.11 pounds

The ruble, which contains 100 kopeks, was worth around $.50 in 1914.

SUSAN P. McCAFFRAY

Fenin and His Memoirs
An Introduction

As a mining engineer in turn-of-the-century Russia, Aleksandr Ivanovich Fenin closely observed the growth of industry in what had only been a sleepy, undisturbed part of the country. A firm believer in the value of technology, Fenin assumed a leading role in the influential Kharkov-based Association of Southern Coal and Steel Producers, witnessed the revolutions of 1905 and 1917, and supported the anti-Bolshevik forces in the Civil War before leaving his country in 1920. Eighteen years after his exile began, Fenin published this memoir, which offers an intimate, astute, and often witty portrait of the many problems that accompanied the industrialization of Russia.

Fenin was one of the few men who had experienced the privileged life of the landed Russian gentry and yet yearned for the Western vision of an urbanized society. Born in 1866 to a "medium-wealthy" family of the Bakhmut District of Ekaterinoslav Province, he grew up in a graceful, unhurried world. While he describes the life of the gentry with some sympathy, his memoir is largely a polite denunciation of his father's world, containing the thinly veiled criticism of one who took up, as he often puts it, "creative economic work."[1]

The steppe country where Fenin's family held land was on the brink of profound transformation in the years of Fenin's youth. Both peasant and noble landowners had mined the coal reserves on their land for some time. But it was state policy that brought big-time industry to the Donets Basin. The trickle of new industry during the 1880s became a flood during the 1890s. After 1855, when Russia lost the Crimean War to industrially advanced foreign powers, the tsars and their finance ministers grew more interested in furthering Russian heavy manufacturing and railroad construction. Such concerns supported Alexander II's decision to emancipate the serfs in 1861 and led to the considerable encouragements foreign investors received from the government in the 1890s through Finance Minister Sergei Witte. Witte strove to attract foreign capital by granting direct subsidies and concessions as well as by erecting protective tariffs for coal and iron producers. He also created a reassuring atmosphere for foreign businessmen by promoting railroad construction, balancing the state budget, and forcing Russia onto the gold standard in 1897. These were the high political decisions that fostered the coal and steel industry of the Donbass, in which Fenin was to spend his professional career. His father, Ivan, must have had some premonition of the future when he sent his son first to the Kharkov Technical High School and then, in 1883, to the St. Petersburg Mining Institute.

Fenin opens his memoir with an account of the time he spent in the great capital city of St. Petersburg. His college years took place in a setting where one might hear Tchaikovsky conduct a performance of his own works, illustrating the exuberant cultural life of the young, educated Russian. In this first chapter, probably the most "Russian" part of his memoir, Fenin passes judgment on the literary and musical greats of Russia's "golden age." It is characteristic of the educated classes of late Imperial Russia that this engineer felt compelled to express an opinion on Turgenev's liberalism, on Chekhov's perceptions of provincial life, and on the efforts of Russia's great composers to create a national musical idiom. His fellow countrymen, then and now, would know much about Fenin, as he intended them to, through the articulation of his cultural tastes.

Here and in the Appendix, which describes the economic development of Russia in the eighties and early nineties, Fenin offers a strongly felt reassessment of the reign of Alexander III (1881–1894), a period commonly viewed by many contemporaries and most historians as one of political reaction and stagnation after the great excitement of the 1860s and 1870s. Fenin strives to convince the reader that Alexander III's reign has been unjustly maligned. We hear the voice of one who wants others to love the years he loved, the years of his youth. But we also hear a rare defense of the slow and careful approach to change that has seldom carried much weight in Russia.

Fenin politely, but passionately, defends the "men of the eighties" as being a conservative, practical, and useful generation that grew up quietly. Fenin distinguishes himself and his friends from what he considers the dilettante intellectuals who wasted their gifts on idle chatter. This is an attitude that pervades the entire memoir from Fenin's account of his student days to his description of his engineering career. His beloved country needed the efforts of hard-working, skilled intellectuals, not of bomb-throwers or politicians. Here Fenin is an example of a new breed, not unique to Russia at the time, of energetic, educated young men who offered themselves as builders of a new world in which man would use technology to conquer nature. Emanating from this technical power they foresaw a social transformation that would banish ignorance, sloth, and poverty from their lands forever. The engineers had faith that the era of true enlightenment was at hand and that its engines were steam and electricity.

The most valuable insights Fenin offers shed light on the process and local politics of industrialization in Russia. For example, he offers a manager's perspective on the workers and their working and living conditions. In the process, Fenin demonstrates the uniqueness of the Donbass workers' predicament. Freed serfs took mining and factory jobs by the hundreds of thousands in the decades following the 1861 Emancipation, driven by land hunger and by the increasing need for cash to make land redemption and tax payments. Single men and husbands who left their families in the villages migrated to the growing industrial centers of St. Petersburg, Moscow, and later the Donets Basin. In these settings, living and working conditions were poor and often brutal, but wages surpassed what most peasants could generate by the marketing of their agricultural surplus. For an increasing number of people after 1861, the insecurities of life in the industrial centers appeared less unappealing than the known adversities of life in the hungry village. Seasonal workers stayed from October until Easter and then returned to their homes to farm. Over time, more and more men gave up their ties to the land altogether, sending for their families and working in the factory year-round.

In the big cities of St. Petersburg, and Moscow, wives, single women, and children could contribute to the family's income by signing on in factories, especially in textile mills. They were paid less than the men, but the expenses of city life required that they take whatever work they could get. However, in the South, where there were few cities and few enterprises apart from mining and steel production, there was much less work for women and children. They took jobs sorting coal at the mouths of the pits, and young boys undertook the deadly yet poorly

paid chore of guiding horse-drawn rail cars underground. A consequence of the relative shortage of work for women and children was
that the pressure on family budgets in the southern coal and steel region
was proportionally greater than that elsewhere in Russia. Moreover, the
South lacked not only social amenities but even such basics as housing,
water, and sewage service, not to mention hospitals and schools.[2] These
problems eventually led southern industrialists to view the question of
workers' welfare differently than did their northern counterparts.

Fenin's memoir demonstrates that these welfare questions generated
considerable tension between engineers like himself, who were the
champions of the new industry, and the region's more established elite,
the gentry. The arena in which this friction manifested itself was the
local zemstvo, and the central issue was that of taxation and responsibility for the welfare of industrial workers.[3] Tsar Alexander II had created
these local governing bodies in 1864, decreeing that they would be
elected by universal male suffrage, albeit one weighted in favor of landowners. He empowered zemstvos to tax property, both agricultural and
industrial, and to provide carefully specified services with the revenues
thus raised. By the turn of the century many zemstvos had become
hotbeds of liberal efforts to improve the educational ,health, and sanitary
conditions of peasants. However, in the southern industrial region
zemstvos resisted extending their services to workers in coal and steel
companies, arguing that firms must provide for workers while zemstvos
provided for peasants. As the bill for providing basic housing and health
benefits to workers steadily expanded during the boom years, southern
managers grew more and more vocal about what they saw as a fundamental injustice: they paid the bulk of the local taxes but received few
services. Recent Western scholarship has focused on the zemstvo and
the agrarian liberals or radicals who tried to use it as a platform for
fundamental change.[4] Fenin provides a grass-roots view of several
zemstvos, thumbnail sketches of zemstvo activists, and generally mixed
reviews on the zemstvos' achievements, suggesting that zemstvo reformers were loathe to extend their programs to industrial workers or to
cooperate with industrialists. This view offers some evidence of the
chronic weakness of Russian liberalism, illustrating that agricultural and
industrial liberals mistrusted, and apparently often despised, each other.

This confrontation was but one of many fronts in the war between
the proponets of either an industrial or an agricultural Russia. Fenin's
book must be understood in this context, too. He describes himself and
his fellows as men who wanted to modernize their country, to replace
the old-fashioned gentry with trained and hard-working industrialists,
and in the process, to create a society in which the common folk could

make a good living and have a better life than had been available in the dark, pastoral Russia of old. This battle was decades old by the time he began his engineering career. Throughout the nineteenth century, educated Russians had contemplated their country's destiny. Virtually all of Russia's greatest nineteenth-century writers, from Pushkin to Dostoevsky, took up social themes and contemplation of their country's problems both in their art and in their correspondence. Most of them suffered for expressing their views. In endless discussions (all the more exhilarating because they were frequently illegal), in literary circles founded by university students, between the lines in journals of literary criticism, in back rooms and tea rooms, in the parlors of country houses, in the sophisticated salons of St. Petersburg, in places of exile at home or abroad, in government offices, in the pages of the greatest novels, Russians *talked*. It is perhaps beyond us to grasp the power of this tempest of talking, or this traffic in ideas about the future. Of course there was censorship of the written and spoken word, but the liberty whose lack was most keenly felt in these decades, a liberty we underappreciate, was the right to assemble. Then, as now, Russians dearly loved assembling, and they assembled to talk.

The boundaries in this long debate about Russia's future shifted frequently, the center-line migrated over time and the nuances imparted to the central question multiplied. At the heart of this long national soul-searching, the same issue remained, however: shall we follow the example of Western Europe? In the nineteenth century, the question of imitating Western Europe involved the question of embracing industry, and the focal point in this debate was Britain. Through her pioneering position in the production of textiles, particularly cotton textiles, by machines, Britain had conquered the world economically. In the space of a few decades at the beginning of the nineteenth century, people on every continent were drawn into a universe held together by British gravity, a force primarily composed of the power of "sail and sale." Contemporaries outside Britain noticed this new configuration even as it was forming, particularly those who were taking up positions in the cold and dark regions of this system, far from the glowing center. Entrepreneurs and strategists from Boston to St. Petersburg coveted the technological secrets that the British Parliament safeguarded by force of law.

Russian observers were among those who perceived that if they could not learn to produce textiles by machine themselves, they would be condemned forever to buy them from British manufacturers. To pay for these manufactured imports, Russians would have to continue in the old-fashioned business of raw material production and export. Many thought that the world was on the brink of being divided into manufacturing countries and agricultural countries and that those nations which sought wealth and great power status must stand with the former. As he argued on behalf of the protective tariff in 1815, Russian bureaucrat Nicholas Mordvinov wrote that, "Agricultural countries stagnate in poverty, lack necessities and most importantly cannot be free peoples because they depend on others for their needs—and they cannot have that political freedom necessary for all who wish to be powerful and independent on their own land. They are deprived of that measure of respect from other countries which is the right of every independent people." For Russia the significance of the British Industrial Revolution was that it spawned a century-long debate about the relative merits of agriculture and industry, a debate that was central to the search for a national identity and that was resolved once and for all only with the unleashing of Stalin's First Five-Year Plan in 1928. Fenin's memoir contributes to our understanding of this central issue in Russian history.

Russians like Mordvinov also understood early on that following England's lead in machine-based manufacturing had implications that reached far beyond economics. The growth of manufacturing would mean larger, more populous cities, inhabited by new classes heretofore only barely present in Russian society: the working and the middle classes. To some, usually labeled "Westernizers," such changes appeared as unmitigated progress. Russia, they thought, could only grow stronger, wealthier and more just by developing according to the Western model. Her people would learn useful and practical skills, abandoning the sloth of the gentry and the inefficiency of the wary and conservative peasantry. They could enter the bright era of enlightenment as industrious, intelligent, and ambitious citizen-subjects. Others, the "Slavophiles," were far less sanguine about westernization. They thought the growth of cities portended a decline in the values and traditions rooted in the soil—deference, religion, obedience—not to mention the twin pillars on which tsarist society had rested for two centuries—serfdom and autocracy. As pastoral mores subsided, the defenders of tradition argued, so too would the influence of those groups long understood to be the backbone of the old regime, the peasants and the nobles. For them, the West represented decadence, empty materialism, shallowness, and poverty of the spirit. Far from beckoning them, the bourgeois culture of the West repelled these Russians, who advocated instead a return to Slavic fundamentals: orthodoxy, the soil, the peasant commune, the ancient assemblage of the estates that had advised the Tsar. The Slavophile read Dickens as a warning from the belly of the beast.

Fenin conveys the loneliness of those who embraced both the Western vision of industrial and urban society and such "middle-class" ideals as hard work, education, and thrift. He asserts that the number of such people in late Imperial Russia was extremely small and that those who did embrace such values felt like outsiders whose considerable efforts were unacknowledged and unappreciated by their compatriots.

Where were those Russians who might have formed a solid middle class? The Russian gentry, even the poorest members of that privileged estate, was ensconced at the pinnacle of the social hierarchy and protected from its chronic cash shortage by the state-funded gentry land bank and by the terms of the emancipation settlement. Gentry families traditionally divided heritable property among all the sons, so that while they became progressively poorer as the generations passed, they rarely became completely landless and dependent upon urban occupations, although there were those who joined the ranks of the bureaucracy in pursuit of a living wage. What could these people gain by committing their funds to risky ventures? They were inherently conservative, and far from investing in new industries, they often resisted the expansion of industry in general. Even the vocal liberal minority among the gentry believed that Russia's salvation lay not in industry and urban life, but in the creation of a more just rural society. Serfdom kept the great bulk of the peasants from amassing even modest savings with which to embark upon speculative gambits; although, there were a few notable cases where the masters let enterprising serfs launch businesses that benefited both master and peasant, as happened in the textile industry of Ivanovo.

The state did its part to limit the growth of the entrepreneurial class, as well. Intricate, restrictive laws strangled commercial initiative among even the modest number of Russians and Russified foreigners who fell into the "urban" estate.[5] The government compelled merchants, for example, to purchase certificates placing themselves in one of three merchant "guilds," each requiring a set amount of capital to join and enjoying carefully specified trading or manufacturing rights. It was difficult under this system for families to establish businesses that might survive for several generations, because one unprofitable year frequently meant the inability to purchase the guild certificate that allowed the firm to stay in business. The Imperial government proved to be at best a vacillating ally to industrialists and merchants. In earlier times, the Tsar acted as the empire's "first merchant," establishing those industries he deemed militarily or financially necessary for the state, even to the point of appropriating prospering private concerns that caught his eye. The state used monopolistic charters and concessions to reward loyal service and otherwise regulated entry into commerce or manufacturing rather closely. In the first half of the nineteenth century the heads of state wavered between the arguments of pro-tariff industrialists and finance ministers and anti-tariff grain exporters, mainly noblemen, who yearned to maintain free trade with their primary customer, Great Britain.

There was something else too. Russians tended not to be greatly impressed by commercial wealth; they might envy the one who had gotten rich in some business, but they also were likely to be suspicious of the entrepreneur. What compromises had this person made to amass his fortune? Whence came the shallowness of character or the poverty of spirit that induced a man to devote his life to material gain? Indeed, the Russians called well-to-do peasants "kulaks," a word that means "fist." This cultural bias against commercial occupations meant that successful entrepreneurs never quite felt secure socially. In this climate it frequently happened that those who achieved financial success aspired not to pass along successful businesses to their sons but instead to secure places for their sons in elite schools or regiments that served as avenues to ennoblement—and consequently to an end to the family's business activities. In other words, although there was a small group of successful Moscow merchant families, many of the most enterprising businessmen in Russia dreamed of getting their families *out* of business and into the nobility. Fenin ably portrays the deep Russian prejudice against businessmen he sensed from all quarters: zemstvo reformers, conservatives, many ministerial officials, landowners, writers, the press, and the general public.

Southern managers did forge an imposing platform from which to defend their industry and to petition St. Petersburg for aid and support, however. They joined the Association of Southern Coal and Steel Producers, a group originally formed in 1874 by small coal proprietors to lobby for railroads and protective tariffs. Successful on both counts, the Southern Association grew with the Donbass, but its character changed by the late 1880s. Engineers like Fenin, who worked for large foreign concerns, increasingly displaced local proprietors at the organization's helm. Under their leadership, the Southern Association became a widely known industrialists' organization, which met annually in Kharkov and published voluminously. This group registered some noteworthy successes, securing from the Imperial government tariffs against the importation of coal and iron into Black Sea ports, improvements in port facilities, railroad rate reforms, pressure on zemstvos to equalize agricultural and industrial property taxes, and permission to organize the coal and steel products markets via the cartels Produgol and Prodameta. Fenin served the Southern Association as the vice-president of its governing council from 1907 until 1919. This work took him to Kharkov and introduced him to the larger issues of national and regional industrial policy.

Aleksandr Fenin and his colleagues among the leadership of the Association of Southern Coal and Steel Producers stood apart from Russia's other merchant and industrial communities in several important ways. Unlike the oldest commercial community, based in Moscow, the Southern managers as a group were greater admirers of things European: they prided themselves on presiding over a thoroughly up-to-date industry, and they admired much about their foreign directors. The Southerners adopted contractual labor relations, faith in science and technology, conviction that Russia needed a strong coal and steel industry to remain among the first rank of nations, and, in time a sense of themselves as citizens who required a forum in which to speak their minds. The Moscow merchants generally had adopted a more conservative, Slavophilic tone, as if to assert that the sacred Russia of Tsar and serf need not change substantially to accommodate the interests of this loyal and respectful commercial establishment. Southern industrialists distanced themselves from their St. Petersburg counterparts, on the other hand, by manifesting a greater preoccupation with workers' welfare concerns than did Northern managers, who were among the most energetic exploiters of worker' time in all of Europe. Donbass managers early on discovered that workers' welfare was not a peripheral but, indeed, a central issue for their industry because labor was in short supply and amenities were few. Fenin's vision of the proper relationship between workers and bosses might be termed *enlightened paternalism*. In language at times condescending and at times deeply respectful, Fenin tries to define a management approach to workers that is less cold-blooded than the one he observed on a trip to Belgium and less benighted than the Old Russian relationship between master and serf.

The native managers of the southern region differed from their compatriots in one other fundamental way: they almost all spent part or most of their careers in the service of non-Russian firms. Originally these foreign concerns seemed a godsend to young engineers entering a tight job market. Gradually, however, as Fenin's generation of native managers was buffeted by the winds of recession and revolution, it dawned on members of the Southern Association that the interests of French or Belgian investors did not correspond exactly with those of Russian citizens eager to see their country progress socially and politically. When many Southern managers came to feel that only as enfranchised citizens could they defend the vital interests of industry in Russia, foreign speculators continued to be content with the status of subject, relying on the old system of ministerial patronage and petitioning the

Tsarist government for assistance as difficulties arose. And as the thorny welfare issue grew in significance after 1905, some engineer-managers wondered how great an investment foreigners would be willing to make in upgrading Russia's "cultural level" and procuring a lasting social peace. As Russia moved toward war and revolution, Southerners like Fenin increasingly felt themselves to be men in the middle, striving to satisfy the perhaps irreconcilable demands of Russian workers and European investors.

Fenin concludes his memoir with an account of the attitudes and events leading up to the Revolution of 1905. The perspective he offers is rarely found in the memoir literature available in English but represents an important segment of contemporary Russian opinion. He chronicles his gradual but irreversible loss of faith in the increasingly inept government of Nicholas II (1894–1917) but refrains from embracing the liberals or socialists who sought to change Russia's government quickly. Fenin takes us to provincial zemstvo meetings at which a constitutional government is demanded, to the exhilarating atmosphere of St. Petersburg salons and restaurants in 1904 and 1905, and to the Donbass during the 1905 Revolution. We see how managers tried to get the payroll in from Kharkov while the railroad workers were on strike in 1905, how they treated one of their fellows who conceded the eight-hour day, how they reacted when the October manifesto created a "Duma," or parliament, for the first time in Russian history. In his description of his rather peculiar motives for joining the Constitutional Democratic ("Kadet") Party, of his selection as an "elector" for the First Duma, and his eye-witness account of the ill-fated Vyborg Assembly after that Duma had been shut down, Fenin articulates the discomfort of one who might be described as a "conservative-liberal." Fenin thought that his government and his country had serious flaws in 1905, but he was not confident that the momentous events he was witnessing would bring the kind of change his country needed. He believed in hard work, a characteristic he felt to be in too short supply in Russia; so he worked. And in this book Fenin pays tribute to those "men of the eighties" whose service to their country, he believes, went unacknowledged and whose fates were often tragic.

Fenin planned a two-part memoir, but the second part was never published. Unfortunately, therefore, this volume ends with 1906. The revolutionary year 1917 found Fenin still in Kharkov working for the Southern Association. The managers tried to find ways to work under the new conditions imposed by the Bolshevik Revolution, but after being incarcerated briefly with other leaders of the Southern Association in 1918, Fenin, like most of his colleagues, threw his support to the anti-Bolshevik Volunteer Army of South Russia in the Civil War. Fenin served as an industrial and trade advisor to the Volunteer Army until his evacuation from Russia in 1920. With his wife and five children Fenin went to Egypt where he continued to work as an engineer. In 1930–1931 he produced his final prospecting report, detailing manganese deposits in the Sinai Desert. From Egypt he took his family to Prague where they settled among the sizeable Russian emigré community there. Throughout his exile years Fenin wrote, including articles for emigré papers and a long piece on the Soviet industrialization efforts. As his memoir attests, he maintained contact with many of his old friends and witnessed from afar the death of several of them at the hands of the Bolsheviks. This memoir was published by the Russian Institute of Prague in 1938 under the title *Vospominaniia inzhenera: K istorii obshchestvennago i khoziaistvennago razvitiia Rossii (1883–1906gg.)* [Memoirs of an engineer: Toward a history of the social and economic development of Russia, 1883–1906]. Aleksandr Fenin died in Prague in 1945, having caught pneumonia, as the story goes, from going out without warm-enough clothes to fetch flowers for his wife on their anniversary. He was thus spared the fate of some of his then quite elderly friends, who were forcibly repatriated after the Soviets occupied Czechoslovakia at the end of World War II. This was also the fate of the Russian Historical Archive in Prague, which was taken to Moscow. What has become of this archive, which may well have included a draft of Part Two of these memoirs, is not known.[6]

Acknowledgments

The story of how Fenin's memoir came to be published in English attests to how small the world of Russian emigrés is. While discussing my reading of Fenin's memoir in the Helsinki University Slavic Library with Duke University Economics Professor Vladimir Treml, Professor Treml asked suddenly, "Aleksandr Fenin?" I nodded, and he proceeded to tell me that when he and his mother had escaped from a German convoy taking them from their native Kharkov to the West in 1943, they and been cared for at the Fenins' home in Prague. Professor Treml offered the further tantalizing information that his mother still corresponded with Fenin's daughter. I was thus able to begin my own interesting correspondence with Marie Aleksandrovna Fediaevsky (née Fenin) who was living in Paris. She was happy to think of having her father's memoir translated when I suggested the project to her. In 1986 Madame Fediaevsky put me in touch with her son Alexandre, also an engineer, who agreed to translate his grandfather's memoirs from Russian to English.

The debts I have incurred in the lengthy process of editing and annotating this memoir are numerous. I am grateful to the worthy historians who have taught me Russian history over the years: Daniel F. Calhoun, Warren Lerner, David MacKenzie, Samuel Baron, and Sheila Fitzpatrick. To Vladimir Treml I owe thanks not only for putting me in touch with Fenin's family but also for lessons in Russian economic history. Professor Treml also provided much helpful advice in the early stages of this project. My deep thanks go also to Thomas C. Owen, who read this manuscript carefully and expertly, who generously gave so much time and good advice, and whose pioneering work in producing a data-base of Imperial Russian corporations has helped me enormously, as it no doubt will many others.

If my husband, Beau, had not provided every possible type of support, this project never could have been completed. My own work in bringing Fenin's book to American readers is lovingly and respectfully dedicated to my father, John Purves, who believes, as Fenin did, that talent and hard work are what his country needs most.

COAL
AND
POLITICS
IN
LATE
IMPERIAL
RUSSIA

These memoirs of Old Great Russia

are dedicated to the dear companions of my life:

my wife,

my children,

and my grandchildren

русскій институтъ въ прагѣ

А.И. фенинЪ

ВОСПОМИНаНІЯ
инженера

Къ исторіи общественнаго
и хозяйственнаго развитія
Россіи
(1883~1906 г.г.)

19~прага~38

Title page of the original edition of
Fenin's autobiography, *Memoirs of an
Engineer: Toward a History of the Social
and Economic Development of Russia
(1883–1906)*, published by the Russian
Institute of Prague in 1938.

Preface

In exile the worst torment is to remember the happy years.
—*Dante*

I n this brief preface I would like to take the liberty of saying a few words about the content and character of this memoir. My subject is the construction of heavy industry in Russia, my recollections about the creators of and participants in this effort, the circumstances that formed the industrial leaders, and the conditions in which heavy industry developed. The scene of the action is southern Russia, the so-called Donets Basin. I myself am not only a witness, but also a participant, since for the considerable period of thirty years I worked in the Basin.

It is well known that the Donets Basin covers an enormous territory of coal deposits, which includes parts of the Kharkov and Ekaterinoslav Provinces, as well as part of the Don Military Region. Russia's biggest coal and cast iron producers were concentrated in the Donets Basin.[1] Kharkov was the economic center of the Donbass, as most of the private and government administrative offices that directed southern industry were concentrated there.

My work deals not only with personal reminiscences about the lives of people who worked with me, such as the engineers, managers of enterprises, and miners, but also with my recollections of the characteristics and peculiarities of the social and economic life of these rich Russian provinces in the period from 1890 to 1914. This was a period of exceptional importance both economically and politically. It embraces the industrialization of the Donets Basin during Witte's administration in the late nineties period, as well as the Revolution of 1905–1906 and the subsequent political and economic reforms.[2] It also encompasses the remarkable prewar period of 1908–1914, when as a consequence of the preceding events the Russian national economy started an unprecedented development in all fields.

As my memoirs reflect my industrial and public activity, I feel obliged to familiarize the reader briefly with the main stages of my career and personal life. A son of the Bakhmut District of the Ekaterinoslav Province, where my father owned some land, that is, a native of the Donets Basin, I finished my education at the technical high school in 1883 and graduated from the Petersburg Mining Institute in 1889.[3] In 1890 I joined the French Coal Mining Company as the assistant to Engineer E. A. Shteding for Shaft No. 19 near Iuzovka. Later, until 1895, I was the manager of the Voznesenskii Mine of P. A. Karpov and, for about three years, the manager of the "Sergei" shaft of the Ilovaiskii brothers' Makeevka Mine. From 1895 to 1899 I was first in charge of prospecting and then of building and operating the Verovka Mine of the Russian-Belgian Company. From 1899 to 1911 I was the executive director [*direktor-rasporiaditel'*] (the "responsible agent") of the former Maksimov Mine, after it was purchased by the English-owned Russian Coal Mining Company.

My public activity began in 1907 at the Association of Southern Coal and Steel Producers, an organization that united all the aspects of the mining industry in the South, including steel and iron production.[4] In that year I was elected vice-president of the association's council, its executive organ. The president who was elected at the same time was my friend Nikolai Feodorovich von Ditmar, a mining engineer who graduated from the Institute the same year as I. We were reelected every year until 1919—the year of N. F. von Ditmar's death and my evacuation from Russia (January 1920). Around 1907 or 1908 Nikolai Feodorovich was elected a member of the State Council on behalf of industry, a position he occupied until his death.[5] In 1907 I moved from the Donets Basin to Kharkov, where I took up permanent residence, paying visits to the mine now and then. I had to replace N. F. von Ditmar for long periods, as he lived in Petersburg for several years and was otherwise obliged to spend much time away form Kharkov. My purely industrial pursuits likewise expanded after 1907. I was not only the executive director of the mine of the Russian Coal Mining Company, but I also became a member of the boards of several other coal mining companies.

If I take the liberty of introducing autobiographical material, I only

do so to show that I know my subject quite well, as my whole professional career was spent working in the industry of the Donbass.[6]

My memoir also contains material about the personal lives of many
of the leaders of the Donbass, often my colleagues and close friends. I
feel obliged to place these often intimate memories near the close of
my text. I do this to enable the reader who is unfamiliar with my subject
to get acquainted with the character of the mining business and also to
understand how the industrial leaders were prepared for their careers
in the Russia of those days.

Among those who are now dead I also mention victims of the Bolshevik terror. It is well known that the absurdities of "socialist" construction along with the inhuman cruelty of the Soviet regime made of the
engineers and industrial leaders of the Old Regime its first blood-stained
victims. Concerning the nature of my recollections of people who were
close to me, I do not want them to be taken as paeans. It should be
borne in mind that I speak here only about one aspect of their lives,
mainly their industrial activities, which naturally narrows the scope of
my memoirs. Besides, I involuntarily lingered over people who showed
exceptional energy, who were able to reach relatively high positions.
Nor would I deny that the period in which these people were educated
and the favorable environment in which they evolved gave rise to a
type of industrial leader very different from that of the preceding generation of the seventies. Their industrial careers in many ways showed
more concern with public industrial matters than with the financial side
of the industry. The foundation of future social development was already
discernable in their eagerness to build up industry "as a whole." In
this quality they illustrated the basic characteristics of the Russian intelligentsia, reinforcing them with their own practical realism, which our
intelligentsia often sorely lacked. In my memoirs I endeavor to give
some evidence of these assertions.

Here in my introduction I must underscore an important characteristic
of both the epoch and its leaders; the exceptional rapidity with which
industry expanded in the Donbass at the turn of the century. This was
an extremely challenging situation for the Russian technical intelligentsia, composed almost entirely of young cadres, as it called for large
numbers of well-qualified people.

Industrialization expanded at such a tempo that coal production in
the Donbass climbed from 300 million puds in 1895 to 700 million puds
in 1900, and reached 1.5 billion puds by 1913. The production of cast
iron over the same years was, respectively, 33 million puds, 91 million
puds, and 189 million puds. The best way to appreciate the speed of
this expansion is to compare the relative growth of coal production in

Germany, Great Britain and, the Donbass in the same period. The growth ratios are 2, 1.5, and 5, respectively. For the same period, cast iron production shows smaller, but comparable, figures.

About 60 percent of the coal and 90 percent of the cast iron were produced in plants owned by foreign companies, but by the very beginning of the twentieth century, the overwhelming majority of the managers in the Donbass were Russian engineers. One had to admit that the Russian technical intelligentsia rose to this difficult challenge brilliantly. As an illustration I have only to mention that when I arrived in the Basin in 1890 there were altogether about ten Russian engineers, but by 1913–1914 several hundred of us were working there.[7]

In addition, the activity of industrial organizations, primarily of the Association of Southern Coal and Steel Producers, which in the boom years of Russian economic expansion included mainly engineers, took on very original forms, rather exceptional for Russia, as I shall explain in the second part of my memoirs. We can only conclude that this period of Russian industrial growth, and particularly of the development of the southern mining industry, deserves attention.

The Russian intelligentsia, represented by her technical cadres, reacted quickly and decisively with an unprecedented display of economic activity to conditions that favored these great industrial achievements. The foreign competition was successfully challenged. This was comparable to the way Russia reacted to the new conditions of land ownership and the new social environment of the Russian peasant in the so-called prewar period of 1908–1914.[8]

Before concluding my introduction I have to mention one of the primary motives that compelled me to take up writing in the twilight of my life. I am neither a political activist, nor a government official, nor a writer, nor a journalist, nor an abstract thinker. I am not even a public figure in the sense that Russians understand this term—my thinking, my feelings, and my whole life have been rooted in practical activity, in the material realm of the Russian economy. Serving the industry to which my close friends and I devoted our lives broadened our insight, through the very nature of our activity, and freed us from any provincial narrowmindedness, despite the fact that most of our activity took place in the provinces. The very nature of our work—creative activity in economic development—brought us into close contact with the interests of the state in general and trained our thinking and our conceptions of society. We realized that respect for law and order were indispensable and that the evolution of the political and social life of the Russian people should be gradual. We were natural enemies of the Revolution, and politically speaking we were people of the center. To Russia's great

misfortune, because of many historical factors, that center lacked sufficient time to develop, much less to become well organized. The cruel
events of recent years, which ruined the Russian state and destroyed
as well the cause we had served, also threw most of us into exile; into
the hopelessness and often the poverty of an emigrant's life. My political
understanding and feelings about the evolution of the Russian state,
which in the prerevolutionary years were based on seeing mainly its
balanced and quiet side, began changing during our general collapse.
As I think was the case also for many of my colleagues, I began to
reexamine old ideas, to reevaluate them and probe them more deeply.
Many things now appeared in a different light. I started to understand
better those grave mistakes that I had witnessed as a contemporary,
which had been committed by the forces that governed the Russian
state. Most of all, in my forced inactivity and advancing years I became
better able to appreciate the kind of people who had surrounded me
and to assess their role in the development of those great historical
events I had witnessed.

To give the reader a better understanding of the environment in which
our activities took place, I thought that it was indispensable to include
in my memoirs a brief account of Russia's economy in those years. This
is the Appendix I place at the end of the first part of my memoirs, so
as not to interrupt the narrative. It might be best to have a look at this
Appendix just after reading the first chapter, in order to have a clearer
idea of the period I am describing.

In conclusion, let me fulfill a pleasant obligation by expressing my
deep gratitude to the colleague and friend who helped me so much in
the writing and editing of this work. I must also express equal gratitude
to the Russian Institute of Prague for their material help and for kindly
agreeing to publish this book under their distinguished banner.

CHAPTER ONE

Student Days

Gymnasium Pupils and Students in the Early 1880s:
The Public Atmosphere and the Influence of Literature

Who, in fact, were the educated youth of Russia at the turn of the century?[1] For it was those young people who had to undertake something altogether new, with a background that consisted of entirely theoretical knowledge. Who were those people who would come to settle in some southern steppe village that had been unceremoniously deserted by its noble landowner? Their new activity, to be sure, was invigorating, but it would contrast sharply with the former coziness and beauty of village life in this "fantastic land of the Donets steppe," with its ravines, its Saurmogila, and its legends about the likes of Zuevka, Khartsyzsk, and Ilovaiskii.[2] What practical experience did the twenty-five- and thirty-year-old educated Russians bring with them in those years?

They had completed the gymnasium course in the late seventies to the mid- or late eighties, and most of them had graduated from the Petersburg Mining Institute in the nineties. Secondary schools, although accessible to everybody, still preserved a lot of traditions and even to some degree the composition of the old gentry schools of the mid-nineteenth century. The "seminary" practices of the mid-century had almost disappeared, and the teachers in both the gymnasia and the technical high schools were quite good.

Most of my fellow students, almost all of them, came from provincial, mainly southern, technical high schools. The programs of these schools were much criticized, and were considered the unfortunate result of the Tolstoi reforms.[3] It was quite true that these schools were not a proper preparation for technicians and engineers' assistants, as they were apparently meant to be. But the technical high schools did provide an excellent and broad preparation for the higher courses in the natural sciences. We had a good knowledge, for our age, of chemistry, physics, and even of such techniques as sugar refining and beer brewing. The general curriculum, which was quite extensive and even included modern foreign languages, was arranged in six basic classes, which were meant to conclude one's general education. A seventh complementary class was intended as an introduction to analytical chemistry, to the principal processes used in industrial production, to intensive physics, and so forth. We finished these six classes by the age of sixteen and the whole school at seventeen, when we were still mere children. I remember some of our teachers who tried to give us courses in a "university lecture" style at the Kharkov Technical High School, when we were in the seventh class. Kindly I. P. Osipov, who later became a professor at Kharkov University, was bitterly disappointed when during one of his lectures on chemistry we all jumped to our feet and rushed to the windows because a military band was passing on the street.

What were our interests apart from our studies, what was our "spiritual outlook" during these secondary school years? I am not exaggerating when I say that both at home and at school there was almost no guidance in this field, that there was no sensible systematic education, and that we grew up untamed. The writers we read the most were Turgenev and Spielhagen. We were delighted when our Russian teacher, N. E. Shevchenko, read us texts from Gogol, in his own admirable way, but we had almost no idea of who were Dostoevsky or Tolstoy.[4] Pushkin was controversial, because of the scathing way in which Pisarev had debunked him. Even now I feel a hint of irritation when I read some of the verses of *Onegin*, as for example:

> Disputes arose between them every time
> And meditations from such subjects spread
> Like plights between some bygone tribes,[5]

or else the rude and jestful way Pisarev interprets Tatiana's letter, which sounds something like, "If you do not come to visit us at least once a week, you cruel tyrant, what was the use of coming at all? If it had not been for you, I would have become a wife and a good mother, but thanks to you I am lost." I still feel it that way, even though I later came to view Pushkin almost worshipfully.[6] Generally speaking, although "men from various ranks" [*raznochintsy*] began to participate in culture from the sixties on, Russian culture was still the culture of the gentry. *Raznochintsy* and persons of non-Russian ethnic origins were equally susceptible to the influence of this "gentry culture." The Pole Krzywicki, the Jew Rabinovich, and the Russian Rutchenko (all schoolmates and professional colleagues of mine about whom I shall say more later) were educated at the same secondary school as I and in exactly the same spirit.

All my heroes developed under the influence of the moving beauty and unforgettable charm of Turgenev's poetry, of the endless Russian horizon, of overwhelming abundance, of the nests of gentlefolk, and of the Russian village. When we arrived in the capital in the eighties, we were young Bazarovs and Rudins, bringing along to mysterious Petersburg from our remote Elizavetgrad, Simferopol, or Kharkov deeply suntanned faces and naive, poetic eighteen-year-old souls.[7] Were we troubled in the least by politics? One may answer with certainty that at that time the average eighteen- or nineteen-year-old provincial youth was not touched by politics. In his mind there was nothing that evoked political tendencies or even that suggested a taste for such things. Frankly speaking, like all young men, we experienced a certain amount of inner turmoil, which was perhaps even more characteristic of Russian youth. We were attracted by noisy, collective actions, probably as a result of the deficiencies in our education. We had some notion of Herzen's call to "go to the people," and we greeted Leo and Tuski, the heroes of Spielhagen's novel, enthusiastically.[8]

Had we been confronted with a different atmosphere than the one we found in the wake of the frightful year 1881, we might have become, to our own doom, "political activists" in student movements such as those which existed in the sixties or seventies, and many of us would have wound up in Siberian exile or in jail.[9] Indeed, I can remember that when I was a schoolboy in the second or third grade, the older students went "to the people" and were arrested. I can see these long-haired students, wearing plaids and carrying heavy sticks—such was the uniform of our populists.[10]

In fact, we were among the first to arrive from our province after the nightmarish final years of Alexander II's reign. Those had been years of social disintegration, almost of collective insanity, in which through some almost pathological obsession a man against whom, one would think, no Russian would raise a hand, was hunted down, persecuted, and, after many attempts, brutally slaughtered by terrorists.

I am not exaggerating about this atmosphere. In his memoirs, De Vogüé (Viscount Melchior), who was secretary to the French ambassador from 1877 on, comments upon the unfavorable decisions taken against

Russia at the Congress of Berlin (following the 1877–1878 war).[11] He notes in his memoir: "The general air of discontent, and near-contempt for the Emperor was striking."[12] It is well known that public opinion assigned all the blame for our failure at the Berlin Congress to Alexander II. De Vogué uses sinister language to describe his impressions when he writes about the twenty-fifth anniversary of the reign (19 February 1880). "[Alexander II's] great day, if such an expression is adequate, was a day of depression and melancholy. In the streets there was the stinking mud of the thaw, everything was grey and dirty, as was the finale of this remarkable twenty-five year reign, which was supposedly being celebrated." He adds a bit later, "Alexander II looked like a ghost. I had never seen him so miserable; he looked aged, strained, and he choked with asthma at every word." After 1 March, De Vogué notes the following impressions: I keep thinking about this poor man, good and weak, who was the sponsor of my wedding three years ago, and who perished tragically, in the blood and shame of a crime. To liberate 50 million people by a single command, and to be killed in his own capital like a hunted beast! What is really undermining us is hatred, which is fermenting right below our feet," wrote De Vogué. "It is a frightful, ill-created world." And there is the eerie, incomprehensible background: "In the streets (after the assassination on the first of March), people look calm and carefree, there is no curiosity or anxiety on their faces." The atmosphere in Russia was then so catastrophic that De Vogué came to the conclusion that the empire would soon collapse.

Another observer, the "red" Russian journalist Eronim Iasinskii, writes the following in the section of his memoir referring to the period preceding 1 March 1881:[13]

> Whenever I came across Voropanov, an official journalist, or similar liberal writers such as Arsenii Vvedenskii or the "bonapartist" Zaguliaev from *Golos (The Voice)*, they inevitably caught me by the hand and, lowering their voice, as they suspected me of being in touch with terrorists, asked me hastily, "will it be soon now?" I asked them in return, "What do you mean soon? Everybody's sick of waiting, it's in the air right now."

Iasinskii says that although he never had direct contact with terrorists, "I felt very strongly, possibly more so than others, that the tragedy was drawing close, and that it was inevitable."

A typical representative of the Russian intelligentsia, and a fine analyst of social moods, E. A. Shtakenshneider, writes this about the 1880–1881 period: "The spirit now prevailing in society can only inspire sadness and awe." She describes the sympathy terrorists inspired within her own circle of acquaintances, who were average, loyal, well-intentioned people. "Hartman (the director of the Lyceum), when he spoke about Lizogub (who had been executed in Odessa), was rhapsodic in describing the latter's intellectual capacities."[14] His daughter used to say that the pronouncements of Goldenberg, another terrorist who was sentenced at the same trial, "were so wonderful and Goldenberg was so appealing, that she could not tear herself from the papers when she was reading accounts of his statements." Concludes Shtakenshneider, "They were unable to speak otherwise because everyone was talking that way."

In his diary Suvorin describes a conversation he had with Dostoevsky: "In discussing these events (Mlodetskii's attempt on the life of Loris-Melikov), Dostoevsky elaborated on the strange attitude of people toward these crimes.[15] The public seemed to approve of them, or more precisely, did now know what to make of them" (*Diary*, p. 15).

These quotations from people belonging to various social strata are a clear illustration of the period that directly preceded the beginning of my student days. But, did we who were by then in our fifth or sixth year of technical school feel in any way concerned about all of this nightmarish unrest, about the tsar's murder and the long-expected uprising, the revolution, which it was supposed to signal among those students who bore aloft "the red banner"? My memory contains no record at all of this period's politics. I was fifteen years old at the beginning of 1881, and I do not remember how the people around me in Kharkov reacted to the events of 1 March. But I vividly remember the morning of 2 March, when our Ukrainian peasant yard-keeper [*dvornik-khokhol*], Vlas Moroka, came into the dining room with the steaming samovar and said to my father, "Did ya hear, sir, they done killed the tsar!"[16] And I can see my father hiding his face in his hands and crying, My God, my God, what is going on?"

I arrived in Petersburg in the fall of 1883. The mood of the students, especially among the young, green provincials who surrounded me, was quite calm. First year students, because of their youth and provincial background, had no political consciousness whatsoever, to use the modern term. But I do remember quite well that the former institute student Rysakov, who was Alexander II's actual assassin, was resented and viewed even by the older students with a sort of muted hostility.[17] Whenever people who had known him spoke about him, it was to mention unsavory features of his character, which was portrayed as antisocial, brooding, and obtuse. There was no hint of considering him a hero.

According to general opinion, the reign of Alexander III from the very beginning was marked by severe political repression, but we young people learned this only much later, when we reached political maturity.

As students, we did not perceive the political aspects of the reaction. We were ignorant of the previous freedom of student life from which we were irrevocably severed by the event of 1 March, which I think made a sharp break in the outlook of everyone except the extremists. All the unrest that had occurred at the end of Alexander II's reign had resulted in something close to a collectively organized murder, and it could not but provoke an inevitable reaction. Maybe because of all this, the reaction was not really conspicuous—it was ubiquitous and not restricted to government circles. It was as though everything suddenly froze in place in the realization of the criminal insanity of what had occurred.

How did the students live? Politically speaking, the period from 1883 to 1889 was exceptionally dull. During the whole six years of my life at the Mining Institute there was not even one political meeting and scarcely any political circles. Our first years were devoted, unfortunately, to our newly acquired personal independence. Having fled the native nest at eighteen, finding ourselves now in the fascinating hurly-burly of Petersburg, many of us wasted a lot of time wandering around the capital, at billiard tables, in cafes, and why lie about it, chasing vodka. Many of us were devoted to music to the point of forgetting all of our duties. This was the golden age of Russian music. I knew students who had never once been to the Italian opera, which was still excellent, but who had listened to "Ruslan" or to "Onegin" dozens of times.[18]

What was our attitude to contemporary literature? Turgenev, whom we had read as schoolboys, was becoming less and less attractive to us. His novels, even the more recent ones like *Virgin Soil*, appeared divorced from life and ceased to interest us.[19] His era had become too sharply and radically cut off from us. Dostoevsky was far more interesting. What attracted our youthful imaginations was not only the mysterious profundity of his characters, the terrifying twists of the plots, and the thoroughly somber horror of his novels, but also the vividly beautiful picture he offered of Petersburg. Many of the events from *Crime and Punishment*, *The Idiot*, and *The Adolescent* are so full of life because they stand against the background of the Haymarket Square, of the New Village and other parts of Petersburg.[20] In many regards Petersburg itself, so mysterious to us Southerners, was one of the reasons we passionately read Dostoevsky, especially in the first years of our student life. And of course, *The Possessed* was far more representative of the spiritual and political atmosphere of the times than was Turgenev's *Virgin Soil*.[21] Did young people read much of Tolstoy's work, did he occupy a great place in our literature at the time? As far as I can remember the answer is no. In any case, he was read much less than

Dostoevsky. Of course, everybody knew *War and Peace* and *Anna Karenina*, but there was no interest in reading them over again, as was the case with Dostoevsky.[22] Certain scenes of *Crime and Punishment* were reread so often that we almost knew them by heart and felt as if we had experienced them personally. Tolstoy's big novels did not captivate us, possibly because generally speaking, they were not very accessible to young people. The intrigue seemed too simple, the heroes not heroic enough, just ordinary people, and the environment of such novels as *Anna Karenina* quite unfamiliar. Tolstoy's deep and true understanding of people and of life slipped past us unnoticed. We became aware of it much later, when we were more mature, and when Tolstoy became, in many ways, the master of our thoughts. I should point out that at the time of our youth Tolstoy had not yet come to his final period of penitence and preaching. "Master and Man," "The Kreutzer Sonata," and "The Death of Ivan Il'ich" all came later. His "Confessions," published at the beginning of the eighties, did not attract our attention.[23]

Among the young writers (in the seventies and eighties), Garshin was undoubtedly the most gifted.[24] I remember that we read a lot of his books. Garshin attracted us not only because of his constant compassion for people, but also because this compassion was almost entirely free of any populist tendencies. He used his great talent for lively sketches to approach some of the "eternal questions" that preoccupy the young reader. The events of the recent war, with the tormenting questions that always arise about deliberate slaughter, were told by Garshin simply, with convincing sincerity. He himself had experienced the Russo-Turkish War of 1877 as a volunteer. He treated one question of social morality, the terrible problem of prostitution, which in those days was called "the safety valve of public passions," in a short story whose hero commits suicide because of his love for a prostitute. Garshin showed his preoccupation with the question of art's significance, its aims and its tendencies in his story "The Artists."[25] I still remember the deep and painful impression produced by Garshin's description of the painting "The Deaf," created by a populist artist (a worker whose craft was hammering rivets inside boilers). The populist who produces this provocative work of art is balanced by another artist who believes that art should not pursue social aims.

Garshin's work was a great departure from the populist literature of the seventies; in fact, it was a rupture. He represented a new trend, separate from politics and especially from revolution. In this sense Garshin was a transitional figure between the mood of the period that was fading away and the bright future expressed in literature by Chekhov.[26] The populist literary tendency toward pity, so conspicuous in the writings of such seventies authors as N. Zlatovratskii and Gleb Uspenskii, was replaced in Garshin's works by a more individualistic love for people, often reaching a painful sharpness.[27] His departure from the "rebellious- ness" of the preceding period is illustrated, for instance, by the way he portrayed Alexander II. Describing the tsar's inspection of departing troops (in *The Memoirs of Private Ivanov*), the hero tells that among the whole brilliant retinue he could see one lonely man on grey horse.[28] "I remember how tears streamed down his cheeks, and fell like glittering drops on his dark uniform. I remember his shivering hands, holding the reins, his trembling lips. Everything bore witness to the fact that he was crying about the thousands of condemned lives he was now saluting." All these qualities of Garshin's work reflected our mood as well. He was very close to us, as the catastrophic events had changed the public mood in a very short period of time.

Chekhov's influence, barely noticed at first, later became enormous. Analyzing now our first impressions of him, one feels that he had no influence at all, and that none of us was willing to identify himself with his "unheroic" heroes. At that time Chekhov did not teach us anything, in contrast to other authors. The life he described was hopelessly hard, but nevertheless we fell under the spell of his talent and, possibly in greater measure, of his soul. Chekhov was a kinsman to us southerners, in one sense, because of his love for nature and for the southern steppe. But there was something else; obscurely, despite our lack of experience, we perceived that he was portraying the era we were entering, in which we were to become "builders of life."

There is yet another reason why we felt so close to Chekhov. Had we not been disillusioned by the previous period? It faded away from us quickly, incomprehensible and alien. All this romanticism of great deeds and vain dreams, drowned in a bloody intoxication, seemed quite strange to us. Unconsciously, instinctively, we were repelled by every- thing romantic, by posing, by anything that looked to us like a lie. Chekhov's pitiless realism, with its new, photographic precision, we felt to be the truth itself, and it matched our mood. "Here is the real Russia, where we have to work and live," he seemed to be telling us, in his own unique language full of indescribable charm, sympathy and poetic sadness. In fact, apart from Antosha Chekhont, whom we already knew, our real encounter with Chekhov occurred during our higher classes, when we were growing into young adulthood.[29] I remember clearly what an acute impression such "southern," stories as "Happiness," "The Steppe," and "The Rolling Stone" made on me: how he evoked the scenery of the southern steppe in such vivid colors, there in the misty and cold dampness of Petersburg.[30] His short stories, which really were only superficially short, such as "Typhus," "Kashtanka," "The Name-Day Party," and others portrayed almost painfully, in their condensed form, all the eternal and tormenting riddles of life, of which we were only barely conscious.

I remember that I attended the first performance of his comedy "Ivanov" with the elder Fortunato.[31] I will not say that we did not understand the play or that we did not like it, but this was a lesser Chekhov, lesser than that of his best stories. The play lacked his vivid colors, and was too schematic. But the impression produced by Ivanov's environment in the godforsaken province where the action is situated was hopelessly painful. The Russian provinces and Russian life did not appear to us as such in those days. I remember that on our way home after the play we were silent, as if stunned. It was only much later when I came to know the Russian provinces better through personal experience that I came to understand Ivanov. But I must confess that I never really liked Chekhov's dramas.

How did we react to the absence of political freedom, or more precisely, to the general disinterest in politics that then prevailed? As far as I can remember, we students did not regret it and had no nostalgia about the lost freedom. Quite the reverse, when I looked back on our student days much later I realized that we, this "grey" mass that in fact included about 99 percent of the student body, had been grateful to destiny for that true freedom we did enjoy, namely freedom from politics, which at that time we found neither interesting nor necessary. We were free, in fact, from the political oppression of the few restless propagandists. It was as if the student body itself, through no outside influence, became able to counterbalance those who only a few years earlier would have become its accepted leaders. The average student was close to completely rejecting what had been the students' political mood just a few years earlier. The "revolutionary unrest" of the students in the sixties and seventies had disappeared, not because "reactionary" conditions had inhibited this mood, but because the "revolution," in its many aspects, had ceased to attract our interest. The new mood of the students reflected youth itself; the "Russian boys" now had the right to express their real, spiritual, nature.

One might think that because of the reaction the oppositional literature would have disappeared completely and that we would have withered intellectually in this literary calm, but this was not the case. Some great authors were part of the opposition, such as Mikhailovskii or Shchedrin, as well as many minor ones. Most of the "thick journals" exhibited, although not openly, a spirit of opposition and resistance.[32] And probably most of us students were readers of such literature, at least of Mikhailovskii and Shchedrin. But the atmosphere already was different and we were different as well. The brilliant Mikhailovskii was a success, his books were captivating, but this was all. Shchedrin seemed artificial and the rest of the journalistic opposition literature simply boring. I repeat that the overwhelming majority of our students was not interested in politics. When I remember the students of the Mining Institute in those days, I realize that only a few of them were involved in politics: the "leftists" were Pogrebov, Golubiatnikov, Sadovskii, Lutugin to a degree, and perhaps Bauman, as well as two or three others whose names I have forgotten. I am not sure they ever formed a group. I remember that after some political event that I have now forgotten, Lutugin, pale and nervous, tried to organize a meeting, but gathered only about eight or ten people.

Student Life at School and at Home

I was living among my southern kinsmen, mostly former schoolboys from the gymnasia or technical high schools of Elizavetgrad and Simferopol. I was the only student at the Mining Institute who had come from Kharkov. My closest friends were the Fortunato brothers, sons of the agent of the Russian Steamship and Trade Company at Yalta. Both of them were very talented youths, musicians and excellent graphic artists, and the eldest, Lev, had a real gift for writing. It is true that Lev Mikhailovich was not at all attracted to the exact sciences, and he even left the institute during the first year, staying away for four years. "I can't stand chemistry," he told K. I. Lysenko, the professor of chemistry. During these four years he went to the conservatory and also attended the Academy of Fine Arts. He lived for a year in the country at a friend's estate, where it was even said that he became the marshal of the nobility.[33] Four years later, after I had graduated, he returned to the Mining Institute where he graduated in due course. He later became a professor of metallurgy at the Ekaterinoslav Mining Institute. Chemistry conquered him.

During the first two years I lived with the Fortunato brothers. Music was the special link among us. We even decided to initiate an orchestra at the institute, like the one at the university, directed by Glavach. A. K. Glazunov, who later became a famous composer, played the French horn in this orchestra. He was then in his eighth year at the gymnasium and was an exceptionally handsome boy.[34] We soon recruited the musicians, but a problem arose about the music that could be found only at the conservatory with the permission of Anton Grigor'evich Rubinstein.[35] So we went, Anton Fortunato and I, to ask Rubinstein for some music; Lev, the future conductor of our orchestra, was too frightened to go. Because Anton Mikhailovich and I did not play, but were just organizing amateurs, we could talk to the famous Rubinstein without apprehension. But I remember that we were quite moved when we entered his office. We had seen him before only at his piano on stage or at symphonic concerts at the recital hall of the Gentry Assembly, where he sat majestically in his special place. We were greatly amazed when we found that the director of the conservatory was a remarkably spry, clean-shaven, jovial, shortish old man, bearing the features of this monument: Rubinstein. He laughed heartily when he learned from us, the nonmusicians, that our "conductor" was too frightened to come. He was very amenable and readily gave us permission to take the music. Our orchestra's first performance was Tchaikovsky's andante for strings.[36]

Among our close relationships of those early years I must mention I. G. Popovitskii, another Crimean, who was never a student but who lived away from home without any occupation—his parents were rather wealthy. Popovitskii was a typical misfit, an aimless daydreamer, a poet with considerable erudition in literature. He was a convinced "pessimist," with a tinge of old-fashioned nihilism. The sum was an absurd, but rather harmless, waste of talent. It was he who first acquainted us with Schopenhauer and Hartmann, who were then very fashionable among a certain segment of the Russian youth.[37]

In fact this pessimism was a legacy of the seventies, a result of the failure of purely political strivings. But by the time we were in school this pessimism, along with some other peculiarities of the fading era, had evolved into an abstract, literary pessimism, in the manner of Schopenhauer and Hartmann; that is, into a far safer form.

Together with pessimism one should examine the subject of suicide, or as people use to say then, of the "suicide epidemic," often debated in the literature in the preceding period. Our generation, as well, was familiar with this sad phenomenon, but it took on different forms, including often a crazy aimlessness, which I will describe later.

Another member of our "musical" circle from those early student years was the kindly Kostin'ka Abraam, a wonderful violinist and gifted musician, who also was quite accomplished on the piano. He was of German descent, but did not speak German, fair haired, with charming blue eyes and a fair complexion. Abraam had been my schoolmate in the very first grade at the Kharkov Technical High School, where I just barely remember him as a sort of child-prodigy on the violin in the school concerts. He apparently moved to Moscow in the third grade, and after that we did not see each other again until we were at the

Mining Institute. He was exceptionally modest and quiet, very cooperative, and seemed to live apart from reality; only music would stir him
up, and I think he lived for the music alone. Our circle wrangled from
the opera management a subscription to the cheapest box for the students. Sometimes it was jammed with over twenty people. Needless to
say, all of us, especially Abraam, were the most faithful subscribers to
the opera. I remember that Kostin'ka was smitten not only with Russian
music, but also with Bizet *(Carmen)*, whose instrumentation he considered exceptional.[38] Abraam remained a close friend even after graduation because he married one of my relatives, Variusha Time, the daughter
of our professor. He started working at the same time I did, first in
Donbass mines and later as a district engineer (in the mining administration) in one of the regions of the Bakhmut District.

   In connection with my memories of various types of "despondents"
I cannot omit G. I. L., a university student who was the son of a wealthy
Bessarabian landowner. Elegant, very well educated, living as a rich
student, L. was introduced to many circles and mainly to Petersburg
military society. I do not remember precisely how and when we got
acquainted and became friends. It must have been during the first years
of my student life, when I was a passionate reader of Dostoevsky and
often dabbled in Schopenhauer, and was more or less officially labeled
a "pessimist" by my circle. I do not remember for what reasons L., a
greenhorn like myself, joined the ranks of the "pessimists." Anyway
he always kept the very *comme il faut* appearance of a regular gentleman.
It should be mentioned that L. was not at all a weak person, nor did
he fall under my or anyone else's influence. In fact, his nature was
stronger and far more active than mine. I think that the burning atmosphere of Dostoevsky's novels had affected him terribly. Perhaps because
of his extremely active nature, L. was not satisfied with purely theoretical "pessimism" and decided to act upon this mood: he decided to
commit suicide. He had no objective reasons to do so, and even his
"pessimism" did not really supply any organic grounds for such a thing,
because it was so removed from his very lively nature. In fact, it was
all deadly bravado, which presumably was the meaning of his real
attempt to kill himself.
   L. lived with his friend who was also from Bessarabia, the student
P., a charming, mild, and good-natured youth, who was devoted to
him. L. took some cyanide powder, dissolved it in water and drank it,
informing the frantic P. what he was witnessing. P. rushed out for a
doctor, but when they came back they found L. in convulsions, unconscious, and foaming at the mouth. The doctor succeeded in saving him,

however. Fortunately the poison was old and had weathered, as the doctor put it. L. said that after drinking the poison he felt as if subsumed in turmoil, and he found himself in a narrow corridor convulsed by a whirlwind. He remembered nothing, felt no pain, and recovered his senses, he said, when he felt the revolting sensation of the doctor's greasy finger in his mouth. L. showed no concern, remorse, or regret, and as usual, he was perfectly calm.

L. no longer wished to take poison after that. He thought up another game to play with death. As he lived on the fourth floor of a building on Pushkin Street, he used to sit on the window sill, facing the street, his legs hanging down, and slide down little by little, as Dolokhov did, until he reached a slight projection in the wall, just barely gripping the window frame. A crowd would gather, the worried janitor and policeman would rush upstairs—only to find L. quietly sitting at his table.

How are we to explain such extraordinary mental agitation, which occurred for no apparent reason? L., like most of us, was not disappointed about anything, nor did he feel any political oppression, nor was he interested in politics at all. It is true that L. was fascinated, and he was not alone in this, by the image of Stavrogin in *The Possessed*. I believe that he wanted to become a man indifferent to fear, and in fact he was such a man.[39] Had he been born 10 years earlier, he might have become a fearless terrorist, or at any rate, the pearl of a group of underground activists. He would have been fascinated by the tense, saturated atmosphere that prevailed then, which corresponded so well with the crazy, agitated feelings of twenty-year-old Russians, which from time to time drove them into outright madness.

This description of the student life refers to the early period of my studies, mainly the first two years of my program at the Mining Institute. I spent two years in the first course because the first year I came down with pneumonia. At this early stage, students usually were just barely interested in the sciences, especially in the natural or technical sciences, which are not very attractive. The urge to study came later, I would say from the third year on, when the youthful rapture faded away and was gradually replaced by the necessity of mastering the numerous serious sciences of the mining craft.

Compared with the sixties and seventies, the student way of life, including its academic aspect, had changed radically. We were given a uniform, attendance at lectures was compulsory, and every morning the famous Inspector of Students, Illarion Illarionovich Tsitovich, took attendance by the racks (that is, by looking at the coat racks on which cloaks and caps were to be hung, one numbered hook assigned to each student). After a certain number of missed lectures, the student was given a demerit and three demerits meant expulsion. The authorities also enforced the wearing of the "correct" uniform. Tsitovich would say to the students: "If you please, what kind of uniform is this? A red shirt under your uniform jacket?" Or "A uniform jacket with pea-green trousers like Mr. Kafka's?" (Kafka was one of my fellow students). But, in reality, no one interfered with students' lives outside the institute, though order had to be respected strictly inside. We were not really compelled to attend the lectures, but only had to be present at the institute, working in the drawing rooms, the laboratories, the museum or else reading papers in the dining room. Once we were inside the institute, nobody really bothered about how we spent our time. Order usually was respected, except in one particular instance.

Two second-year students, Bisarnov and Shirkov, while sitting idly in the dining hall, came up with the idea of betting who could eat the most *zakuski*.[40] This silly bet was met with curiosity by the bored students, and ended with one contestant vomiting. The unexpected result of this bet aroused laughter and disgust. The students would soon have forgotten this whole affair, to which in fact they paid little attention—especially because the loser, Bisarnov, was a "merry idler," though a good fellow whom most of us liked. But our "leftists" decided on a "trial" of the "criminals," made speeches, and voted a public condemnation—to which the "criminals," I might add, paid no attention. But what amazed me, tenderfoot that I was, was the hatred, the heavy, deep, unforgiving hatred shown by the leftists. I remember as clearly as though it were yesterday, the dark-haired "prosecutor," Sadovskii, full of animosity, with his bulging eyes, hissing as he spoke. This hidden hatred was characteristic of contemporary leftist youth. Their recent activism had been paralyzed; their moods had been driven underground and made an appearance only as eternal irritation and malevolence toward everybody, not only toward people with different convictions but also toward the indifferent, who were then the overwhelming majority.

As I have already mentioned, among the leftists there was L. I. Lutugin, the long-term treasurer of student organizations, my fellow student, and the future well-known geologist and political leader.[41] Here are a few more recollections from my later life, concerning this kind of hatred. I did not know Lutugin very well as a student, but I came to know him very well later, when we both were engineers, and Lutugin used to spend whole summers in the Donets Basin studying the geology of coal-bearing seams. Lutugin had a wonderful sense of humor and great insight. He became friends with almost everyone, as he moved from one mine to another, one engineer to another, living at the expense of various people. "By the end of the summer," he used to say, "I'll be a real scoundrel." Lutugin was unable to hide his feelings, and this is why he was on close, almost intimate, terms with most of his summer friends. Consequently, much later, I would once again be amazed by the hatred that appeared in Lutugin whenever he was on the path of his leftist public or political activity. I remember a technical meeting held in the early nineties, in Petersburg, that quickly turned into a political demonstration, as was much the fashion in those days. I remember Lutugin making a speech. He was by nature a very good debater, a rather outstanding figure at political demonstrations. When he left the podium he was pale, almost trembling, with quivering nostrils, and he aroused tumultuous applause.

During the break I joined him to share the very sad news I had just received about the sudden death of one of our closest acquaintances, S. F. Ianchevskii, the executive director of the big Shcherbinovka Mine.[42] Lutugin knew him and his wife very well, as he had spent long spells in the summers at their house. Lutugin greeted my announcement with quite an unexpected reaction, to the effect that this did not interest him at all. True, at the next meeting he was remarkably attentive to Ianchevskii's memory, but the first impression could not be forgotten. I also remember how Lutugin and his friends attacked the dissertation of V. V. Murzakov, a mining engineer I knew well, having worked with him at the Makeevka Mine. Murzakov was seeking a higher scientific degree in order to obtain a professorship in mining technology. Lutugin suspected Murzakov of belonging to the Black Hundreds and also of mistreating the miners, all of which in fact was not true and based upon absurd rumors.[43] Murzakov failed ignominiously, although the official critics declared that he deserved the scientific degree. I saw Murzakov soon after this deliberate decision to fail him. He was in a state of complete despair because of this undeserved humiliation, the result of senseless hatred.

Once, while wandering with Lutugin through the steppe country of the Slavianoserbsk District making geological observations, we happened across an abandoned mansion quite by accident.[44] Beyond the deserted yard and the shut windows we found ourselves in a wonderful abandoned garden, where beneath the invading weeds an old fountain was still visible. "Look, Leonid Ivanovich," I said, "here is an abandoned 'nest of gentlefolk.'"[45] A loud spit was Lutugin's only reply.

Hatred, this dreadful feeling, was already fermenting, right below our feet. And hatred already governed Lutugin, in spite of his ability to understand and even to love people with different opinions. Hatred had caught most of Russia in its net, like some kind of spell.

May I be forgiven for this digression. Lutugin was such a flamboyant example of Russian life, though even more so later on.

Returning to my description of student life, I have to say that one should not imagine that the life of either my colleagues or myself was that of secluded, lonely bachelors. We were frequently introduced to families and often met there. Almost every Sunday both the Fortunatos and I were invited for lunch by Elena Nikolaevna Potapenko, the wife of the well-known author Ignati Nikolaevich Potapenko.[46] A relative of the Fortunatos, dear Elena Nikolaevna was of Greek descent. She did not live with her husband. She was not a good-looking or attractive woman, but good-hearted and exceptionally friendly. Her small, cozy, quiet flat was filled every Sunday with the sounds of lively conversation and music. She had a piano; Lev Fortunato played quite well; and I sang, like all men with poor singing voices, in a faint baritone. But why hide the fact, the greatest attraction was her incredibly tasty meals, her cabbage pies and soup. In fact, we were often hungry, and I remember the compassionate, kind glances from Elena Nikolaevna's nearsighted eyes during the meals. We sometimes went to the house of Ivan Nikolaevich Lampsi, her brother, or to her sister Mariia Nikolaevna, the former wife of admiralty barrister Fisher. There we found more music, conversations that were more interesting but more restrained, and an atmosphere that was neither gay nor captivating. Lampsi and his wife lived grandly, spending, or should I say, wasting, Ivan Nikolaevich's rather considerable fortune and doing literally nothing but attend theaters, concerts, balls, and so on. We poor bohemians were not in their league. Fisher was brooding and presumptuous and we avoided him.

I also visited my aunt Varvara Valerianovna Time (née Fenin), the wife of our Professor Ivan Avgustovich Time and the mother of a dramatic artist who later became the famous Elizaveta Ivanovna Time.[47] Varvara Valerianovna herself was an excellent singer who had sung on the stage of the Mariinskii Theatre as a mezzo-soprano; she was reputed to be the best romance singer in Petersburg.[48] Time's nephew, Ivan Nikolaevich Temnikov, lived with them. He was a student in the same course as I. We later became great friends. I remember a sad situation that drew me closer to Varvara Valerianovna and her family. Before I came to Petersburg I did not know them at all, and at the beginning of our friendship I maintained a studentlike, reserved demeanor. When I was about to enter my third year, I had to retake an examination in chemistry. Having passed it in mid-August, I had a whole month to spend in solitude and boredom in Petersburg before the courses started, because I had not planned to return home. This is why I enthusiastically accepted the invitation of Chetverikov, my "colleague" in the reexamination, to go hunting in Kursk Province where his wife owned a small estate in the Fatezh District. When I joyfully announced this to Time, Ivan Avgustovich asked me to escort his wife who was going to her brother's place at Izium. He explained that Varvara Valerianovna had been suffering from nervous troubles ever since the birth of Elsa (the future singer, then an eight-month-old baby) and wished to rest in a different environment. In the course of the trip poor Varvara Valerianovna became completely insane, her condition having worsened to the point of violence. Chetverikov and I spent two painful days caring for her, until we reached Kursk where we entrusted her to her father whom I had telegraphed. After a long treatment in Kharkov, Varvara Valerianovna fortunately recovered completely.

I cannot fail to mention what tragic fate awaited I. N. Temnikov, whom I mentioned earlier. After having graduated with honors—he was always a very serious student and gifted man—Temnikov returned home to the Urals where he was engaged as an engineer at the state-owned Perm Factory (at Motovilikha, near Ekaterinburg).[49] The events of the second revolution found him there, where I believe he was the manager of the factory.[50] In 1917 or 1918 he and his son, also a student at the Mining Institute who was home for vacation, were arrested by some revolutionary workers' committee. I do not know the details of this crime, but I know that both were brutally tortured; their hands chopped off, then they were locked in a bathhouse overnight where they bled to death. It should be added that his workers had no reason to hate Temnikov, a kind and just man. His "execution" as an "enemy of the proletariat" was performed by workers who came from somewhere else.[51] And so here is one more shudder in the face of yet another horror from the Russian people's history of criminal insanity.

The Academic Life

The Mining Institute's imposing facade was about a century old, the work of a famous Russian architect, Voronikhin, and it faced the Neva River. Two gigantic allegoric figures guarded the main entrance. Our alma mater, with its auditoriums, drafting rooms, museum, chemical laboratory, lectures, and professors, absorbed most of our time. I remember those yellowish grey Petersburg mornings in the fall and winter perfectly, as I do that brisk, youthful state of mind, that sharp curiosity for everything that was happening. First I see the narrow provincial streets of Vasil'evskii Island, where I lived almost the entire time that I was a student in Petersburg, then the Neva embankment with its grand, European-style houses, the building and grounds of the institute, whose front door we were not allowed to use for some reason, the narrow, old, subterranean corridor, the crowded cloak room, the old janitor Sakharov, and finally the auditorium, gaslit in the early hours of the day.[52] To this day, I can recollect all the professors of the institute as they pass by, most of them reputed experts in what someone among us called "the learned sciences."

In the junior courses every professor had his particular "story," mostly invented by the students. The "terror" of the students, the physicist Kraevich, was a yellowish, elderly man, always wearing an academic black scull cap, and still not a full professor. This was due, according to the students, to the fact that a certain Zolotarev whom he had sacked long ago, would inevitably reappear every time he was defending his thesis and make him "mess up." Students were so afraid of the physics examination that even when they drew a question they knew by heart, they would often do no better than a "2," from pure fear.[53] Lectures in crystalography and mineralogy were given by Professor Eremeev, a small, skinny, hoary old man with a very ugly face, trimmed whiskers, and sharp eyes. He was a brilliant lecturer, and we listened intently as his minerals and crystals became almost living creatures. If by chance he felt after two hours that we were getting tired he would tell us amusing anecdotes, such as the one about his trip to Italy where a group of Russian ladies, not suspecting that he was a compatriot, called him an "old monkey" in Russian, adding the accusation that, like every Italian, he probably considered himself irresistible.

Mathematics were taught by impetuous Professor Georgii Avgustovich Time, who had the nervous habit of whipping himself and his students with the expression "Now then!" over and over again. Georgii Time, as people called him to distinguish him from his brother Ivan Time, gave the impression of absentmindedness, of being unaware of his surroundings, of being the type who could not even recognize his own students. He was so impatient and apparently so confident of his students' knowledge that they passed his examinations without knowing anything about the questions on the test. "Now then!" he would say. "You just draw a polygon, a-b-c," and then he would explain exactly what the student was supposed to say and invariably give him a "3." Some people claimed that Georgii Time was subject to sudden fits of madness, in which he dressed up in women's clothes and went walking along the street.

The "legends" about professors disappeared in the higher courses, but oddities were still discernable, and I realize now, strangely enough, as I try to reminisce objectively about those figures who vanished long ago, that many of them really were curious people. I remember our chemical laboratory, where we spent long hours, with its cupboards and working tables full of flasks and test tubes. This was the the domain of Professor Konon Ivanovich Lysenko, our inspector, a gray-haired, skinny old man who paced with an uneasy half-lame gait and invariably wore the uniform jacket of a mining general. A professor of chemistry and an excellent musician, brother to a well-known Ukrainian composer, Konon Ivanovich was undoubtedly a great character, and what I remember best about him, of course, are his oddities.[54] Upon entering his office, one would often find him squatting on a stool, a notebook in hand, whistling a tune with all his might; for a long moment he would not realize that anyone was there nor would he answer questions, even when repeated, for a long time. He had difficulty remembering students' faces and used to ask one's name over and over. He asked one student, Khovanskii, to tell him his name, and when he learned it, he gestured grandly and pronounced that that was not possible. A few days later he approached Khovanskii working at his desk, and muttered simply, "in fact, it is possible," Upon questioning Konon Ivanovich we later learned that the princely Khovanskii clan had become extinct long ago—our student was only a Cossack Khovanskii.[55] Once when I was filtering some liquid chemical Konon Ivanovich stopped near me, stared at me for a while, and then he said, "Mister (this is how he addressed everybody), what you are doing is useless; you might as well give up chemistry and start writing stories." When I asked the reasons for this strange advice, he just answered that I resembled Kantemir.[56]

But now I turn to the very image of perfection: stately in his outward appearance, our beloved Professor Ivan Vasil'evich Mushketov, the geologist and well-known explorer, who studied and described the geology of the mysterious Turkestan.[57] He was very charming, always attired in civilian clothes, a brilliant lecturer, and he always had a crowded auditorium. It was not only him we liked, but also the subject he taught, his descriptive, poetic geology. This truly dignified image of a professor and his teaching was enhanced by the summer geological excursions Mushketov conducted on the banks of the Volkhov River. We would gaze with fascination at the beauties of northern scenery, at the bedding of the geological seams and at Ivan Vasil'evich himself, who, with his large black hat, his field boots and his geologist's hammer in hand, was gracefully leading us. I have preserved a fond memory of Ivan Vasil'evich Mushketov and of the science he taught.

We also greatly appreciated and respected our professor of mining mechanics, Ivan Avgustovich Time, always benevolent and attentive to us, accurate and clear in his science. With him our attitude was confident and simple, and we had no fear, quite unlike our experience with other professors. We tried to do well studying and understanding his subject. I remember a typical incident. One of my classmates, M., asked his brother, who already had graduated as an engineer, to calculate and draft a project he had to do for his final examination. M. was so lazy and careless that he did not even review the project and just handed it to Time. He almost fainted when he saw his draft at the examination, just penciled in, with the following note on it from his brother: "I'm sick of this, the hell with you—do the ink draft yourself." Underneath this ran the following red ink remark from Time: "Who is responsible for this?" I do not remember how, exactly, all this ended, but I know that Ivan Avgustovich did not report it to anybody.

We were unlucky with the main subject: mining technology. Both our professors, Romanovskii and Kotsovskii, were poor lecturers. Genadii Danilovich Romanovskii, an old mining general, was a big, heavy-set man who, even for those times, had a rather primitive knowledge of the subject. His teaching was boring and he used to draw endless, detailed schemes of timbering and excavating on the blackboard, putting us to sleep with his deep monotone. We would sit there listening, sketching, taking notes (our professor refused to print his lectures), and we got to thinking how Romanovskii lived all alone in his big flat, where students used to say, after a few drinks his greatest pleasure was to roll a heavy, iron dumbbell on the floor. Professor Wojslaw, a nervous and bilious Pole who lived in the flat below, used to jump out of bed and rush upstairs to try to reason with this unhinged old man.

Nikolai Dmitrievich Kotsovskii used to teach part of the mining technology course as well as surveying. He was very accurate and conscientious in his approach to his subjects, but he was utterly unable to communicate his knowledge. His courses left the impression of hopeless chaos.

I will not mention the host of other professors, among whom were great scientists such as the paleontologist Laguzen, the geologist Karpinskii who taught historical geology and later became a famous academician and chairman of the academy, the metallurgist Iossa, and the chemist Sushin.[58] All of them were men of great knowledge, but they lacked that elusive fire of true creativity capable of exciting an audience, which I. V. Mushketov possessed in such abundance.

Ultimately this "dabbling" at science was not so funny, because when we left the institute we really did not know much, partly because there were too many subjects to study. It is sufficient to mention that the curriculum of the institute encompassed both mining as such and metallurgy. Soon after we left, this was split into two separate departments.

The National Mood in the Era of Calm. Our Longing for Real Work and the Possibilities of Realizing It

Did we students have any nationalistic feelings at that time? What was our attitude toward our country? One might think that Russia did not interest us at all, that we were a gray, dull mass indifferent to everything that did not concern us directly. Such an opinion could be justified partly by the outer conditions of our life. Nothing of our inner feelings was visible, and there were no outward manifestations of them. Our life was devoid of any activism, whether social or political, in contrast to the youth of the seventies. Political or public activity in fact was absent, but, I insist, it was neither because we were oppressed by "reaction" nor because we were spiritually empty. General conditions, and even more than that the general atmosphere of the period, separated us sharply from the pattern of the preceding generation of students. Unexpectedly, we found ourselves spiritually free. We were free to express and draw upon our "inner selves," guided by our own characteristics and by that elusive "something" that Russian life had to offer in those days. For, without outside constraint or intervention, Russia at that time was consumed by its incredible possibilities, which not only the young perceived. We young people were surrounded by Russian talents unsurpassed either before or after, primarily in the arts. We witnessed virtually first-hand the greatest musical creations of Tchaikovsky, Rimskii-Korsakov, Borodin, and Glinka, who was revived primarily through *Ruslan and Liudmila*.[59] Operas of unprecedented brilliance and real artistic richness were performed by such exceptional singers as Mel'nikov, Stravinskii, Vasil'ev, and Slavina.[60] We witnessed new stars rising, such as the Figners, Iakovlev, Mravina, and Dolina. At the peak of their careers such people as Varlamov, Davydov, Savina, and Strepetova performed at the Aleksandrinskii Theatre. Contemporary painting also was producing stars. Repin was being heaped with glory;[61] people were troubled by the mysterious Nestorov; and then there were the wonderful landscape painters such as Levitan, Krachkovskii, and the painter of seascapes, Aivazovskii.[62]

And in every facet of this art, which was as brilliant as the sun, there was Russia; her themes, her nature, her history old and new. All of it spoke, breathed Russia, and only Russia. With what feverish youthful enthusiasm we listened to the magic sounds of Rimskii-Korsakov's musical rendering of the charming tale of *The Snow Maiden*,[63] and how deeply we felt Pushkin's presence in Tchaikovsky's inspired interpretation of *Evgenii Onegin*. His musical translation preserved the very essence of Pushkin's creation, the spirit of the epoch and the life of its heroes. I will not linger over Glinka's *Ruslan and Liudmila*, this mighty Russian epic, developed with a musical splendor that Lizst himself envied.[64] Even now I remember the shiver of excitement we felt when we watched Tchaikovsky during concerts at the concert hall of the Gentry Assembly or at the Mariinskii Theater where he directed the jubilee performance of *Evgenii Onegin*. I still can see his timid eyes staring out from under his brows, and his face, which seemed to us full of indefinable charm.

And our singers! Mel'nikov was the very incarnation of this great Russian epoch, from his figure and his face to his wonderful acting and his incomparable voice: the immortal figure of Ruslan, of Prince Vladimir in *Rognede*, or of the old boyar from *The Enchantress*. Stravinskii (the father of the famous composer) was excellent in his classical acting and singing of such roles as Farlaf, Eremka *(The Power of Evil)*, and Mephistopheles.[65] Even the enormous talent of Shaliapin in later times was not able to obliterate those unrepeatable impressions that were due, I think, to the musical genius of Stravinskii. I also remember the great impression left by the debut of Figner performing in *Aida*. This may have been the first time that the public was presented not with the puppetlike hero of Verdi's stilted opera, but with a poetical image of the young Egyptian warrior Radomes—expressed with such musical grace that even Figner's peculiar voice seemed charming. I remember that the audience stood up, quite an unusual occurrence for so formal an audience as that of the Mariinskii Theatre, to give Figner a hearty ovation at the end of his first big aria. But this ovation was not only for his perfect artistry, but also for Figner as the descendent of a hero of 1812 (Figner's grandfather, General Figner, had been a hero of the Fatherland War).[66] Even in the midst of this musical feast, the spirit of the times was perceptible.

I will not go into how we reacted to other manifestations of Russian art. I do not think that it would be exaggerating to say that all these impressions so passionately felt by a provincial youth produced an enthusiasm and rapture followed by exultant national pride. It was a pride in Russia; in her talents; in the strong, unyielding calm of her government; in her might among other nations; in her tsar, powerful and just, with his olympian serenity; these were not just the impressions of greenhorns such as we, but also of a large circle of society in this unjustly overlooked era.

These same impressions were reinforced every summer, when we left for the holidays, to have a closer and more direct contact with Russia. Even the trip itself, which was then quite long (three days and nights to reach Kharkov), although tiresome, was varied and for a young eye, an introduction to the splendors of the Russian landscape. The straight line of the Nicholas Railroad, the deep forests with the occasional village and fields, the carved wooden huts, quite strange to us, then the massive square stations, quite in the spirit of Nicholas's times, and even the damp chilly air of the North, with its bluish, grayish, transparent nights and dawns—all of it was subtly charming.[67] Moscow appeared garish, noisy, and after Petersburg, very dirty, when we had to rush early in the morning, feeling brisk but tired, from the Nicholas Station to the Kursk Station in some shaky carriage.

The road to Orel and Kursk was quite different. This was no longer the North; there were just a few forests, and the eye welcomed the hills, the frequent bell-towers of the village churches, and now and then the poetic contour of some mansion with its shady garden and stone-walled estate. Everything was peaceful, full of poetry, and one did not even wish to sleep in spite of the almost always rough night. And then at last, the whitewashed huts of the *khokhols*, the bright sun, the heat, the dusty village roads, Kharkov: I was home.[68] I usually did not stay long with my parents who still lived in Kharkov and flew off further south to my uncle's in Ekaterinoslav Province. The Bakhmut steppe: what a limitless horizon and what a fragrance of wormwood and other wildflowers of the steppe greeted me. From the railroad station to my uncle's estate was about 50 versts. My uncle was then visiting a neighbor near the railroad station, so we drove home together, in a tarantass equipped with springs. The road was smooth, the bells were ringing, and the steppe was like a carpet with the blue-gray waves of feather grass and bright red dots of wild peonies. This was the steppe untouched by the plough, as moving as the native song, the chime of countless larks.

Life on the estate of a steppe landowner of average wealth was quiet, almost lazy: early in the morning taking fragrant tea with cherry marmalade or thick cream with my uncle, during the day either relaxing in the garden or wandering through the fields taking in the fragrance of the black southern earth and the blossoming wheat. In the evenings friends would come to visit and play cards—the inevitable vint. Conversations were leisurely and quiet, about crops, rain, hay mowing, and every now and then some innocent teasing of the student from the capital by some neighboring landowner. On the other hand, they might talk about God, the creation of the world, or the domestication of the old "nihilism," all in quite colorful *khokhol* language. One might step out into the garden, into the darkness and the dry, fragrant air as smooth as velvet. The steppe starts right here, with the neverending music of the grasshoppers and the night sounds that were occasionally impossible to define. When the moon shines everything is touched by a deep, silvery, still light, bearing no resemblance to the pale, transparent, clear nights of the North, which seem now like some remote dream. And here once again is endless, quiet, wonderful Russia. Like Bunin's Rostovtsev you feel a shudder of emotion when you hear or recall Nikitin's verses: "Under the high tent of the blue skies I see the endless steppe. . . . This is you, my Russia, my mighty, Orthodox fatherland."[69] Yes, even among us youth this genuine poet, this singer of the Russian landscape and of Russia, this divinely talented gem was much appreciated. These sentiments about great and "powerful" Russia, if not universal, were shared by many people who belonged to the quiet, balanced Russia and these people were the overwhelming majority.

This consciousness of Russia's power and pride in it permeated most of the student body. This "mood," which ultimately was much more than a "mood" was deeply felt as a love for everything that represented Russia at that time, although it was devoid of political consciousness. This gave me and many other young people a solid foundation, which spared us many bitter disappointments when, almost as adolescents, we had to face the often rather uncouth Russian province, where it was our fate to carry out our professional work, our "real life." This almost universal mood was reflected in our great literature as well.

Someone labeled the eighties a transitional period, a pause between the crests of two waves. True, it was as if Russia had thoughtfully stopped to take a last deep breath of the old Rus air, the air of that strong and mighty Russian history, of true Russian nationalism. This era in many ways is poorly understood and unappreciated, and still awaits some impartial historian. Our celebrated historian V. O. Kliuchevskii makes the following observation about Alexander III, and indirectly about this period, in which he guessed the "historical significance of the direction taken by the Russian people."

> This Tsar reigned just thirteen years, and no sooner had death's fingers closed his eyes, than did the astonished eyes of Europe open wide to recognize the worldwide significance of this short reign. . . . Europe realized that the country she had considered a threat to her civilization was and is in fact her guard, realized that she understands, appreciates and defends her foundations just as their creators do; Europe has accepted

Russia as an organic, indispensable part of her cultural being, a natural blood-relative in the family of nations . . . and bearing the coffin of the Russian tsar to the grave, Europe mourned him as a European sovereign. . . . Who knows, perhaps this recognition will give Europe's international life a new direction. In any case, the path of Russia's historical thinking becomes clearer and easier. Death, which has just closed the eyes of the deceased emperor has thrown a shining light on his people's sense of history and has restored Europe's feeling of spiritual unity.[70]

V. B. El'iashevich, now a professor, who was a student at Moscow University at the time, recalls the impression made by Kliuchevskii's speech, which he delivered during his first lecture after Alexander III's death.[71] "After he had finished the mournful silence lasted for a few minutes. The audience was visible shaken. The speech produced on us such an emotional impression and entered so deeply into our memory that once we got home my friend Ivashchenko and I were able to reproduce it entirely without having taken any notes." It is well known that Kliuchevskii's next lecture was met with hostile demonstrations and whistles. El'iashevich says that he was "at once struck by the unusual appearance of the audience. Besides the usual students sitting at their places, there was a crowd of unknown students standing along the walls. These were all people who did not usually attend Kliuchevskii's lectures. When Kliuchevskii entered they greeted him with deafening whistles." El'iashevich says this demonstration was organized by "The Association of Fellow-Countrymen," who were unwilling to accept Kliuchevskii's description of Alexander III. This marked the beginning of the rising of the second wave of opposition after thirteen years of tranquillity.

Here is how Chekhov reacted to the general spirit and political mood of the epoch in his letter to A. N. Pleshcheev (9 February 1888), about his recently written story "The Steppe."[72] Speaking about one of his characters Chekhov says, "such natures as the mischievous Dymov are not made for dissidence, for wandering or for a settled life, rather they are directed straight towards revolution. There will never be a revolution in Russia, and Dymov will end up a drunkard, or else in jail. He is a superfluous man." This suggests the extent of the feeling of great peace and security that suffused Russian life at that time—to such an extent that so keen an observer as Chekhov was able to make statements that now sound quite naive.

In *The Life of Arsen'ev*, Bunin says this about Rostovtsev who lived in a small provincial town and with whom the high school student Arsen'ev shared an apartment. "Pride frequently echoed in Rostovtsev's words. Pride in what? Pride of being Russian, purely Russian, that we live a special, very simple, modest life, which is the true Russian way of life, and that a better life does not exist." This life is "the incarnation of the true Russian spirit, and a country richer, mightier, and more glorious than Russia does not exist. Later on Bunin has Arsen'ev say, "I realized that this pride was very typical of the times, and was felt strongly not only in our town." Arsen'ev concludes, "I know for certain that I grew up in a period of a substantial growth in Russian power and of a general consciousness of this fact."

The memory of these perceptions from the distant past brings that period back to me, just as I lived it. Later on I was able to "sum it up" rather more consciously. In my view, the great majority of the youths of the eighties—the "men of the eighties" as we were half-contemptuously called later by Russian liberals—differed sharply in their political orientation from those who preceded or followed us, although I do think that the generation of the nineties was closer to us.

The epoch of the eighties and nineties was not only that of "the reactionary reign of Alexander III." It also was inevitably the era of the liquidation of old ideals, of old fancies, of Bazarov's nihilism or Nezhdanov's "going to the people."[73] The various shades and forms of socialism were fading away and, at least during this period, losing their appeal. In this Chekhovian twilight at the end of Alexander III's reign and the beginning of Nicholas II's (1894–1917), an original, but rather crude, even primitive, Russian nationalism was developing. The era then beginning was one of unprecedented international importance for Russia, and one of equally noteworthy economic construction. The huge task of social and economic reform initiated by Witte contrasted sharply with the period of socialistic or other wishful thinking: the former required real work and realistic ideas.

The young generation of the Russian intelligentsia, especially the technical cadres, faced great responsibilities, a task greatly complicated by the lack of continuity because the older generation for the most part was incapable of giving us adequate guidance. Men of our fathers' generation during the whole course of their lives brought very few tasks to completion. Bunin is right to have Arsen'ev observe about his father: "He realized a few things about him, for instance, he realized that he did nothing at all, that he spent his days in this happy idleness which was so common then, and which characterized not only the Russian village nobleman, but in fact, the Russian in general." The author of these memoirs made similar observations, as did the majority of his contemporaries. It fell to him to be one of the first to embark on some major undertaking.

What spiritual environment greeted the younger generation when it set out into the real world? Here is what that incomparable portrayer of this period, Chekhov, says about it in an 1892 letter to Suvorin:

> We have neither immediate nor distant aims, our souls are as empty as a void. We do not have any political opinions, we do not believe in revolution. Is it sickness, or is it not? Definitions do not matter, but one must admit that we are in a tight corner. I am not to blame for my sickness, and I do not have to find a cure, because one has to suppose that this sickness has some hidden good in it and that it was not sent without reason.[74]

In 1888 he had written to Suvorin about his comedy *Ivanov:* "Disappointment, apathy, weak nerves and lack of resistance are the result of overexcitability. . . . Take it as a given. Socialism, another sort of excitability —where is it now? It is in Tikhomirov's letter to the tsar. Nowadays all the socialists have gotten married and are criticizing the zemstvo. Where is liberalism? Even Mikhailovskii says that the checkers are all mixed up."[75]

Russia's intelligentsia was at a turning point, on a razor's edge in those days, where old ideals were ruined or discredited and there was nothing to replace them, the "checkers were all mixed up." We were sick of the old inconsistencies, of our everlasting "alienation from our surroundings." The Russian intelligentsia did not yet have anything real to do, and at the same time aimless dreaming had now become boring. This is why *intelligenty* sought health through some creative "cause," in any field, so long as it meant action and creativity—but they still were unable to find it. And in fact, this very intelligentsia was transfigured when it did find a real cause, even one so fleeting as fighting the cholera epidemic, as Chekov himself pointed out. In 1892 he wrote to Suvorin, the intelligentsia is working diligently on the cholera, sparing neither its money nor even its life. Every day I am moved when I watch them. In Nizhnii the doctors and the cultured people in general are working miracles."[76]

It is noteworthy that together with other trends, the public perception of engineering was evolving quickly, at least among the young. Just ten or fifteen years earlier the very word *engineer* had been synonymous with "money grubber," if not with "shameless plunderer." This had been a consequence of the great railroad boom of the seventies. The literature of the seventies and early eighties referred to engineers only as plunderers. Garshin was no exception. He himself had begun his education at the Mining Institute, but left it during the war, and afterwards attended university courses as an auditor, as he was unwilling to become an engineer.[77]

The economic reforms of Alexander III, about which I will speak later, significantly improved the public attitude toward engineers, and thereby greatly changed the environment in which they worked, particularly transport engineers, who had faced great temptations in the past. As for us mining engineers, especially those who were eager to return to the South, we knew full well what awaited us: hard work in the rough environment of our own province and in the poorly developed industry of those days.

In conclusion I will add a few words about the opportunities afforded by Russian life to young *intelligenty* in the area of practical work and industrial construction. The main "business" of the Russian intelligentsia was agriculture, which was almost entirely in the hands of the gentry and which showed all the symptoms of terrible impoverishment. Half of the land in fact was abandoned by its owners and farmed in the economically senseless system of short-term leases. Competent agricultural management was the exception. I shall not elaborate on the reasons for this phenomenon, but I must say that it cannot be explained entirely by the Russian gentry's lack of business sense and by its inept management. Certainly a major legacy of serfdom was the congenital inability to save, or more precisely, a tendency to squander.[78] This established a poor foundation for agriculture, which must be built up through small savings by thrifty people. Apart from these reasons, which perhaps are exaggerated—after all, noblemen often worked successfully in other areas of the economy—there were other, perhaps more important economic reasons for the desperate state of agriculture. The working of small or medium-sized holdings in Russia was always unprofitable. Russian grain prices remained incredibly low, because of our dependency on German orders.[79] For historical reasons the technical level of small or medium grain production was also very poor and slow to improve. The terribly weak domestic market that stemmed from the country's generally low cultural level and the absence of commercial or agricultural organizations, all made agriculture a hard, unrewarding, and often ruinous activity. The only people who managed to make ends meet in agriculture were a very few, exceptionally talented, landlords and the *kulaks*, who profited from their ruthless and many-faceted exploitation of the peasants.[80]

Chekhov described agriculture from his own personal experience in a letter to Suvorin in 1895: "The toil of your hands and the sweat of your brow, if you work on an estate, will feed you only on one condition:

that you work by yourself, like a *muzhik*, without even a thought for rank or sex."[81]

Our government supported the gentry in many ways because it was the military, socially representative class, but did little to ensure it a sound economic base. Cheap credit through the Gentry Bank was about the only government economic measure on the gentry's behalf, and this was far from sufficient for its needs. The government's incapacity to organize and support this vital part of the Russian economy is even more conspicuous in comparison to the constant efforts of the German government to improve that country's agriculture. This sector of the economy did not attract much attention from the Russian intelligentsia.[82]

The traditional Russian industry of those times was primarily textiles, which was almost entirely in the hands of the merchants. It was a peculiar trade, deeply rooted in the traditions of the Moscow manufacturers, and it functioned in most cases with exceptionally little guidance from the intelligentsia. Its management was old-fashioned, harsh, and rigid, and held little attraction for a young educated Russian. Finally, this ancient Russian trade, along with the whole Russian merchant estate, entered into a deep crisis that shook its leaders. So said a representative of one of the greatest merchant clans, V. P. Riabushinskii, in *Russkii kolokol (The Russian Bell)* in 1928:[83]

> The founder of the firm, a man who had emerged from the depths of the common people, maintained until his death the life-style in which he had grown up, even though he amassed considerable wealth. The son of the founder usually resembled his father in many respects, but he was generally more talented, bolder, and smarter. He was the one who guided the firm onto the broad road and make it famous all over Russia. The spiritual impoverishment of the merchant aristocracy began with the grandsons and their contemporaries, mainly because of their fascination with the intelligentsia culture that surrounded them."[84]

I will not add anything to the author's reasoning. In any case, this old branch of the Russian economy began to break down for purely internal reasons. There was nothing a newcomer from the outside could do for it.

The rest of Russian industry, including that of the Urals and Siberia, was still poorly developed until the nineties, and provided little opportunity for those eager to make some big contribution to the country's social and industrial development. In fact, in this period that kind of contribution could be made in only two fields: in the railroads or in the South Russian mining industry, which, because of the intervention of foreign capital, showed promise of strong and rapid development. These two major sectors of the economy were closely linked. The mass production of inexpensive coal, iron ore, and flux, which often had to be transported over considerable distances, required an equally well-developed rail network. I do not wish to dwell on the work of the Russian technical intelligentsia on the railroads; that is not my area of expertise. I will say only that the development of the European part of the Russian railroad network and its operation grew hand-in-hand with the southern mining industry, often with the close cooperation of the southern mining industrialists represented by the Association of Southern Coal and Steel Producers.

This is how a part of the young Russian intelligentsia at the turn of the century, trained in the technical sciences, found in the southern mining industry what the Russian intelligentsia had previously lacked: invigorating work in pursuit of a practical "cause." This technical intelligentsia had no industrial experience and only a very limited experience of real life. The Donets Basin from 1895 on developed very rapidly, and its demand for technically trained personnel increased greatly; the old local industry was insignificant, from the standpoint of its size, its organization, and its technique. There were no industrial or technological traditions there. The foreign technicians brought their own habits and techniques, which almost always were inappropriate for Russian conditions. There was an urgent need to create some kind of synthesis from all these difficult and peculiar conditions. It fell to the young Russian technical forces to resolve these thorny problems.

Looking back on these bygone times one may say that these men accomplished their task well. Now let us consider the curious and original tactics by which they achieved their goals.

CHAPTER TWO

My Early Career
in the Donets Basin
of Yesteryear

Life is not a trifle, not a joke
Life is not even a delight . . .
Life is a hard toil . . .
Fulfilling one's duty is the
thing one should care about.
—*Turgenev,* Faust

*I*mmediately after graduating from the Mining Institute, I had to fulfill my military obligation. I served in the Voronezh Infantry Regiment at Kharkov. Upon completing this service and qualifying as a reserve ensign, I started to look for an engineering job in one of the Donets Basin mines. All I could find in the fall of 1890 was a position as head miner for the "French Company" (the Rutchenko Coal Company) in their Shaft No. 19.[1] It was almost impossible to find an engineer's position in those days, as the industrial boom in the Basin started much later.

My first impressions of the mining life were rather distressing. Shaft No. 19 was the French Company's biggest producer, with its 1000–1200 workers and its large staff of junior employees, in spite of its old and worn out equipment.

My direct superior, mining engineer Ernest Aleksandrovich Shteding, who had been only two years ahead of me at the institute, departed just a month after I arrived.[2] This placed me in the senior position at that shaft and imposed upon me enormous responsibilities, as it seemed to me, because I had no experience either in the technical aspects of mining or in dealing with workers and employees. I remember being afraid of everything and sleeping horribly. I feared that the boilers would blow up, that gas would explode, and the shaft would cave in, that the

cable would snap; in other words, I imagined that every mining catas-
trophe could befall me. Almost every night I dreamt that as I descended
into the shaft the cable broke, plunging me into the pit, and every night
I woke up sweating.

My fears were well grounded in the realities of the situation. The
winter of 1891 was exceptionally cold and the main shaft that housed
the cage (we called it the *trunk*) was frozen solid much of the way down.
The outside air that ventilated the mine came through this shaft, and
it was extremely cold in the winter. The walls of the shaft were always
wet, either from leaching water or from water splashing out of the tanks
with which we removed water from below: instead of using pumps we
lifted the water up in iron tanks suspended from the cages. Consequently, that winter the shaft was so frozen that the cages, which
hung on special cables, sometimes jammed in the ice on their way
down. In that situation they were supported by the ice alone above a
400 foot precipice (the whole shaft was about 650 feet deep). One of
my duties as head miner was to inspect the trunk before the 6 o'clock
shift began. The cage would descend slowly so that the mine's carpenter,
who accompanied me, and I could inspect the walls of the pit carefully,
estimating the amount of overgrown ice. Sometimes the cage would
stop, and we would notice that the cable (made of a heavy alloy) was
coiling on the roof of our cage. This meant that we were being supported
by the ice alone, and that if the weight of the motionless cage, combined
with the weight of the cable, broke that ice, then a fall was inevitable
and the cable would certainly break. In such cases, when the mechanic
above noticed that the engine was turning idly and the cage was standing
still, he would reverse the cable's direction, lift the cage to a certain
height, an then let it go crashing down at full speed to break the ice.
We would fall headlong, barely able to protect ourselves from the horrible jolts. All of these "manipulations," unavoidable given the kind of
equipment we had at the time and the round-the-clock operations, were
frightfully dangerous and, at the very least, extremely unpleasant. It is
a wonder that I did not dream of that precipitous descent every night.

On Sundays and holidays the ice was knocked down the shaft. Two
carpenters would take up their positions on one of the iron tanks I just
mentioned, which were attached to the floor of the cage by long, flat
iron bars. With miner's hacks the carpenters chopped at the ice, which
fell crashing down the shaft with a tremendous roar. Up above, the
mechanic carefully lowered the cage or stopped it as signaled by the
carpenters. On one occasion when I went to the shaft during such an
operation, I found the *verkhovoi* in a state of great agitation. The carpenters had not signaled in a long time, had not answered to his shouts

and in fact, had given no sign of life whatsoever. The *verkhovoi* was a senior miner who had command of everything at the top concerning traffic, including the movement of the cages: no mechanic could move a stopped cage without the *verkhovoi's* order. Only a very experienced and authoritative workman was appointed to become a *verkhovoi*.

His concern indicated how serious the situation was. Really, the lack of signals from below could mean only one thing: the carpenters who had stood on the edges of the tanks, all slippery with ice, had fallen into the shaft. While I stood there no answer came from below, in spite of our calls, so we decided to lift the cage, with great care and very slowly; if the carpenters were still on top of the tank they would surely let us know. But there was no signal at all, and our worst fears were confirmed when we lifted the cage all the way up and found nobody standing on the tank. This meant that the unfortunate carpenters had indeed fallen the length of the shaft, to a certain death. I was in complete despair. This was "my" first accident, and it was such a terrible one. Suddenly, to my amazement, the *verkhovoi* rushed to the tanks shouting curses, which seemed most strange under the circumstances, and a minute later both carpenters appeared from inside the tank, looking ghostly in their frozen cloaks. As we later learned, instead of splitting the ice they had been sleeping in perfect safety inside the frigid tank. "Kindly forgive us your lordship,[3] we drank a bit, and then the wasps started buzzing in our heads, so we took a little nap."

Generally speaking, the reaction of the miners, especially the experienced ones, to the often mortal dangers of this work was incredible flippancy or even bravado. I remember that one time the executive director of the mine, the French engineer Barbier, told me that it would be a good idea to have a look at the old ventilation gallery, which might be blocked with rubble. He warned me not to crawl into any conspicuously dangerous sections under any circumstances. So I picked my way through the gallery together with the airman (the foreman in charge of ventilation) until we reached a point where all the timbering was ruined and where the slightest mistake could produce, if not a total collapse, at least an avalanche of loose rocks that would bury both of us. So I decided to give up, and ordered the foreman to go "uphill," as the miners call the ascent to the surface. As I later learned, after accompanying me to the trunk, the foreman returned and crept through the ventilation gallery. "At certain places," he reported, "I had to force my way through broken timber, and it cracked all around me like shots." God knows why he did it—nobody had sent him, and he certainly was not looking to gain favor. Most probably he had been attracted by the novelty; even novelties such as this helped to break up the monotony of mining life.

The boredom, the monotony, of this exceptionally dull life were truly debilitating. All around was the steppe, flat as a board, lacking even so much as a gulch, in the winter blindingly white, in the spring all black except for patches of snow. It was fair only in early summer when the wild peonies tinted the steppe red, and the song of hundreds of larks rang almost like chimes. But even this beauty was marred by the deliberately prosaic setting of the mine, which seemed incompatible with spring—especially the great mounds of grey-white rock, reeking of sulphur, where, through pale smoke, one watched the jerking outlines of the workman's figure, endlessly emptying wagonloads of rocks. I recall the strange sense of bondage that often seized me in my first years at the mine, most acutely in spring. I felt a strong urge to run away, and I was weary to tears.

A young engineer's private life was exceptionally hard in those days. My flat consisted of one room, divided in two by a wooden partition which did not reach the ceiling, on the other side of which lived an old servant. I had no horse for transportation, and the other engineers lived far away. I remember how once I was delighted when a horse needed to be taken out of the mine for a rest, and I was able to ride him. The ride was an uneasy one, however, as the horse was unused to the light and the features it disclosed; it was scared by everything and skittishly dodged mounds of snow or even shrubs.

My social circle consisted of poorly educated people, the junior mining staff. Their manners were such that once two of the "ladies" started a quarrel that led to blows. Even worse, the offended party came to me to complain, as I was the acting manager of the mine during Shteding's absence.

On Sundays the other engineers and I used to have lunch with the director, Barbier: being obliged to speak French, with foreigners, was not very relaxing. From time to time we could rest in our own environment; for example, when we went to Iuzovka[4] to visit the cultured family of Iuzovka's doctor or some other educated Russian family, but such people were rare in our neighborhood at that time.

Six months after I arrived, I departed the French Company for Karpov's mine,[5] where I was a sort of manager. The work was hard, mainly because of Karpov's character, of which I shall speak later. The living conditions were different—I had a flat and horses—but the environment was the same as before. A year later I took a post as the manager of Ilovaiskii's mine, of which I shall speak in detail later.

This dreary and difficult situation continued until 1895 when I departed to work for a big, new Belgian operation. The first five years of my career passed as a kind of nightmare. In such circumstances Russians often become alcoholics, and I know of not a few such cases, especially among mining engineers. But neither I nor my close associates and neighbors, with few exceptions, abandoned mining for the more sedate life of a civil servant. The work of a mining engineer yields a certain amount of spiritual satisfaction over time, if pursued persistently and methodically—qualities infrequently found among Russians, frankly. First of all, we were very close to the workers. By and by we felt them to be a sort of undifferentiated mining collective, bound to us by invisible but sturdy threads. This body, composed of barely distinguishable individuals, possessed all the characteristics of the simple Russian people and, once these were understood, working with them was not only easy but often pleasant. Moreover, constant work in a given location produced a feeling of kinship with the mine itself, as it was the place of one's creativity. Every aspect of mining work, even the peculiar air of the mine, had its invigorating charms.

Few people are aware of the conditions under which the mining engineers lived and worked. For this reason I shall describe the work and way of living of the mining engineer and also that of the coal worker, this "miner" who was perceived as a threat to peace and order both at the mine and in the village.

First of all I must underscore one of the main characteristics of the Donets Basin mining engineers' outlook: among South Russian engineers, professional ethics required unreproachable loyalty to the owner. Throughout my long career, where I was in touch with hundreds of mining engineers whom I observed under everyday conditions, I never came across dishonest people, with only one or two exceptions. Such people immediately became social outcasts.

Relations with the management, with subordinates, and with colleagues followed a distinctive pattern in the southern mining region. These relations were influenced neither by tradition, which did not exist, nor by Western European models brought in by the many Europeans who flocked to the Donets Basin later on. Such typically Western features as coolness and the inflexibility of disciplined obedience insulted the Russian sense of freedom and were silently discarded. Under Russian conditions the rigor of ranks was replaced by a form of partnership that reconciled the strictness of labor discipline with the need to respect the subordinate's personality, even in the details of everyday routine. In addition, I can confirm after observing foreigners working in Russia for many years, that they quickly submitted to the soothing influence of the Russian atmosphere.

There was another way in which the Russian engineers' attitude toward workers differed even more sharply from that of the Western Europeans. The relationship between the workers and the engineer was direct and personal, due to the absence of labor organizations, and to the fact that most workers were peasants who had not entirely severed their links to the land and who came to the mine seeking wages on a seasonal basis, some in the summer, others in winter. The small contractual or *artel* organizations did not interfere with this relationship, as they were very short-lived and often fell apart only to reappear with a new composition.[6] Finally, the Russian workmen liked and appreciated this direct sort of relationship, and I may say with no exaggeration that the mining engineers were able to win the strong sympathy of the workers. The overwhelming majority of engineers paid close attention to the workers, and could not avoid paying attention to the often depressing details of the workers' living conditions. The worker brought from his village all the peculiarities of the *muzhik's* way of life, and inevitably he darkened this with the characteristics of the "mining life." If Chekhov found that in the village, people "guzzled vodka hellishly, and that there was a horrible lot of filth both moral and physical," there was much more of all this in the mines, and this is why the miner had such an unsavory reputation. I must say, after years of close relationships with Russian miners, that this reputation was not really deserved. Basically they were neither worse nor better than the Russian *muzhiks*, with all their defects and all of their often exceptionally fine qualities as well. Chekhov describes this Russian *muzhik* excellently:

> The majority of them were nervous, irritated, offended people. Their imagination was depressed, they were ignorant, with a poor, dull mental outlook, with the same unceasing thoughts about the gray earth, the gray days, the black bread; they were cunning people, but like birds used to hide only their heads beside a tree; they were unable to count. . . . It is true that there was filth, and drunkenness, foolishness, and cheating, yet one felt that the *muzhik's* life in general grew from a strong, healthy stem . . . upon a closer look you felt that there was something fundamental in him, something highly important . . . that is . . . he believed the essential thing on earth was truth, that his own salvation and the salvation of all the people is truth alone, and this is why he loved justice above all.[7]

Indeed, the Russian miner appreciated justice from his superiors, and he was able to understand it, even in those cases where justice contradicted his own interests. In this sense he was quite steadfast and reliable. This unusual, and I might add, peculiar, quality of the Russian people made working with them easy even in the miserable conditions that prevailed in the mine settlements at that time. The workers' sensitivity to fairness compelled one to stay on his toes, as there was no label a Russian worker could bestow more insulting than "unfair."

Another thing eased the relationship between the intelligentsia and the "simple people," between the *"barin"* and the *muzhik*.[8] To the *muzhik*-miner, the engineer was not a *"barin,"* or at least he was not a *"barin"* who was hoarding much-needed land. The engineer was not seen to be confiscating anything from the miner. Moreover, the engineer wielded considerable authority, as he paid a good salary (both a larger and a more reliable income than any other) and supervised a dangerous and complicated network of operations almost incomprehensible to the individual worker. The engineer often behaved, in his own way, like a fair and good *"barin."* Doubtlessly the "closeness" of the worker and the engineer was enhanced by the fact that the work was not only continuous but carried out in the workers' own backyard, that all were united by the darkness, the dampness, and the discomfort of the mine, as well as by the utilitarian costume everybody wore.

In these primitive and inevitably harsh conditions, and with the ever-present dangers looming over everybody, individuals of quite different background grew so close that there was no longer "miner" and "engineer"; we felt this closeness deeply in the course of our work. In the special conditions of coal mining there were no grounds for the rough and scornful attitude toward the "little brother" all too common in Old Russia.

Some almost forgotten vignettes may illustrate the actual relationship between engineer and worker.

The time was about 1892 or 1893, the place was the Makeevka Mine, owned at that time by the heirs of the well-known Ivan Grigor'evich Ilovaiskii, a very rich and very original Russian character.[9] He was represented by Chekhov in his story, "The Steppe" as the character Varlamov—a man always touring the limitless steppe, a man everybody needed to see, whom nobody could ever get hold of.

At that time I was the manager of the "Sergei" pit, supervising about 1000 workers, almost all of whom were Little Russians from the provinces of Kharkov or Voronezh. They had typical Ukrainian features and the usual Ukrainian sense of humor, but an utterly inadequate understanding of the discipline needed for mining. They worked seasonally, so that there was a complete turnover of miners at Easter and again at *Pokrova* in October, during which times all the shafts stood idle for two or three weeks while virtually all the workers were away.[10] This unique system of "going away for wage work" involved whole villages and was an integral part of the village economy. These people were not the kind of "itinerant miners" typical of Tula or Orel.[11] Almost all of my seasonal miners worked well, exerting themselves especially hard for two to three months before their departure.

After the Easter break the newly arrived workers would register personally at the engineer's office. I would sit at my desk—the mine's office, like my house, was a converted workers' barracks; before me was a small window opening into the workers' waiting room. Smiling brown eyes inspect the room and light on me, and a man asks, "So is everybody alive and well? I'm here for a job!" "O.K., what's your name?" The man is offended: "How is it you don't know me, I worked for you last summer—Syrytsia."

And so it went with almost all of them, not the slightest awkwardness or pretense when dealing with their "superior."

At Trinity we would have a seasonal game: a "strike."[12] Every year at Trinity workers demanded a pay increase, which just as regularly was refused. But the strike was a tradition, it was impossible to avoid it. The strike always followed the same ritual: a week before Trinity, the workers who all lived in barracks without families forsook these quarters for the steppe, where they set up a sort of real gypsy camp. In this encampment littered with bags and baggage the miners ate dinner, slept, washed, dressed in their work clothes or on Sundays in their "clean" clothes. In the evenings they played games accompanied by lots of noisy howling and whistling, boisterously egging each other on in every conceivable way.

Every evening I had to cross this colony on my way home from the main office. I would be on horseback, a custom in this Don Cossack region. Every evening they would stop me, surrounding me in a narrow circle, start to complain about the poor wages, and threaten to leave for agricultural work. They always requested a discussion with the actual "owner" [*khoziain*]. This tradition also had to be fulfilled. But the faces were calm, even jovial, as I would try to explain to them that their demands were unreasonable because the wages had been established at Easter for the whole summer, and that they had accepted them. Nobody paid much attention to me, however—the steppe was so wonderful, the evening air was so mild, it was so good to be out in the open air after the filthy barracks—I would just touch my horse, the men would step aside, and I would slowly ride away. The crowd would break up with a commotion, as the men returned to whatever occupation my arrival had interrupted.

The meeting with the owner, one of Ilovaiskii's sons who was a partner in the mine, usually would be arranged for the third day of Trinity before the work started; the setting would be a large square in the fields between the shafts. Workers from all the shafts gathered there at the appointed time, as did I and my neighbor, the engineer M. M. Kovan'ko, manager of the Capital shaft, each of us leading our own miners, as was the tradition. Not only were we the "eyes" of the owner, but also we were the responsible experts in case conflict occurred. Surrounded by a retinue of subordinates the owner arrived in a cavalcade, imparting a touch of solemnity to the scene that our Ukrainians obviously appreciated. There were no "delegates" to address the boss, as relations at that time did not require delegates. If the demands were serious enough, if there were complaints about irregularities, then the complainers themselves spoke out; if there were no serious complaints, then the crowd shouted out a demand for a general wage hike. This the owner refused with a joke. After two or three hours this ceremony usually would end peacefully.

I do recall, however, a certain Trinity when the miners' mood was more serious, as I could discern in advance. The "game" could turn violent under these circumstances, because a crowd after all, is a crowd. In this case it was necessary to invite a detachment of Cossack soldiers to this meeting with the boss ahead of time. The next day work always resumed as if nothing had ever happened, and it continued without interruption throughout the summer until October.

The Great Russian workers with whom I had to work in other mines (usually from Tula or Orel) were less sociable, more gloomy and much rougher than the Little Russians; and during strikes the former were much more unpleasant. But even among them the engineer's personal authority was very high, and only in exceptional cases did a confrontation result in personal insolence, which the other workers usually disapproved on the spot.

I recall that once I happened to be present at a discussion between striking workers and my neighbor and friend, engineer L. G. Rabinovich.[13] One of the workers standing in the front row was not only smoking during this conversation, which in those days was considered insolent, but he was not averting his head when he blew out the smoke. Rabinovich yanked the cigarette from his hand and threw it away. I saw in the eyes of the people that they not only understood Rabinovich's action, but approved of it.

Rabinovich was a Jew, and it is noteworthy that our people, the workers as well as the local peasants, never singled out his Jewishness in any way—they all appreciated and liked him as a fair and simple *"barin."* In fact, the peasants of Chutino village, where Rabinovich lived and managed the Maksimov Mine, took it into their heads to build a church, and appointed him chairman of the building committee; thus the Jew Rabinovich came to construct an Orthodox church.

*T*he plague of the miner's life was heavy drinking after the monthly paydays; sometimes work stopped for two or three days. Engineers who were managing the mines had to fight this ubiquitious Russian evil in various ways, starting at the village level, but often without result. We struggled to have the village inns closed on paydays, and later even the state-owned liquor stores—we bribed the neighboring villagers to enforce closing orders against the stores. Finally, we resorted to the measures practiced at the Makeevka Mine, where the traditions established by old Ilovaiskii were still in place. We stopped paying workers their entire monthly wage, even though the law required us to do so, giving them instead small sums for their everyday expenses and sending money to their families from the office. We paid the full balance only twice a year, at Easter and at *Pokrova* when the workers were in such a hurry to get home that even with relatively big sums of money in their pockets, there was no drinking. This illegal practice was the most efficient way to combat alcoholism, but it gave the engineers a lot of extra trouble.[14]

Later I will speak at greater length about the valuable cooperation with the Russian worker that I experienced during the construction of the Verovka mine between 1895 and 1899. I can say right now, however, that when I look back on the long course of my professional life, in spite of the harshness of the Russian way of life, I feel only a sincere sympathy for the Russian worker, and especially for the mining "master," a category in which I would include all those workers who had some responsible position. Such men invariably were gifted mechanics, endowed with an all-round talent and able to learn quickly. I would watch as some clumsy young peasant, who arrived staring in amazement at this oddity that was the mine shaft, transformed himself in a two- or three-year period into a first-class coal hewer, an excellent timberman, or a foreman [*desiatnik*], a perfect master of the mysteries hidden in a coal seam. With great ease and poise this master coal hewer or timberman could show you his work. Or the foreman would guide you, his chief, through his quarters; and in the mysterious and often sinister darkness of the mine you would feel that it was he who knew better, more certainly, this business he had mastered almost to perfection.

The miner who became a "man" [*vybravshiisia v "liudi"*[15]], a master—whether he was a foreman, a mechanic, a hewer, or a timberman—often was just a simple worker, but steady and self-controlled. Such a person was part of the minority, of the spiritual aristocracy of the mine. His demeanor quickly changed: his dwelling would most likely be an individual flat or a small house, shining with its white-washed walls, decorated with some pictures, some decent furniture, and around the house some flowers and young trees made their appearance. The master of the house donned a coat when he was not on duty. Yesterday's peasant was now crystallizing into an industrial worker.

The rest of the mining "brotherhood," the majority of the miners, the hopeless bumpkins, lived in barracks: these were the unskilled workers. They usually had strong links with the village; they were in fact, really just peasants seeking seasonal jobs. For them the mine was a foreign place, just a place to earn a few extra rubles. A somewhat different category were those cases like Makeevka, where whole villages worked a mine seasonally. For the most part, however, those who sought mining jobs were the ones who had been squeezed out of the village by overpopulation, those whose farm work could easily be done by someone else. These, in a sense, were the superfluous folk of the village—the victims of agrarian overpopulation. Such people were left with the confused feeling that they were useless to the village, that they were cut off from their natural surroundings and their family. They could not cope with the new work and frequently took on the outlook of vagrants, becoming untidy both in their inner life and in their personal appearance. They were always ready to drink or even to get drunk, they worked poorly, and they were often absent. Only very strict discipline could keep such people in order.

This type of miner exhibited all the defects of Chekhov's or Bunin's *muzhik:* a depressed imagination, a dull brooding frame of mind. It seemed as if these people lacked something essential, strong, and basic: perhaps the *muzhik* way of life had never given them any kind of economic "upbringing," which was the root of the peasant psychology. They were incredibly ignorant; it seemed that neither religion nor tradition had left any trace on their souls. They were somber, and if not empty, at least they were not touched by anything, living more by instinct than by reason. It is worth noting that the miners' life was in a way repeating the stratification that existed among the village *muzhiks.* This was clear in the consequences of such stratification: the mine was producing its own *"kulaks,"* that typical phenomenon of the Russian village. The accession of a lucky or a gifted miner to a higher situation often resulted, especially in those days, in moral corruption. As soon as he acquired a bit of power, a peasant began to plunder, abuse, and ruthlessly exploit his lesser "brothers," reserving the best positions for his close relatives and bestowing positions on strangers only in exchange for bribes. When one of these former "brothers" wielded executive power in a mine, as often happened in the smaller concerns, exploitation and injustice could reach monstrous proportions. Let me illustrate this with an example. When I went to work at Makeevka (Ilovaiskii's mine), I was appointed as head of the big Sergei shaft, which had been directed by an illiterate, self-made man, Pankrat' Kovalenko, a former foreman. He was a typical *muzhik-kulak*, who had grown incredibly fat. His relatives and pals ran the whole "administration." Miners regularly had to pay for the better working positions. This Pankrat' had grown so lazy that he never even descended into the shaft. He had devised a system of signals to be given by a specially appointed watchman for coping with unexpected visits from superiors. When he got the word that "they're coming!" Pankrat' rubbed his face and hands with coal and waited with a mining lamp in his hand at the entrance to the mine: the zealous manager was just "returning" from the mine.

The uncleanliness and filth in the barracks was so awful that, when I decided to inspect them in my first days as manager, the above-ground senior miner [*poverkhnostnyi*] warned me threateningly: fleas. In fact, after visiting three or four such barracks, I had suffered innumerable bites and noticed with horror that the tops of my high boots were alive, so to speak. I had to struggle long and hard to rid the mine of Pankrat''s legacy. It was a difficult and unpleasant task.

The life of an unskilled miner living in the barracks was undoubtedly hard, but was this not due in large measure to his own peculiar outlook? Were the way of life, the tradition, the outlook of the village any better? I am inclined to think that the lifestyle of the Russian village was very often, if not always, much harder. The mine offered enormous advantages, the main one being a good and secure income; an able man with a strong and tenacious character, whose will had not been dulled by the *muzhik* mentality, had a good chance of making it. If family housing was lacking at the mine, he could always rent a flat in the neighboring village for a small sum, which often was done. The miners' living conditions improved every year, and the number of small private houses for families was growing very quickly. The wage of even an unskilled miner in the nineties was about 1 ruble per shift, which was far more than the annual income in the villages.[16]

And how did people live in the village? If one's own observations, or those of Chekhov or Bunin, lack color, village life is described with pitiless realism by Pod"iachev.[17] Himself a *muzhik*, he says:

> Everybody not only avoids each other, in fact they all hate each other with incredible viciousness. If someone is grieving then the others are glad. It is an inexhaustible theme for conversations. Everyone is watching

everyone else, where did he go, what did he do, what did he eat, what did he drink?

Vodka, what's vodka in the village, and how do they drink it? Vodka, that's everything. . . . For vodka one would do anything. . . . They drink because no one is sure of his own life, no one is sure of standing on his own feet.

The fear of life compels one to drink; indeed, if there's only one hour left, at least it's mine . . .

In my memory there are a few similar recollections. Sometimes I was able to get close to the life of the village, as I was not the type of person to inspire hostility. I remember how in the early 1900s during the summer I had to do some surveying near a small steppe village in the Bakhmut district, which was populated by half-Great Russians [*poluvelikorossami*] (there are such people). Before I was situated in my own accommodations, I had to spend two or three nights at the home of the *muzhik* considered to be the cleanest; in fact, in spite of all possible precautions, I could barely close an eye because of the stuffiness, the unbearable stench and a whole assembly of creeping and biting insects. I had to spend most of the night sitting outdoors—a joy, the nights were wonderful. My landlords slept just as badly. The master of the house used to follow me to the yard, take up a seat next to me and entertain me with conversation. What did he talk about, in a sort of confidential whisper? In the village I was not only a new man, but an interesting one as well, because I brought with me the opportunity to make some easy money. Naively, in an effort to gain my confidence, and considering me an utter simpleton like every *"barin,"* he told me what thieves and drunks his neighbors were, and what drastic caution I should take when supervising the surveys: "they'll carry everything off and drink it up."

When I sent the old village elder to the nearby town for some shopping with 50 rubles, people shook their heads: "he'll drink and bring back nothing—oh no he won't, the old woman went along to keep and eye on him." Sure enough, the old woman did go along, and the next day they returned safely, the old man only slightly drunk.

About two months later, having almost finished the survey, I was preparing to leave that village—which in fact was no worse than any other—when I was struck by an unusual agitation that had seized this normally sleepy population. *Muzhiks* and *babas*[18] wandered from house to house in groups, arguments broke out, and there were more drunks than usual. Finally I saw the railroad station policeman, with two witnesses, going worriedly from house to house. I finally learned that our village collectively had plundered an entire freight car full of goods from the nearby station, and the commotion I had seen had resulted from trying to divide the spoils. My host turned out to be one of the leaders of this enterprise.

True, the living conditions in our villages were often very hard—an inefficient agriculture carried out on plots of communal land or else on expensive rented holdings, poor harvests, a miserable income, seasonal work outside the village entailing long separations from families, petty and often brutal personal relationships, all against a backdrop of ignorance and hopeless poverty.[19] Money was a rare luxury in the village. Whenever there was any, it was safest to hide it from the master of the house, as the temptation to drink it up was just too strong.

*R*ussian public opinion was often, if not always, rather biased in this regard, and therefore usually unfair. It considered the miner's life tantamount to imprisonment with hard labor and dwelled on the unsatisfactory living conditions, particularly the poor housing at the mines. In fact, housing often was poor, especially the barracks. This can be explained by the fact that the Donets Basin coal operations were located in an area of sparse population, where people had never before worked in mines; therefore the mine had to build living quarters for all of its workers. These expenses, which were unknown in the West to such an extent, were a serious drain on the enterprise's capital. One should also keep in mind the physical uncleanliness of our peasant, especially if he were a bachelor. He was capable of turning a decent lodging into a virtual cesspool, as was the fate of the model barracks built at the Verovka mine.[20]

The public conception of the profits earned by the coal companies was equally unfair. Although the public thought our profits exceedingly high, in fact, the Donets Basin coal mines (except for a few individual cases, especially the big joint-stock companies) came close to being unprofitable. For example, in the exceptionally favorable year 1911 the coal companies' average profits reached about 6 percent of basic capital, according to *Mining and Metallurigical Industry of South Russia* by Professor P. I. Fomin.[21] Such a small return must be considered a virtual loss for coal companies, which bore so much risk. Generally speaking, none of Russian heavy industry could be profitable at this time, for many reasons, whereas certain branches of light industry could be. The main problems were the weakness and instability of the domestic market and the economic policy of the government, which itself was a major consumer, especially of the products of heavy industry. The government was the greatest consumer of coal and iron, which it used to supply the state-owned railroads, the navy, and the army. The state took advantage of its position to depress prices, mercilessly driving down the prices for other customers as well.

We mining engineers of the Donets Basin greatly resented this public hostility, whose ostensible cause was the alleged exploitation of the workers. In the public mind our real fault was that we were industrialists.

The mere presence of the mines, their accompanying life-style, and what they brought to the life of the region—all these were perceived as an evil. This was a typical example of the Russian intellectual's age-old hostility and even hatred of industry, of any kind of accumulation, and of wealth, which always aroused suspicion. They always combined this hostility with the obligation to shed a sympathetic tear for the "little brother." This irresponsible attitude contained a good deal of ignorance and deliberate willingness to ignore the facts. The cities, and especially the capitals, knew nothing about the provinces, indeed, knew nothing about Russia.

We engineers, who were devoting almost all our lives to establishing a healthier, sounder Russian economy, were in a position to view the life of the people more realistically. Our view of Russian life as it was lived in the villages was devoid of romantic populism; together we were trying to prepare people for more responsible and skilled labor, and to some extent for a new way of life, in spite of all the conflicts and difficulties imposed by the old habits. It seemed to us that our people were almost completely devoid of what is usually called *culture*. But deeply hidden inside these people there usually was some excellent foundation, which only needed a strict education in some alternative way of making a living. The old way of life had not given them schooling of any kind.

The bulk of the Russian peasants were far from the cultural level created in Western Europe by centuries of steady, if often rote, teaching. Specifically, the Russian was almost hopelessly behind his Western counterpart in the way the latter carries out his work systematically and stubbornly—and almost with exaltation. For the Russian peasant, in fact, for Russians in general, work is still God's punishment. But the Russians have a wealth of "good nature" that will enable them to overcome many difficulties. Says Korolenko[22] in his letters to Belokonskii, "The Russians have little culture, especially the culture of morals, but that is life. The Russian is good at heart, although he is still too inclined to vice."

CHAPTER THREE

Russian Heavy Industry
in the Old Days

Makeevka Mine (1892–1895)

I had the chance to observe two sharply distinct periods in the mining industry of Southern Russia; up to 1895–1896 it was dull, with insignificant production, scarcely noticeable growth and habits conspicuously reflecting the out-of-the-way mode of life of a remote province. There was no new construction, everything was conducted in an old-fashioned, small-scale way; there was no foreign or even new capital in the industry whatsoever. Coal and iron were scarcely needed—there were no consumers, almost no factories, and the railroad network was still very weak.

The mines had poor communications, nor was there so much as a neighborhood nearby. People at the mine lived in heavy boredom, the only entertainment consisting in paying one another visits for cards and vodka. The majority had no interests; the regular "provincial" was moved only by a drink of vodka, lovingly referred to as his "glass-warmer," and by the macao card game renamed "makakusha." For me this characterized the Ilovaiskii brothers' Makeevka Mine at the beginning of the nineties. The head of the mine was then Dmitrii Ivanovich Ilovaiskii, who had a mining engineer's degree, but had never practiced.[1]

Dmitrii Ivanovich—a very good-looking man, but with a heavy, massive sort of masculine handsomeness, aged thirty-five or forty, a Cossack-aristocrat with a bovine stare, curly hair, and a stern appearance—was in fact the independent master of the enterprise; his father, the well-known Ivan Grigor'evich Ilovaiskii, a very rich landowner of the Donets region who had founded the mining business, was dead by then, and Dmitrii Ivanovich's brothers did not interfere in the mine's direction. Formerly, before my arrival, the duties of the director had been accomplished by Andrei Nikolaevich Glebov, a transport engineer very well-known in the South. He was the Ilovaiskiis' partner in the ownership of the mine. I never met him, but heard a lot of legends about his management. Living about 25 versts away from the mine at Ilovaiskii's country estate, Zuevka, Glebov used to arrive at the mine in a wild troika amidst great uproar and ringing of bells, either late at night or at dawn—these unexpected visits were the way he "controlled" the works.[2] Glebov loved to embarrass his employees by oddities, surprises, and tricks, but never with malice (he was good natured in spite of his extravagance). People told how one summer morning he arrived at Khartsyzsk railroad station, encountered the director of the Mining Department enroute to the Caucasus, and invited the director to visit his mine. The director (a high-ranking person in the mining profession) was a very well-known person, privy councilor K. M. Skal'kovskii, and as a result of this visit he had to wait several hours for the next train.[3] The head engineer [of Makeevka Mine], Sutulov, was considered the manager, so to speak, but he never ran the mine in reality, as he was exceedingly lazy. Living near the main office, far away from the shaft, Sutulov used to wake up very late and (so people said) sat sunning himself at the entrance of his house in a sort of "negligee," covered only by his wife's bed jacket.

"Vladimir Grigor'evich," says Glebov as he approached the manager and noted his costume, "I will introduce you to the director of the Mining Department who has just arrived and sits in my office."

"We know you well, what director?" said Sutulov, rising and moving toward the office, persuaded that, as usual, Glebov had prepared one of his tricks, and that he was about to encounter a contractor, or even a supplier who was a Jew, instead of Skal'kovskii.[4] When he realized his error, Sutulov, who was terribly scared of any authority, disappeared like smoke, and in a few minutes was back, to be presented to Skal'kovskii in full uniform, his sword hanging at his side. Whenever he recounted this "trick" of Glebov Sutulov invariably added, "On the other hand, nobody ever presented himself to the director of the department as I did."

Sutulov also was no longer at the mine when I arrived—he had left to become a civil servant, a position that suited him better; he served as a state mine surveyor at Iuzovka.

In fact, we engineers at the Makeevka Mine had no real boss—Dmitrii Ivanovich Ilovaiskii seldom came to the mine, fully trusting us, and never interfered in current operations. Whenever we met, he limited himself to a few questions and bits of advice, but never gave instructions or orders. A calm man, rather lazy, tall, and a genuine *barin*, Dmitrii Ivanovich disliked any sort of disturbance—during my stay he never once descended underground, in fact he never even went to the shaft. And in spite of all this Dmitrii Ivanovich was an exceptionally capable administrator and a clever businessman—he knew perfectly how to select the people he needed and put them to work almost jokingly; we valued his approval highly, he had a great knack for selling coal (which he did all by himself), and all in all he directed this big firm expertly. But for all that he was virtually a stranger to us, because of the infrequency of his visits to the mine, because of the scale on which he lived, and because of the sphere of his personal relationships, about which we knew nothing.[5]

Our life at the mine was quite different. The social environment for junior engineers such as M. M. Kovan'ko and myself was restricted both at work and after work to our colleagues, mainly four childless couples, all older than we were: the head of the main office, A. G. Obraztsov; the cashier, I. A. Tomanovich; the doctor, A. I. Datskov; and an engineer who had the same functions as Sutulov and who performed them in a similar spirit, D. D. Ornatskii. All of them were married, so our society included four ladies . . . and no children. This was odd, and underscored the strangeness of our "life-style"—we had married people, but in fact there were no families. We met, sometimes in different combinations, almost every day—it was too boring for Kovan'ko or myself to sit alone at home after the monotonous and tiresome mining work. Melancholy and boredom drove us out *anywhere*, and even if we did not ride beyond the outskirts of the mine, which happened only rarely, we found ourselves come nightfall at the "estate," where the office was and where the employees lived, or at the hospital, or else, most frequently, at the home of the accountant Obraztsov or the doctor Datskov. Both were rather smart, cultured people who read a lot; it was interesting, especially at the beginning of our visit, to have a chat or a discussion with them. Both of them were philistine leftists, but in different ways: Obraztsov use to "fill his soul" with Shchedrin, but was not only utterly indifferent to the people, he even used to make disgusted faces when talking to the miners. Datskov was rather a populist while a student, having been brought up on Mikhailovskii and *Russian Wealth:* he considered mining work an inevitable evil and used to mourn over the miner's fate. Both hated Alexander III and his regime—Obraztsov could not bear Witte, who was then a rising power, and called him "Wittie," for some reason. These were moods rather than confirmed opinions, and although lasting, were quite inactive in the given environment and absolutely harmless; they were a sort of respectable intellectual suit of clothes, a subject for conversation around a glass and a game of vint, a diversion from the overwhelming boredom and the callous indifference of everybody to everything.[6]

Nevertheless both of them, characters quite typical of those times, deserve some attention, especially Obraztsov who later worked many years for me as the head of the commercial division at the Maksimov Mine.

A. G. Obraztsov, or Abra as my children, who were great friends of his, were to call him, was almost an old man when he was at Makeevka. He had features reminiscent of Vasili Shuiskii, a typical Russian of the northern provinces, with a thin beard and whiskers—a "clever courtier" as malevolent people used to call him.[7] He was scrupulously honest, very competent in business, and a skillful accountant; he was not at all a favor seeker, but was genuinely affectionate toward positions and people who were his "superiors"—those who took on the responsibilities of professional life with its stresses and hurly-burly, all of which were unbearable to him. At Makeevka he was Dmitrii Ivanovich Ilovaiskii's faithful servant and later was inseparably attached to me, although I was much younger than he. He was something of a sybarite, admiring precision, order, and above all, calm, both in his private and in his professional life. He was a liberal because at the time this was easier and more convenient, which explains his toleration of the wicked, cold, rather indifferent satire of Shchedrin. His wife (whom he had married in the civil ceremony fashionable at the time), Varvara Mikhailovna, was a wonderful, simple, cultured woman with a very interesting personality, who later became a dear friend of my wife's and our whole family's. After her husband's death she came to spend a week at our house, but never left and continued to live with us until she herself died.

Quite a different man was Aleksandr Osipovich Datskov, our mine doctor. Educated in the spirit of the active "populism" of the seventies, but a cunning *"khokhol,"* he would have been "eager to fight" had there been the slightest occasion for it at the mine. Had he been a zemstvo doctor, especially one of those in charge of dealing with epidemics, where conditions demanded a real "struggle," he would have been an eager opponent and enemy of the very "order" he had accepted.[8] From his point of view we engineers were involuntary slaveowners, and his attitude toward us was somewhat condescending, although in a Russian, good-hearted way, especially when his beloved "glasswarmer" was at hand. His wife, an "incorruptible populist" as she liked to describe herself, was far more intolerant and fanatical.

When people gathered at the Obraztsovs' they usually played cards, almost always gambling games, which Obraztsov and Kovan'ko passionately enjoyed; the latter, with the Olympian calm of the true gambler, was able to lose everything, and he lost some evenings up to a few hundred rubles, out of a monthly income of 200 rubles; happily, because the game continued, he usually won again and the balance was not so catastrophic.

At the Datskovs' house we did not play cards—he and his wife viewed card games with utter disdain. But there, to keep in tune with the people, we "drank well," in Datskov's affectionate phrase, swallowing each time "forty eighths of an eye."[9] After dinner with vodka, and the resulting pitiful conversations, people sang, usually Nekrasov's verses.[10]

Other members of our community, such as the Tomanoviches and Ornatskiis, people with no ideological convictions, lived similarly, of course. Tomanovich, the kindest person in the world, was a Montenegrin and spoke Russian poorly and with a thick accent, although he had lived in Russia for about three decades. He and his wife (Klavdiia Il'inishna), Kisia,[11] as he used to call her, were exceptionally open-hearted and hospitable, both were simple and kind; he did not like drinking, but was a passionate gambler, although he preferred vint to the Obraztsovs' makakusha. I can still picture him in front of me with his glittering black eyes, nervously petting his beautiful side whiskers after a masterfully played rubber.

The Ornatskiis were typical "homebodies," probably because the restless Dmitrii Dmitrievich preferred drinking alone. Indeed, he was quite unbearable if even slightly drunk, and he loved drinking.

When a larger crowd gathered, including young men and young ladies from neighboring mines or plants, there was less drinking, no card playing, often some dancing, and sometimes debating—as Chekhov wrote about the mining life of those times, "the youth always hotly debated things which they did not understand, and these debates turned out badly. People argued noisily, but it is peculiar that nowhere else could one find people who were in fact so indifferent and carefree as they were here. It seemed as though they had no country, no religion, no social concerns." Such was the course of our life—absurd, in fact, and for a young man, even dangerous.

I leave Makeevka, Marry, and Look for a Job

When I ponder the sum of my life at the mines in those first years of my engineering career, I see that after my student years, after the brilliant atmosphere of Petersburg, I was obliged to spend long years in the rugged conditions prevailing in the provinces in those days. Russia's political and spiritual life progressed far away from us, unnoticed and ignored. It was only gradually, thanks to changes in my personal life, that I started to become more conscious of a different Russia, mainly the capital and the big cities. A happy circumstance helped me to escape from this provincial bog.

That circumstance was my marriage. Here I am obliged to disclose purely personal memories, which are outside the scope of my assignment here. So I shall limit my story to a strict summary of the facts, even if this is in sharp contradiction to my wishes.

Having married the niece of Iuzovka's factory doctor, I left Makeevka and went with my wife to Petersburg to find a job.[12] I had almost no money and did not want to ask my parents for any, as they were not rich people. Nevertheless, I did not want to stay in Makeevka, as I felt that neither my future career nor my new private life were compatible with the Makeevka environment.

Both I and my wife, a twenty-year-old woman who had been brought up in a very protected family circle, were absolutely inexperienced concerning the realities of life. She and I were overwhelmed by a feeling of disarray when, after "crossing the Rubicon," we found ourselves all alone in the growing darkness of the railroad car. We bid farewell to our old life, which I had no reason to regret, and hailed the unknown future. So ended the first part of my mining career.

We remained in Moscow for about a month, living in the Great Moscow Hotel. Here I was in Moscow with my wife, after the mining life that now seemed centuries away! In the morning we visited the Iverskaia, the Kremlin, the Tret'iakov Gallery, then lunched in the big white dining room of the hotel, with the waiters all dressed in white in the Moscow fashion, the band playing. In the evening there was the opera, the Malyi Theatre. All around us the wintery glittering of that wonderful town, and Russia was reborn after a long, dull hiatus. Everywhere, both outside, but especially inside of ourselves, it seemed a splendid holiday after the endless days of humdrum work.

In Petersburg the holiday gradually faded away—it having become urgent to find a position; not only had the money grown scarce, but having pawned my fur coat I was going about in a topcoat—fortunately, spring was at hand.

At this period, in the beginning of 1895, when foreign capital was just starting to penetrate the southern mining industry, it was very hard to find a mining engineer's position. Professors from the institute with whom I was on close terms, both the Times and our famous geologist Ivan Vasil'evich Mushketov, who liked me very much, were unable to help me at all. In the South there were only one or two foreign enterprises and they did not hire Russians at that point; in other regions, nothing was going on.

The Fenin family, circa 1910. Seated,
from left, the author (Aleksandr),
Leonid, Mme. Fenin (Karlotta),
Aleksandr, and Hella. Standing, from
left, Theodore and Marie.

A view of old Kharkov, the city where
the Association of Southern Coal and
Steel Producers had its office.

Sédim. Tert. et Crétac
Grès Supérieur
Calcaire   Carbonifère
Grès Intérieur
Granite et Diorite
Failles.

Fenin (seated, center) with a group of
bedouin chieftans at the Egyptian
manganese mine where he did his last
prospecting work. Seated second to his
right is his son-in-law, Fediaevsky.

Fenin's geological sketch of manganese
deposits in Sinai (shown on facing page)
was published in his article "La Formation
Geologique des Gisements de Minerais
de Manganèse au Sinai" in *Bulletin de
l'Institute d'Egypte*, vol. XIII, 1930–1931.

Aleksandr and Karlotta Fenin in Prague, 1924.

Aleksandr and Marie Fenin in exile, circa 1930.

Aleksandr and Karlotta Fenin in
Marienbad the year his memoir was
published.

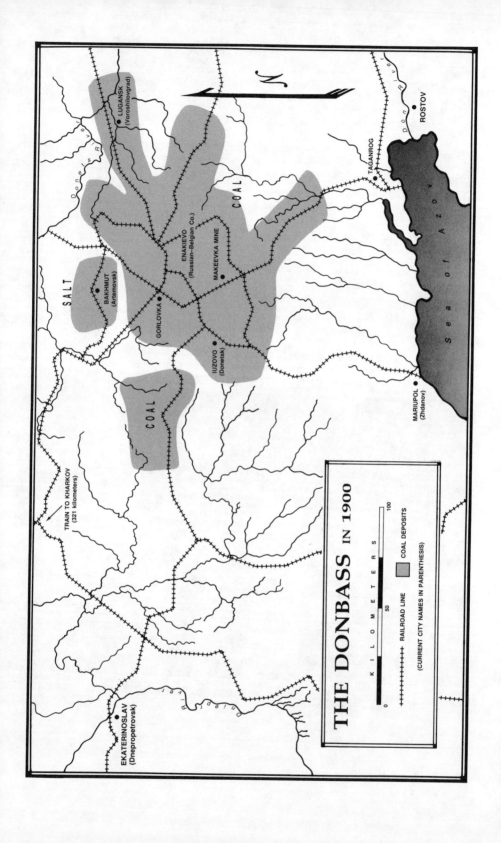

THE DONBASS IN 1900

K I L O M E T E R S
0   50   100

╪╪╪ RAILROAD LINE

■ COAL DEPOSITS

(CURRENT CITY NAMES IN PARENTHESIS)

LUGANSK
(Voroshilovgrad)

TAGANROG

ROSTOV

Donets R.

Don River

Sea of Azov

COAL

SALT

BAKHMUT
(Artemovsk)

ENAKIEVO
(Russian–Belgian Co.)

MAKEEVKA MINE

GORLOVKA

IUZOVO
(Donetsk)

COAL

MARIUPOL
(Zhdanov)

TRAIN TO KHARKOV
(321 kilometers)

EKATERINOSLAV
(Dnepropetrovsk)

Dnieper River

N

I. V. Mushketov and his wife Ekaterina Pavlovna greeted us as though we were close relatives. Ekaterina Pavlovna, née Iossa, knew my wife's family quite well—her father, the mining engineer Pavel Andreevich Iossa had owned a small mine near Iuzovka for a long time. Kindly "Auntie Katia" had known my wife since she was a child and called her *Totochka* and *ty;* from then on Auntie always treated her as a beloved daughter.[13] Ivan Vasil'evich Mushketov, a brilliant professor who always won young people's hearts with his wonderful, open face and matching character, met us with a bracing, warm welcome.

During my quest for a position, which I immediately began in Petersburg, I got in touch with the mining department. The director was then the very same K. A. Skal'kovskii whom I mentioned earlier. He listened to me while he signed papers, being very clever and talented, but having careless, almost rude, social manners. Noticing that I was ill at ease and had stopped talking, he just whispered, "Go ahead, I'm just signing these papers, not reading them." He offered me a post as a district engineer on Sakhalin Island, saying that he had nothing else to propose.[14] He recommended that I see the well-known General Kononovich, former governor general of Eastern Siberia, who was living in Petersburg at that time. He added carelessly, "It's true, Sakhalin is Sakhalin, but why shouldn't a young engineer go there?" I was not much attracted to Sakhalin, but I did pay General Kononovich a visit, and discovered to my amazement that this lofty bureaucrat was a very simple and accessible man—he obviously really loved that territory; he kept describing the richness of Eastern Siberia and Sakhalin with great enthusiasm all evening, recommending that I not be afraid and go. Kononovich had almost convinced me when, fortunately, chance saved me once again.

The Russian-Belgian Metallurgical Company had just been founded at that time and bought a huge tract of coal-bearing land in the province of Ekaterinoslav.[15] The chairman of the Board of Directors, which included both Russians and Belgians, was transport engineer A. A. Bunge, a big railroad contractor; another member of the board, transport engineer Feodor Egorovich Enakiev, well-known in Petersburg, was the director of operations at the site. The plan was to build simultaneously a large steel mill, including a rail rolling plant, and a coal mine that could produce great quantities of coal. Enakiev was looking for a mining engineer to prospect the coal deposits and build the mine. By chance the brothers A. and V. Keller from the Crimea, who were close to my wife's family and nephews of the then prominent mining engineer A. P. Koeppen, were in Petersburg at that time. They knew we were there and suspected our difficult situation. As a result, Koeppen recommended me to Enakiev. I was appointed after our first meeting to a virtually independent position with an unexpectedly high salary.

The members of the board of the Russian-Belgian Company belonged to a stratum with which I was not familiar—they were financial and industrial wheelerdealers, people of an older generation in their fifties or sixties—a generation that hailed from the railroad business of the 1870s, the era of the first big Russian railroad building and equally big speculation. At any rate, these were every enterprising people, used to large-scale, primarily financial operations. Among the members of the board there was a well-known person in Petersburg business circles, already quite an old man, Nikolai Nikolaevich Sushchev, chairman of the board of the Russian Foreign Trade Bank. Sushchev had had a long and diversified career, first as a high-ranking official and chamberlain, then as a promoter of railroad building, the founder of a bank, industrial companies, and so on.

Except for Enakiev, whom I had the occasion to get to know in my later career, I became best acquainted with this man Sushchev, as he asked me to give him a few lessons about the layering and exploitation of coal, saying that he was not used to working in a business he did not understand. I had to come a few times to his enormous apartment, furnished in a unique but rather heavy style, and acquaint him with the technology of coal mining in the Donets Basin.

Sushchev in many regards was an original and imposing character, starting with his appearance: an old man, with a white face and crooked nose, with a flame red beard and the enormous belly of a glutton: with his heavy figure and short legs he was so fat that he could scarcely move. He looked almost ugly—not even his clever, attentive, if cool eyes could add any charm to his face.

He was exceptionally intelligent and sharp, an excellent "pupil," even in the new field of mining. I sometimes attended board meetings, where he astonished and almost oppressed the others by the sheer power of his businesslike mind. He always produced the definitive formula, just the right phrase that had utterly eluded the others in his absence. On the board he was considered an oracle.

When he was bored with a lesson on coal, if he was free and in the mood, he would ask me pointed questions, trying as it were to gauge me with his piercing eyes, or else he would narrate something of his own—thus on one occasion, having kept me for lunch and offered me a delicious wine that he liked very much, Sushchev told me how once when he was a civil servant he had had the composer Tchaikovsky in his department for a brief period. Tchaikovsky was a young man then and a very inadequate employee. Sushchev use to say, "I drove him to music."

I remember that when the Verovka Mine was completed Sushchev, who had come down with the whole board to inaugurate the plant, insisted on descending into the shaft to see the coal in the earth personally; and I recall that this wish of his was not fulfilled. His footman, who had served him for many years, upon examining the cages that ran up and down the shaft, was struck with such terror that he declared to Sushchev that he would block the entrance and never let *barin* go down that precipice to a certain death. Thus Sushchev never saw how the coal was "growing" in the earth.

CHAPTER FOUR

The Constructive Revival
of the Basin

Construction of the Verovka Mine:
Prospecting and Purchasing the Land

Now, unexpectedly, I found myself to be the virtually independent creator of a big coal mine. It was joyous and challenging work, in fact the only truly creative engineering work of my whole career, carried out from beginning to end, from the prospecting and purchase of the land to the construction and starting up of the mine—four years at the Russian-Belgian Company passed before I knew it.

To establish its rail-rolling mill and the adjacent coal mine, the Russian-Belgian Company bought quite a large piece of coal-bearing land that had belonged to Prince A. S. Dolgorukii. This piece of land straddled the border between the Bakhmut District of Ekaterinoslav Province and the Don Military Region. Both the mill and the mine were constructed on the Ekaterinoslav side, near the Volyntsevo station of the Catherine Railroad.[1] The factory was officially named Peter, after the old Peter Factory that had been constructed on the same land in, I believe, the early nineteenth century. That factory had been meant to run on Donbass anthracite, soft coal being virtually unknown in the Basin at that time. However, the factory was never put into operation. I found only the ruins of two small blast furnaces.

I remember how operations started in the spring of 1895, with the erection of the factory and the beginning of the prospecting for coal seams. We needed an enormous staff to build the mill—the majority were Polish transport engineers. We had nowhere to live and I was alone there, my wife having stayed in Petersburg. We were three to a room in a barrack hastily constructed between the mine and the mill. There were about thirty or forty of us at meals. The chief, Enakiev, already had been on the site for a long time. The general spirit of the work and the relationships were no longer those of the old mining days—one could feel both the tension of the task and its grand scale. Where the factory would be at the moment there was only surface digging and grading. Enakiev, who loved theatrical gestures, used to climb to the top of the neighboring hill to show off the anthill, with its hundreds of carts and white digging figures, to visitors and to his Belgians, who up to now had been occupied only with the plans. The scene was an impressive one, and certainly new to the Belgians.

From morning to night I would tear about the steppe, identifying and marking the limestone deposits, indicating the direction in which the ridges should be dug for prospecting the coal seams so we might estimate their quality. My wife arrived in the middle of the summer and we were provided with an old landowner's house—quite a mansion—Aposhnianovka, with a big garden, a brook, a horse stable, and horses. We started living like true landlords; the house originally was too big for the two of us, but it was naturally filled up when my relatives and my wife's mother arrived. Only then did I feel that a new life was starting, altogether different from the previous chaos. Everything suddenly became beautiful and calm, against a background of a wonderful country village—matching well my current preoccupation with prospecting which was carried out in the bosom of nature, temporarily far removed from the noisy industrial invasion. Our life was almost idyllic.

The coal deposit measured about 12 versts, stretching along the extent of the seams, close to the main "anticlinal fold" of the Donets Basin, where the beds dipped almost vertically and where they were so closely stacked that in my prospecting I found almost all of the classical coal-bearing sequences of the Basin. I had to prospect the entrails of the earth, choose the most suitable area, and construct a mine capable of enormous coal production. This was a huge assignment, altogether new for me, very interesting and full of responsibility.

The responsibility was increased by the fact that the deposit had a bad reputation—this coal was said not to yield coke, which the company needed for the metallurgical factory it was starting to build. I remember how once on a train I met the old mining engineer A. F. Mevius, a recognized expert on the Donets Basin, and how he cautioned me seriously about the well-known inadequacy of the deposits I was prospecting.[2]

Also interested in these prospections was a colleague and friend who I have already mentioned, L. I. Lutugin, who was at that time working in the Donets Basin as a geologist for the Geological Committee.[3] Lutugin visited the prospecting often, and I gave him the data. He almost always brought along his assistant-servant, already well known in the Basin, a self-educated peasant geologist from Lisichansk named Moses Gorlov, or simply Moses, as everybody called him. Moses must have been about fifty years old. He had a long greyish beard, intelligent, attentive eyes, and an exceptionally gentle and winning face. He always wore a grey lustrine suit and had a grey cap on his head, high, almost peasantlike boots, and a long stick in hand—such was the famous "Lutugin's Moses." When Lutugin was away from the Basin, a prospector confused in the identification of the layers often would summon Moses. I had to call on him as well. Moses would stride across the doubtful places, we would consult, and then he would almost always locate precisely the limestone bed that had escaped detection (limestone beds were the orienting lines of the Donets Basin). "This, Aleksandr Ivanovich, can only be the 'Mother-in-Law' seam," he would say, pointing out the limestone's incontestable diagnostic signs, which sometimes were visible only to him. Before he established a complete classification of the geological strata of the Basin, designated by figures and letters, Lutugin used temporary names related to the most characteristic place where the seam had been found—so the "Mother-in-Law" limestone showed up splendidly in Moses's mother-in-law's kitchen garden; "Liubimovskii" was the limestone outcropping on Liubimov's land, and so forth.

Moses was a remarkable representative of the real Russia and its modest simplicity. There was no pretense in his attitude toward "his science" or toward the variety of people, all his superiors, whom he and Lutugin were advising. In his wisdom Moses did not resemble the conventional inhabitant of a professor's study, who had learned like a parrot the Latin names of his specimens. Moses often had to draw his own conclusions from his observations, and he was rarely wrong in his "scientific" determinations. In his attitude toward people Moses was neither servile, arrogant, nor self-centered—he had found that middle line so characteristic of the Russian. Everyone addressed him familiarly, but no one ever invited Moses to his table, so Moses unpretentiously ate in the kitchen; still, no one would speak to him with contempt or disrespect, except once. Lutugin told me this story, which is worth mentioning.

A rather well-known character in the South was mining engineer K—ov; with the face of a daring cab driver, he was a tough fellow, always ready for a drink.[4] His manners were provocative to the point of rudeness. Once, contradicting Moses during a discussion at which Lutugin was present, he seized Moses by the beard and scornfully shouted at him, "Hey, you beard!"[5] Moses bore the offense silently, but long afterwards, while strolling with Lutugin along the limestone out-croppings and discussing "gentlemen-engineers," Moses expressed doubt that K—ov should be placed in this category: "he ought to be sent back to the *muzhiks*." Such was Moses—he was not a real miner when we first came to know him, but came from the unskilled workers, and it is a pleasure to start my narrative of the great project that the workers and I undertook there with this remarkable, "simple" Russian man.

By mid-summer it became clear that the very center of our coal de-posit, virtually the place where the first shaft should be dug, lay partially on the neighboring property. It was indispensable that we buy this piece of land or else the enterprise would become complicated and expensive. The land belonged to a well-known old mining engineer, then retired, a rich landowner from Poltava, Nikolai Nikolaevich Letunovskii. I knew him only by reputation, as the discoverer of enorm-ous salt deposits in the Bakhmut District. Rumors described him as a strange man, now absolutely cut off from life, with no human contacts. He and his wife lived almost as recluses, in their beautiful, luxurious mansion near Poltava. For some reason his wife was considered a bit "off." Enakiev assumed, quite correctly, that it was useless to try to buy land from such people by an ordinary procedure such as going to see them or sending a broker. Some special "approach" had to be discov-ered—he decided to send me, accompanied, of course, by my wife. I was a mining engineer, a brother-in-arms, a newly married young man— Enakiev felt that we would be more likely than anybody else to find intuitively some common language with Letunovskii. This is exactly what happened; the poor old people, half-sick, almost on the brink of death, greeted us as if we were their own children— we spent two or three days with them, most of the time in their incomparable park. I do not remember precisely through what negotiation the indispensible land was purchased, at an exceptionally low price. This was the bright side of the coin. The dark side appeared only too soon. Letunovskii wrote to Enakiev that he had only sold the land to the company for our sake, insisting that I should be paid the usual commission for a completed purchase. Of course, because I was so inexperienced in such things at the time, I never received any such commission.

A Trip Abroad

My work equipping the mine was carried out at the site, almost independently of the factory's administration, which simply paid the estimated expenses. But I had to deal with Belgian engineering consultants, such as old Durand, a long-time head of the technical part of the Belgian Société Générale, and his assistant Kersten, a man of my age. I will not describe the construction of the factory—its technical aspects were managed by two reputable metallurgical engineers, the Belgians Philippart and Haller; the administration was in Russian hands, directed by Enakiev, who often came to the site and remained there for long periods. The local managers shifted quite often—in two years' time there were three of them: transport engineers Tvardovskii and Hirshman, and mining engineer Podgaetskii, none of them metallurgists. As I have said, I had no professional relationship with them.

I completed the exploration of the deposit by the fall of 1895. I found it to be excellent, because of the quality of the coal, and because of the remarkable regularity of the seams, spreading straight as lines through the whole 12-verst area. At that point I went to Belgium with a set of coal samples. My wife accompanied me, of course. Foreign countries still seemed like fairyland to Russians, and we felt this as soon as we crossed the border. The contrast was sharp indeed. Russian railroad stations (and this got even worse toward the border) were clumsily and thoughtlessly designed, the surrounding landscape almost a desert. Now all of a sudden, we were passing through railroad stations that appeared neat and lively, almost festive looking. We could not take our eyes off the cozy, clean little villages and towns, with the elegant, trim gothic architecture of their churches, quite new to us. Everywhere, order, cleanliness, apparent well-being: for us, a real holiday. This first trip abroad together with my wife really did seem like a fairy tale. I remember my first impressions of Brussels—the luxury, as it seemed to us, of the Grand Hotel, the truly charming main square with its ancient town hall, surrounded by impressive historical buildings—we came across this square quite by accident one night, and discovered it under the light of a fantastic moon.

Almost all of my time in Brussels was devoted to the mining project I was working on with Kersten. Given the arrangement of the coal seams, we decided to design the mine as two huge twin-shafts, a system very popular in Belgium, of which there were many examples. Besides my work on the project I had to visit Belgian mines together with Kersten or Durand.

Closer contact with the people and their habits started to shake my festive impressions of Western Europe. I remember how I was shocked by the cool and dry relationship between the directors and their junior engineer subordinates—nowhere was there even a hint of friendly partnership; almost everywhere there was strict order and unquestioning obedience. This was carried to such a point that in one of the mines I saw a junior engineer taking off his hat to address his director. It was out of the question for a junior engineer to sit down in the presence of the director or to shake hands with him. In the family setting I was amazed by the marked inferiority of the wife, by her subordination to her husband. At one of the mines I visited with Durand, the director who had invited us for lunch wished to entertain us with some music while we had coffee and liqueurs after the meal, so he asked his wife to play the piano. To her timid protest he answered with a brief, *"Vite, vite, allez jouer"* [Quick, quick, go and play]. At another place, where the after-dinner entertainment was to shoot some wretched rabbits in the director's garden, his wife had to load the carbines and hastily pass them to us. When family groups went to restaurants, which was quite common, wives would hand the overcoats to their husbands, and even to me. The Russian sense of constraint in the presence of women was so lacking, as were all of those little tributes of respect for a lady, that things even went to the point, both at home and in restaurants, of using the toilet in their presence. All outward, visible aspects of family life seemed purposely simplified so as not to embarrass the husband, the head of the family, in his working life. The husband, the man, was the unchallenged chief, his "career" was the most important thing in his life—to the wife remained the kitchen and the protection of her husband's peaceful working environment from the children. For us Russians all of this seemed novel and unusual; having personally experienced Makeevka's informality, I found the strained working attitude of the Belgian engineers, which at that point I thought to be exceptional, quite strange. In the short span of my visit to Belgium I was not able to understand fully the attitude of the Belgian engineer toward the workers. But even in that amount of time I found it astonishing how strictly disciplinarian and formal these relations were; not a shade of paternalism, not a hint of sympathy toward "the people"—everywhere, if not harshness, there was at least dry formality. Housing at the mine sites was good, but not sufficient, and the rents were very high; almost everywhere the overwhelming majority of workers lived in private flatlets in the villages and small towns, which were plentiful in densely populated Belgium. Likewise, the workers had to pay for the coal they used to heat their houses. At the same period our workers got their houses (quite rudimentary, of course) and the coal to heat them free of charge.

I will now say a few words about Durand and Kersten, who were my colleagues more than my superiors. Durand was already an old man, and he was obviously withdrawing from an active role as an engineer; for our project his assistant Kersten was far more important. Kersten, a very gifted engineer, was a far from ordinary man; his personality was very complicated and he was fanatically Catholic. I suspect that he must have been educated by the Jesuits. His religious feelings were from our point of view more than strange, bordering on fetishism. Kersten always carried in his waist pocket a tiny statue of his patron St. Joseph, seriously asserting that without it he would not be able to cross the street.

Two months later we returned to Russia along with Durand and Kersten; they were back for only a short stay, to inspect the coal deposit and make a mutual decision about the precise locations of the shafts. I remember how we were amazed, my wife and I, to see the two Belgians take off their wedding rings just before crossing the Russian border. I never was able to get an accurate explanation for this kind of behavior. I am afraid that, along with the firm conviction that the late Emperor Alexander III had been the only virtuous man in the country, they fancied that the Russian girls threw themselves on every bachelor's neck. While living in Russia, at least at first, they were terribly afraid of the simple people and rapid horse-riding drove them into panic—they were also uneasy about our hellish way of driving trace-horses. Generally speaking, the first steps of my Belgians on Russian soil were every bit as ridiculous as those of our own tourists abroad.

Durand and Kersten paid us "inspection visits" faithfully twice a year, remaining at the mine for from two weeks to a month. Besides the fact that they had full faith in my work, they were not much attracted by the dull atmosphere of the Russian village.

Construction of the Mine and Start-up Operations

I am trying to recall how the Verovka Mine was constructed. Both shafts were sunk in the winter of 1896, and in the spring the construction of the mine was in full swing. My closest collaborators, in addition to the young engineer M. M. Bronnikov, were head miners [shteigers] I. N. Gladkii and A. V. Babakov, simple people, without much culture or education but with sufficient experience in mining. The young Belgian engineer Tille who was given to me to "keep order" by the Belgian members of the board was of little use, as he was unable to speak Russian, and had no experience—nevertheless he was a quiet and obliging man and readily carried out my instructions concerning the supervision of the works.

I was then thirty years old, and had five years experience—for one year I had been the manager of the fairly large Karpov Mine. Two and a half years after the prospecting the Verovka Mine was working at full capacity, producing about 2 million puds of coal per month and employing about 2000 miners and a whole staff of technicians and other employees.

It was the first time that a mine of the Donets Basin had been equipped with two enormous elevating engines, each of 1000 power.[6] A huge Gibal ventilator 12 meters in diameter (an exceptionally large one) was assembled, although such ventilators already were outdated and usually replaced by smaller, quicker engines. Compressors and equipment for boring galleries mechanically (crosscuts) were erected, together with big steam boilers—in other words, in the midst of the unspoiled steppe there now stood a modern mine of the West European type. All this was directly realized not only by the strength, but also by the minds and talents, of often only semiliterate Russian craftsmen, mechanics, blacksmiths, carpenters, masons, and even drifters. In fact, my role as the leading engineer was limited to general supervision and administration; I simply had no time for technical oversight. I remember with what amazing speed our team of Iaroslav carpenters was able to comprehend the drafting and master something as complicated as the wooden coal-sorting device that in the plans had looked like a spider web. The team was led by Semikhin, a *muzhik* full of talent but scarcely able to write his own name. The mine's superstructure, about 20 meters high, shielded the shaft's metallic head frame (a purely Belgian system). It was designed with only one transverse wall and constructed with almost mathematical accuracy out of untrimmed blocks of sandstone, which had no regular shape, by simple bricklayers who had never done anything like this. The young head miner, I. N. Gladkii and the blacksmith-mechanic Kostenko, an almost illiterate *muzhik* with no education but with quite a knack as a fitter, supervised laying the complicated foundations for the engines and assembling mechanisms.

True, during the fitting of the engines, mechanics from the manufacturer were there to supervise, but once the engines were in operation, Kostenko had to do the whole job with his own people, who were simple Russian workers. All these engines, which were rather complex for the time, were set up and attended by our workers and functioned perfectly with no breakdowns or interruptions. Subsurface work was designed and initiated with a similar precision. Seven coal seams had to be crosscut, then worked out. This complicated and specialized task was conducted principally by head miner Babakov and a whole army of foremen in a typically Russian fashion, which demanded from the workmen much talent, efficiency, often personal courage, and an ability to become mentally oriented to mining work very quickly, for an accident was always to be feared, because of the primordial danger of mining. The Verovka Mine, I believe the biggest in Russia, was established by a mutual effort, by a cooperative creative effort, which included the simplest workers.

However, things did not run that smoothly for me personally, and I wish to recollect an episode that caused me much nervous tension, an episode quite typical of mining.

The mine already had been established, digging had reached the first coal seam at a depth of 60 sazhens (a 2-meter thick seam that I named "the twins"), and enough coal had been extracted to load the new high furnace of our factory (4 versts from the mine). The coal was solemnly transported and fed into the furnace. Twenty-four hours later, when the coke was to be unloaded from the furnace, it appeared that there was no coke at all, the coal did not "bake," that the furnace contained only useless coal ash. All my work and prospecting, all the mining equipment I had chosen for the site, appeared to have been a fatal mistake. Enormous sums of money, close to 3 million rubles, had been wasted; my head began to spin, particularly because I had been given full initiative in this affair. The words of old Mevius now echoed as a sinister prophecy. The Belgian builders of the metallurgical factory, Philippart and Haller had never been among my supporters, resenting my sense of independence. They immediately attacked the executive director, old Bihet, saying, "This is what comes of your blind confidence, you chose this inexperienced young Russian engineer and the whole business is completely ruined," and so on and so on. Bihet was the model of a broad-minded, fair administrator, and he had full confidence in me. "So, Mr. Fenin, what is the matter?" he sternly asked me when he summoned me to his office. I answered that I could not understand it myself and asked for two-weeks in which to find the answer. He granted me the two weeks.

I was quite sure that the coal deposit was of good quality, and I felt that I was facing here some geological riddle I had not foreseen concerning that particular coal bed, or more precisely, that particular point at which the crosscut gallery intersected the seam. I sent a telegram to Lutugin who luckily was then in the Basin. For two days we both ran like madmen through limestone and sandstone outcroppings and found an almost invisible fault of the sandstone at the top and the bottom of "the twin" coal bed. The fault hung almost at the precise spot where the crosscut met "the twin." "The blame must be shared," said Lutugin, relieved, but somewhat embarrassed that he had not discovered the fault earlier, though the reproach certainly concerned me as well. The fact that the coal of "the twin" bed did not bake was explained by the fault. The sandstone at the top and bottom of the bed was not firm enough to protect it, so weathering could proceed in three directions, and the coal was affected to the unusual depth of 60 sazhens. The area of bad coal was discovered to be very narrow, and two or three weeks later we reached excellent coal, which yielded one of the best cokes in the Donets Basin: the honor of Russian arms was restored.

I will add some words about the establishment of the workers' colony. The problem was complex, as it was essential to build houses for at least 2000 workers, and with their families this meant building a whole settlement. Building a sufficient quantity of houses nice enough for family life would have permitted us a better selection of personnel, but it was very expensive, and the Belgians did not agree. Building barracks, even of an improved type, that is, with wooden floors and individual kitchens, was far cheaper, but bachelor workers, the "barrack-dwellers," were undoubtedly the worst type of workers. Personally, I wanted to provide the mine with the best possible hewers and organize the basic mining work correctly.

When the coal seams are quite steep, which was the case at Verovka, it is technically impossible for teams to do the hewing, and the work must be done individually. Consequently, it is essential to attract a suitable contingent of miners. The compromise we reached was to build individual, but inexpensive, houses. This compromise had already been effected long ago at the old neighboring Gorlovka Mine, which also had steep coal seams. The "Gorlovka House," designed for individual families, consisted of one room that also served as a kitchen and an attached entrance-way, constructed of slabs thickly coated with clay on either side. The circumstances compelled me to repeat the "Gorlovka compromise," but better to protect the house from cold, I made walls out of two rows of rough board, filling the gap in between with clay as much as possible. The result was a sort of warm adobe house. Inside and outside the walls were plastered with clay, or sometimes white-washed. Of course, from a European point of view, such houses seemed too crude, or simply bad, but they could be kept sufficiently warm in the winter by burning the free coal in their stoves constantly and by the frequent plastering of the walls by the *babas*. They gave the colony a tidy look. When young trees and flowers appeared near "one's house," and sheds and pigstys stood in the courtyards, the colony began to look cozy and even smart. It must be pointed out, in all fairness, that the married miners and their *babas*, when given a house of "their own," always kept it perfectly clean.

The family settlement with its hundreds of little houses sprawled out on one side of the Verovka Mine. On the other side stood the barracks for bachelors. Houses for the staff and the director's house were constructed about a verst away from the mine on better, less stony land, near a small hill of thick sandstone. There was a little garden near each of the houses, and the ridge that ran beside them was graced with trees and benches. The mining colony originally stood on sparsely covered coal-bearing rocks, that is, on almost barren clays and sands, but within two or three years, through constant care, the land was green with gardens, a sight rarely encountered in that region.[7]

In contrast to many of Chekhov's characters, "who in their whole life never planted a tree or a bunch of grass," I felt that I could take at least part of the credit for what this formerly barren steppe was now producing. I could not help then or now feeling proud of this accomplishment. My ego was especially gratified when I watched the long line of miners hurrying off to their shift or when I observed the enormous three-floored cages steadily hauling to the surface their cargoes of six full coal carts. This coal had been produced through my efforts and as the culmination of a complex technological process. First it had to be located, then reached via a network of underground galleries, then extracted from the seam, and finally lifted to the surface continuously in mass quantities.

I knew that similar achievements, on a previously unheard-of scale, were being carried out elsewhere in the Donets Basin during this feverish period, by many of my colleagues, young Russian engineers; my personal pride was related to a feeling of national pride. But the reader must not imagine that our "pride" was in any way nourished or even supported by public opinion. Neither the unique scale of our activity nor its usefulness for the country, alas, attracted the slightest interest from contemporary Russian society. The intelligentsia was not interested in industrial or purely economic achievements.

The Social Isolation of Donbass Industrialization

In spite of our geographical remoteness from Russian society and our lack of social experience, we perceived that southern industrialization was being carried out in a kind of strange isolation, almost as if it were in a foreign country. We heard and knew that in many parts of the Basin they were constructing steel mills, excavating great coal mines and laying railroads; we could measure the extent of this enormous industrial expansion, but we never found any written account of it in the press, or the faintest echo in society when we met it, or the slightest sign of interest in what was going on there. Even in Kharkov, in the council of the Association of Southern Coal and Steel Producers, whose president was the very elderly Mevius, we encountered an organization living entirely in the past—innovation was not their concern. Our senior colleagues, executive directors such as Enakiev, Sushchev, and Bunge, preoccupied with their own affairs, seemed not to realize the magnitude of the boom that was going on in the South.

Looking back at this remote period, it is noteworthy that this indifference to economic progress on the part of our social leaders in the late nineties coincided precisely with the dawn of their involvement in political struggles. Opposition to the government was on the rise, after the political disengagement of Alexander III's reign. It began with the petitions addressed to Nicholas II upon his ascension to the throne, and his famous answer about "senseless dreams."[8] The first sign of social unrest was the student disorders that began with the futile clash between Petersburg University students and their rector. Eventually all Russian universities joined a general strike in solidarity with the Petersburg students. The Russian public and press reacted strongly, entirely in support of the students. The movement gradually became politicized and took on the oppositional character. The culmination of this unrest was the first terroristic act in many years—the assassination of education minister Bogolepov by the student Karpovich in early 1901.

Now the second revolutionary wave to wash over Russia swelled up at the beginning of the century. The educated public and the press, preoccupied with the political struggle, cared little about economic achievements or, of course, about us.

But not all the strata of Russian society were seized by political fever. Some elements were calmer, let us say, "businessminded," and these men could and should have been interested in the industrialization developing so broadly throughout southern Russia. Having personally observed the composition of our society at that time and later, I noticed that at least provincial society (which I could observe most closely) was devoid of this particular "stratum" that could react in a positive way to the industrial development then seizing Russia. Our "agrarians," the class of noble landowners who might have turned to business, were highly prejudiced against the idea of establishing big industry in Russia. I do not even mention a real "industrialist" class, as no such group existed in Russia at that time.

The prevailing opinion, which was expressed by virtually the entire press, was that Russia was an agricultural country, that most manufactured goods could be imported cheaply, and that our own manufactured goods were rendered unnaturally expensive as the result of harmful protective tariffs. Finally, they argued, large-scale industrial development had been promoted artifically by the government, to the detriment of Russia's real interests. Even such a broad-minded scholar as Professor Maksim Kovalevskii believed that "our industry was by no means developing independently, but only as the result of the government's protectionist tariff policy."[9] This short-sighted opinion was then very common, and it irritated Witte greatly. He wrote in his memoirs: "They say that I take artificial measures to promote industry. What do they mean by this stupid statement? How else could one develop industry except by artificial means?"[10] Witte, the main promoter of state-led industrialization, acting on the government's behalf, wrote bitterly in his memoirs, "Up to now the significance of industry for Russia has neither been understood nor appreciated. The only person who understood this was our great scientist, my faithful friend Mendeleev, who collaborated with me right up to his death."[11]

Even then, close to the end of the nineteenth century, we have to admit that in the field of state economy, the only "European" in Russia was the Russian government. This bitter truth, which Pushkin had pointed out in the thirties under Nicholas I, was still applicable. Reality demonstrated that Pushkin was still right in the early 1900s, and it is more than obvious that this sad statement did not apply only to economics.

Intellectual Trends in the Field of Economics: Marxists and Populists

Speaking of the climate of public opinion and the press in the mid-nineties, I have to mention a new trend of thought that concentrated on the desireability of economic development for Russia. This "economic materialism," as it was then called, was based on Marx's teachings. Its main promoter was a young Petersburg scholar, Petr Berngardovich Struve.[12] These ideas were soon actively discussed in society and in the press under the simplified label of "Marxism" and were opposed to the receding "populism" that had been proclaimed by Mikhailovskii, Zlatovratskii and other publicists.[13] The essentials of Struve's "Marxism" can be summarized by the following statements. "Social advancement is conceivable only on the basis of capitalism, and cannot be reconciled to obsolete economic forms." "The economic picture of nineteenth century Russia is one of developing capitalism." "Only the capitalist training which develops the country's productive forces can produce cultural progress," and further, "only this training can promote class consciousness and establish complete clarity in mutual class relations." "The significance of capitalism for the development of class consciousness is one of essential points of Marx's teaching."

In this manner Struve elaborated on Marx's ideas, which were more or less new to Russia at the time. The teaching of the "populists," on the other hand, offered a very negative view of capitalism, as they considered the conditions of Russian life ordained a very different course for the country's economic development. These conditions included the uniqueness of the Russian peasant, who embraced the idea of an almost natural economy, of primitive equality, of community, and of harmonious organization where the "rights of the weak and the poor are guaranteed."

The fundamental contradictions between these two teachings led to passionate disputes: first in the press, primarily in the thick journals which presented such ideas; later in the economic and philosophical societies such as the Free Economic Society; and finally, in various student circles in the capital.[14] Hot debates arose on every aspect of contemporary opinion. The populists reproached the Marxists for being "the lackeys of capitalism" and for having become "apprentice capitalists." On the other hand, the Marxists accused the populists of hopelessly confusing concepts, of belief in the "phantom of an omnipotent classless intelligentsia," and in their own role in procuring political and economic progress.[15] Ultimately, in the restless atmosphere of the capital, both teachings furthered the same political aim among students and scholars. Marxists were saying "only the development of capitalism followed by the expropriation of the expropriators by the proletariat, strictly following Marx's recipe, would promote future happiness."[16] The populists maintained that the "theoretical understanding of the laws of Russia's historical development must be considered the foundation of all efforts to overthrow the present order, and must be integrated into the movement immediately." So both of these abstract currents pointed Russian thinking in the capital toward the path of inevitable struggle against the existing government order, indeed, toward the revolution that the leading Russian intelligentsia, unfortunately, was seeking.

The highly theoretical nature of these intellectual trends, as well as their remoteness from reality, can be illustrated by two different, ongoing social phenomena. On one hand, there was an enormous economic advancement in the country, resulting from the government's initiative, an initiative that neither the populists nor the Marxists would acknowledge or even notice. On the other hand, one could observe something remarkable in Russian literature: Chekhov, in spite of his striking descriptive precision, never so much as mentioned these two currents of thought among the intelligentsia. The almost brutal realism that characterizes his celebrated "Muzhiks" [The peasants] written, incidentally at precisely this time (1897), is a severe reprimand to the ephemeral teachings of the populists.

It is not easy nowadays to describe the impressions that arose in those confused days of nascent revolution. We were too remote from intellectual circles, not only those of the capital but of the province as well; we were too busy with our practical preoccupations to spare any time for abstractions. We knew about Marxists, and of course about populists, out of books—most of the mining staff subscribed to various thick journals. Sometimes we were told about what was going on in Petersburg by visitors—especially by Lutugin who came frequently during the summer months. I remember having formed some general opinions about what was going on in the Free Economic Society, to which Lutugin always was connected, and about the statements of "big people" whom I knew from newspapers, such as Iarotskii, Chuprov, and others.[17] I knew about the strange goings-on in lecture halls, mainly among young people, and even about scandals. But I scarcely remember Lutugin ever mentioning Marxists or populists in his accounts. Lutugin was too much of a skeptic to be involved or even to be really interested by such teachings. What he took from them was only their mood of overall commotion, agitation, turbulent discontent; he was not conscious of the coming revolution, which was just dawning. What was really heating up was the merciless hatred of the existing order, of the government—this was possibly Lutugin's only political credo.

I, like other provincial engineers, listened to these and similar conversations with intellectuals from the capital whom we encountered. We were not moved by them but we did not contradict them. The roaring stream rolled on far away from us—at that time it was entirely alien and had no effect upon our lives.

"Promotion": An Off-shoot of Industrial Construction

I must mention another undertaking that accompanied the build-up of the South: the so-called promotion. The value of enterprises was inflated by brokers speculating on shares, and similar gains fell into the pockets of the founders as well as those of establishments or individuals who risked their money in these transactions. This phenomenon is inevitable in all industrial activities, especially large-scale ones, as it is the main stimulus for commercial initiative; in fact, speculation was not all that rampant in the construction era of the nineties. Its alleged scale was greatly exaggerated by public opinion, which took a very negative attitude toward "promoters"—a quality readily suspected in every engineer. At any rate, this speculating could not even be compared to that which went on in the railroad building of the 1870s.

As for investments in foreign enterprises—those who "made money" in difficult and often very technically demanding ventures, of course, were the presidents and members of the boards of the corporations, Russians as well as their foreign colleagues. People who were involved in setting up the industrial enterprises always made even more money, and they usually did not remain after this initial stage.

I cannot avoid mentioning here one of the most successful of these "promoters," the well-known southern mining engineer Aleksei Mikhailovich Goriainov, the director of the Briansk Factory.[18] Most of the Belgian business passed through his hands, including the selling of the Maksimov Mine, in which I later worked, to English interests. Goriainov's popularity among the foreigners who rushed to Southern Russia as to a Klondike, was such that Belgian visitors used to go first to Ekaterinoslav to shake hands with Monsieur Goriainov. It should be noted, though, that Goriainov was not at all the common type of broker, the "money grubber," agreeable to any proposition for the sake of his personal profit, as were many of these organizers. Goriainov, an excellent engineer and an expert in the southern mining business, was a modest, amiable, urbane man—perhaps these qualities accounted for his exceptional success. His appetite for money was rather modest; he grew rich on the sheer quantity of affairs he arranged.

Neither Goriainov, Enakiev, Bunge, nor even Sushchev or any of the other great industrialists of this era ever made such fortunes as Poliakov, Von Derviz, and the other big-shots of railroad building in the seventies. Needless to say, we younger engineers working at the scene took no part whatsoever in the financial end of the business. We were occupied exclusively with the local administrative and technical tasks—the financial fever, because of our youth and our lack of connections, passed us by.

The quiet atmosphere of the university, and later the bleak, isolated provincial life, transformed us into "no-nonsense" characters, capable of carrying out the demanding tasks of actual construction from start to finish. We, the Russian technical intelligentsia, the "men of the eighties," were able to build factories, mines, and railroads in a simple and practical way, without any of the disastrous Russian tendency to deviate toward political illusions and wishful thinking. I am not exaggerating when I say that we were virtually the first of our intelligentsia to participate in this kind of real economic, constructive work.

My Life at the Verovka Mine

How did we live, my family and I, during the four years during which I worked for the Russian-Belgian company constructing and operating the Verovka Mine? At first I was completely isolated socially speaking, even professionally, because the work itself was so intense during the construction; and this isolation persisted later because the mine's output went to our own factory, a circumstance that restricted outside contacts. Our sphere of personal acquaintances was limited to a few employees of the factory, mainly the family of my brother-in-law, K. F. Wagner [Vegner], the company's head doctor, and his few friends, as well as some of my subordinates from the mine.[19] The first I should mention was my assistant, the young mining engineer Vasilii Aleksandrovich Stepanov.

After the departure of my first assistant, M. M. Bronnikov, who did not remain long in the South, as the mine was completed, I hired V. A. Stepanov who later became a well-known political leader. I believe he was a member of the Duma, beginning with the Second Duma, as a member of the K.D. [Constitutional Democratic or Kadet] party.[20] During the Provisional Government I think he was a government inspector, a position he occupied again in the Volunteer Army under the government of General Denikin, when we were once again collaborators after years of almost complete separation.[21]

Stepanov was exceptionally cultured and had an excellent education, as well as being a straightforward and unquestionably fine person. He worked in the mine with me for about two years, and remained there for a short period after my departure. Our relationship when we worked together and later on was good natured and friendly. After I left the Russian-Belgian Company, as he later told me, he insisted that the mine should be given my name, as I was its founder, and not the name of the chairman of the board, the Belgian Depré, as the directors wished. When he failed in this, he took great pains to have the mine named after Verovka, the nearest village. This in fact was the name that stuck.

At the beginning Stepanov lived at the mine with his mother and his aunt, Baroness Engelhardt, both charming old ladies and great friends of my wife. Soon afterwards Stepanov got married in Petersburg, and I recall that he returned with his wife Magdalena Vladimirovna, née Pokrovskaia, a very well-proportioned, beautiful young woman.

Unfortunately his marriage was not solid, and a few years later they separated in Petersburg.

The staff of the Verovka Mine was not numerous, just two or three cultured families—including my colleagues from Makeevka who had followed me to the Russian-Belgian Company, Obraztsov and Tomanovich.[22] Along with the families of Stepanov and the foremen Gladkii and Babakov, this constituted our entire social circle. Along with these people, my brother-in-law's family and two or three families of the factory staff, we hardly visited anybody else. The mine took up all my time, the children took up all of my wife's—the melancholy and boredom of Makeevka were only memories—although I devoted almost four years of service to the Russian-Belgian Company, virtually without a break. Oddly enough, card playing was now out of fashion even with Tomanovich and Obraztsov, so strong was the influence of this new environment. In the evenings, especially in winter, people used to read aloud; in the summertime, after returning from the mine, almost everybody was busy with his garden—gardens proliferated and bloomed everywhere.[23]

A vivid memory now emerges from that time: an early morning in May when my wife gave birth to our eldest son. The midwife who had been living with us for two weeks woke me at dawn, saying, "It is time to ring up Karl Feodorovich." My brother-in-law arrived, as always, bringing along his doctorly reassurance. "Come, Sasha, let's go into the garden and let Totka (as he called his sister) have her baby." In spite of the stress of the "event," this was a wonderful morning for me. It is only in our land, in the unspoiled steppe, and only in the spring, that one can have this feeling of complete splendor: the mild, tender, dry air, the sky still dark but quickly turning blue and then radiant, the steppe fragrance and the larks, larks singing endlessly. I remember I stood for a long time, all alone near our low fence. Karl Feodorovich, himself an excellent horticulturist, was earnestly discussing some point with our gardener. I was contemplating the steppe that beyond a small slope rose again to the horizon. The sun was just beginning to rise. I was full of concern for what was going on in "there," in our house, and at the same time, conscious of the mysterious beauty of the springtime steppe. I was not really afraid for my wife, as this was her second delivery, she was so young and healthy, and she yearned for children—and all around me everything seemed to radiate the triumphant beauty, health, strength, and fertility of nature. Happy, bygone times.

I also remember troubling, painful events in the life of the Verovka Mine, fortunately short-lived. The construction was not yet finished, but we were already living in our home at the mine. The mine office was still in a provisional wooden barrack, closer to our living quarters than to the mine. During one dark autumn night, the watchman's hurried knocks at the window woke me up. "There is trouble, your lordship, please come," he said, trying not to scare my wife—mine accidents, unfortunately, were quite common. I dressed quickly and came out. "The office was robbed, the guard killed and the safe stolen—the burglars came with three carts," he reported. In fact, a band of gypsies was then making daring raids, especially on mines. They used to attack at night with shouts and roars, shooting at the electric lights, plunging the mine into darkness and the guards into panic, then plundering with impunity. At the Berestovo-Bogodukhovskii Mine the director, Engineer Tsemnolonskii, had been killed as he came out of his house to see what the noise was all about. I knew all of this, but I still had to go. So I gave my coachman a pistol and set him on guard in the entrance way of our house, and taking another pistol with me, I set off cautiously with the watchman through the total darkness of a November night. We had to cross about half a verst of empty land to reach the office. Of course I said nothing to my wife, and she learned about the murder the next day. There, I confronted the typical scene of a robbery: lamps put out, the unfortunate office guard lying in a pool of blood with a bullet through his skull, the iron safe hauled away.

The robbers, of course, were long gone. Although they had heard shots, the unarmed miners had not dared to leave their houses. The safe was found next day in a gulch, broken and the money, fortunately only a small amount, missing.

Back home I found my poor coachman Osip almost mad with fear, his hands shaking so much that the pistol was threatening to fire by itself. It is worth mentioning that all of our security personnel, from our watchmen to the guards recruited from among former soldiers, in fact were incredible cowards. Our security and that of our families, one might say, was in God's hands. Because of the robberies and our inadequate protection, many of us hired Circassian night watchmen, but this proved to be quite unsatisfactory. Those born "assassins [*ubivtsy*]," as they were later called, eventually organized a series of robberies of their own. Our neighbor at the Maksimov Mine, the land owner Savel'ev, had to defend himself for a whole night from an armed siege by somebody's Circassian guards. Savel'ev was saved only because on this night his two student sons were with him—they were great hunters and excellent marksmen. The shooting lasted all night and in the morning they found a gigantic Circassian lying shot in front of the window: he was still in the throes of death when they found him. Even though one of the aggressors had been killed, the police were unable to arrest the gang.

And thus we lived at the mine, in this not altogether refined atmosphere, at least as far as elementary security was concerned.

After a four-year period at the Verovka Mine, I left and joined the Maksimov Mine. I will explain my motives later. Bihet, our executive director, did not want to let me go, offering to make me his special assistant for the entire enterprise; that is, the mine and the factory. But I was not much attracted to the factory, which I knew little about because I was primarily a mining engineer, and where I would work would be exclusively with Belgians. So I departed for Maksimovka. I was sorry to leave the operation I had more or less built from scratch and the colleagues with whom I had built it and with whom I had lived very agreeably for four years.

True enough, but still, the new place did attract me because of its independence and its really large scale. My colleagues and the senior miners gave me a touching farewell—there were speeches, an address, and the kind gift of a full-sized silver miner's lamp, which was specially ordered from the Wolf Factory in Zwickau, Germany. I was glad that my work had been recognized there, on the site, with a sincerity that I could not doubt.

The next year my work received more official recognition, as I was awarded a personal medal for the construction of the Verovka Mine by the Paris 1900 Exhibition Committee. Our district engineer Evgenii Nikolaevich Taskin had insisted that my work be exhibited.

CHAPTER FIVE

Directing an Industrial Enterprise, 1899–1906

Maksimov Mine and the English-owned Russian Coal Mining Company

*I*n 1899 after four years' work at the Russian-Belgian Company, I was offered a post as executive director of the former Maksimov Mine, which the Russian Coal Mining Company had just bought. The mine was located in the Slavianoserbsk District of Ekaterino-slav Province, near the Almaznyi Station of the Catherine Railway. The situation offered to me was that of an independent director of an industrial enterprise. Among the director's duties were the entire administration of the mine as well as the sales of the coal and coke. At that time there were no coal marketing cooperatives in the Basin.[1] The Company's Board of Directors was in London, and I was its plenary representative in Russia, the so-called responsible agent.

I changed employers with some hesitation, as I was intimidated by the magnitude of the business and its attendant responsibilities. But the almost total independence of the position was so attractive that I signed a several-year contract.

I was not deterred by either the small coal reserves, albeit of exceptionally good quality, or by the company's tremendous amount of capital, which was out of proportion to the modest potential annual production—only about 12 million puds. I was fascinated by the possibility of grasping the whole of an industrial business, which allowed me a chance to go beyond the local technical or administrative interests of a mine, to which I had been limited at the Russian-Belgian Company.

Technically speaking, the Maksimov Mine differed sharply from the Verovka Mine I was leaving. Because of the big intervals between coal-bearing strata and the narrowness of the coal seams, this mine had to be constructed as a number of small shafts. This also explained its technical backwardness. But a great advantage of the Maksimov Mine was its high production of coke—the mine boasted 200 coke furnaces that produced the best coke in the Basin. The mine also had the advantage of a substantial railroad spur about 25 versts long, which was used to ship the coal to the Almaznyi Station. This spur also served the neighboring Golubovka Mine. This "Maksimov Spur" operated separately from the mine, having five locomotives, an engine house, and a workshop.

Life at the Maksimov Mine was far more interesting than at the Verovka, because of the work itself. The living conditions, frankly, were more or less the same—the comfortable life of a company director. But the business of conducting all the activities of the mine was new—especially in the early 1900s, a period of coal shortage that raised coal and coke prices sharply and kept the commercial part of the enterprise very lively.

The trips to Kharkov, Ekaterinoslav, or Moscow themselves for sales or on mining business were very frequent, especially at first. These trips were a diversion from the everyday mining routine, and for me, the novelty of visiting such towns without bearing any of the expenses was altogether charming. The mine's location, the so called Almaznyi region, was one of the most active regions of the Basin. Within a radius of about 5 or 6 versts were seven big mines, four of which belonged to foreign companies—Golubovka, Irmino, Briansk, Krivoi Rog, Kamenka, and Maksimov Mines were all managed by Russian engineers.[2] Only the Kadievka Mine, and only during her first years, had a Belgian director, Poncele, who quickly and quite readily participated in Russian life.[3]

In fact my personal life had changed sharply since the Verovka days. We already had three children when we moved to the Maksimov Mine, my mother-in-law lived with us, and my parents often visited. My family lived the happy, secure life of the old Russian village. Our house stood quite a distance from the mine, which, with all of its industrial stress, really existed for me alone—the other members of my family scarcely felt it. Our house was surrounded by a newly grown but very nice garden and the endless, almost always sown southern steppe.

Our close neighbors were the other young families of my colleagues—subordinates or directors and staff of the nearest mines. Among them we found lasting friends, and I found collaborators in my public industrial work. I will say a few words about them.

In the immediate neighborhood were some of the remaining landowners of the region. Ten versts away was Victor Nikolaevich Radakov, the president of our zemstvo, who lived on his estate Iur'evka.

Both he and his wife were cultured Russians, but their attitude, though modern, still bore the stamp of the landowning nobility. Elena Petrovna Radakova loved archaeology and at that time was gaining a name for herself in archaeological literature. We maintained a close relationship with this family, who were distant relatives and friends from my childhood. Their home was a place of spiritual peace in which to rest after the tiring, hurried pace at the mine. The Radakovs were quite aware of the intellectual and political trends of those days, and it was interesting to be there for a lively chat, especially in the summers in their wonderful old garden, where an antique arbor shaded a big garden table on even the hottest days. We visited them frequently in the summer, along with our whole family.

Closer to us lived a rich landowner, the brother of Elena Radakova, Artem Petrovich Elenev, whom we simply called Artem in our youth. He was a few years my elder and had studied at the Petersburg Technological Institute, but for some reason had never finished his studies. In my memory I preserve an image of an extremely scrupulous, timid, man with beautiful blue eyes full of kindness. I remember an anecdote about him which sounded very plausible. People said that once, when he was a student, he found a thief in his room, who was just lifting a topcoat from a portemanteau; Elenov averted his gaze so as not to embarrass the thief. The Krivoi Rog Mine of the French Company was located on Elenov's estate and the company paid him an enormous sum for his land, almost 2 million rubles. As far as I remember, ever since the war he had lived in the Crimea, in a big house he had built in Yalta.[4] He became Yalta's mayor for a term or two. After the 1917 Revolution, Elenov remained in Russia and was mysteriously murdered in 1920 while hiking form Simferopol to Yalta. During the Bolshevik era he and his family had a very difficult life. One of his sons, Nikolai Artemovich, a gifted writer and art critic, now lives as an emigré in Prague. I seldom met Artem Petrovich in those years as he only came to the village for brief periods.

Before describing life at the mine itself I would like to summarize the impact of such mines, especially the big ones, on the once lazy atmosphere of village life. I shall speak about the relationships between the Maksimov Mine and its neighborhood, as they stood even before my arrival.

The mining engineer, when directing an independent unit (that is, a mine) was necessarily in contact with the nonmining world on the outside. The links were business related. When I was directing the Maksimov Mine, I represented an independent and rather important economic administrative-cultural entity, particularly for "my" peasants, of Nikolaevka and Chutino villages, as well as for the local priest, the head of the zemstvo, the zemstvo council, the local police, and so on. I had a whole network of necessary contacts with these people. My relationship with the peasants took on an out-dated sort of noble-land-lord character, perhaps a bit standoffish, but generally speaking broad and rich. Besides the land owned by the mine, we rented some of the acreage needed for excavation from these peasants (we did not rent the surface). So peasants were tied to the mine by this lease as well as by other contacts. In fact, as the rentals were part of the communal budget they did not interest the peasants very keenly; peasants were far more interested in our own surface land, which they could rent quite cheaply. The mine, on the other hand, was far more interested in maintaining good relations with the locals than in extracting high rent for its land.[5]

For all of the these reasons, I was an unusual *barin,* in many regards far more pleasant than the old landowners. This is why my relationships with the peasants had that old-fashioned but definitely improved pattern. The first two years before a house was built for me I lived in the old landlord's mansion in the village itself. This tightened my bonds with the peasants but created some specifically rural discomforts that now and then interrupted our "idyllic" relationships.

Peasants loved to come in whole groups to chat at great length, often about trifles, and they left only reluctantly. They used to come to pay their respects very solemnly on major holidays, when it was traditional, alas, to give them some money "for vodka"—there was no escaping it.

A special ritual was the kiss in Chirst's name at Easter.[6] I had to follow the tradition of their former landlord, the nobleman Prokopovich (a very odd character), and sit in a big armchair on the balcony while the peasants, under the direction of their village elder who stood at my side, came up one by one, to give me a red-stained egg and to exchange three kisses. When the elder noticed that I was growing weary—a natural enough reaction if one appreciates that the peasants had already found the time to get a bit drunk—he would direct them, "Not on the lips, kiss him on the cheek."

Our village priest, Father Arsenii, was a somewhat modern rural parson. With us he had to cope with the demands of a wealthier and more demanding parish than that of the village. In public he used to wear rustling silk robes, speak in a studied way, and was very strict about the payment of church offerings. Generally speaking, Father Arsenii was a mild, pleasant person, with the cultural level of the average village priest.

Our company subsidized the Maksimov Mine's school entirely, as it had for a long time, although it was still technically a parish school directed, if only in theory, by Father Arsenii. The curriculum compared to the expanded government curriculum. Two experienced schoolmistresses who had been at the mine for years gave the lessons. The school accepted not only the children of the miners and some of the staff, but also the peasants' children, free of charge, of course—there was just a small parish school in the village.

The local land captain was our neighbor.[7] A barrister by education, Georgii Petrovich Savel'ev had recently graduated from Kharkov University. In spite of his youth Savel'ev knew both the village and the life of the peasants very well, as he had grown up in the village—which was often the case in those days with young noblemen who had not severed their connection to the land. He was fairly practical and very reserved. Overall he was a calm, positive, average man, with no political inclinations, indeed he was virtually a stranger to politics. He got along perfectly with the peasants; despite his youth, he was an authority among them. It is well known that the institution of land captains was especially odious to our political "vanguard." The harsh conditions of Russian life combined with the hardened and often dark outlook of the peasants created situations where the paternalistic tutorship of the land captain, primitive though it was as it combined both executive and judicial functions, was more helpful, or at least safer for the peasants, than the local police administration. It was fruitless to dream of socially united districts, as in fact there was no social unity, especially in our region. I personally knew many land captains, and the overwhelming majority of them were efficient, fair, average people who doubtless undertook many useful measures on the peasants' behalf.

Links with the District Town, Provincial Leaders, and the Zemstvo, Especially Radakov and Kolokol'tsov

Because of the mine's affairs I was directly tied to our district town of Lugansk, where the various branches of the mining administration had their offices. Recalling the provincial life of the turn of the century,

I now realize how dull it was in such towns as Lugansk and Bakhmut. It lacked any kind of animation, even in the activities of our district zemstvo in Slavianoserbsk (the zemstvo office was in Lugansk because the district town of Slavianoserbsk was too far from the railroad.) The president of the zemstvo board, my neighbor and great friend Victor Nikolaevich Radakov, was a very cultured man who eventually became a member of the State Duma as a Kadet representative. He and his colleagues on the zemstvo fully understood the significance of such public work for Russia. They all participated, as the saying goes, not from fear but from the dictates of their consciences, although in the end little came of their efforts.

Our zemstvo's main concern was public education, and it blanketed the district with a network of well-constructed schools. But the teaching staff, the most basic component of public education, was transferred from place to place terribly frequently, and in some schools as much as every year. Schoolmistresses, who were in the majority, roamed from school to school. Mostly from the urban intelligentsia, they failed to establish lasting relationships with the peasants, the local school inspectors, or the local priests. They remained "outsiders," although, in theory, they were full of love for their work and for "the people." They were consumed by their loneliness and the hopeless boredom of the village. I was well aware of the unsuitability of many of the zemstvo teachers, as I was the trustee of many zemstvo schools and had my own school at the mine, where conditions were different—partly because the mine itself provided a more intellectual atmosphere. The outside of the zemstvo schools, although nicely built, remained fenceless, littered with heaps of sand and stone left by the bricklayers and devoid of trees for years after they were finished—evidence of their lack of comfort and the absence of a real "master."[8]

In the fields of medical, veterinary, and agricultural assistance for the population, the zemstvos had a difficult and unrewarding task. The results were very poor. Hospitals were scarce, and the struggle against epidemics and cattle disease in the conditions of our villages, with their paucity of means and insufficient medical staff, was virtually hopeless. I remember that in one village where I had to stay for some time almost all the children died of diphtheria within a month or two—the medical assistant [feldsher] in charge of epidemics was able to arrive only at the end of the epidemic. Agricultural assistance to the population in fact was restricted to facilitating the purchase of farm machinery.

Only just before the war did the Slavianoserbsk Zemstvo set up an experimental field and invite district agronomists. I was personally able to observe more than modest results of zemstvo agronomic aid elsewhere, in Poltava where I had a small estate. The Poltava Provincial Zemstvo had the best experimental field in southern Russia, conducted by a well-known scientist, agronomist Tret'iakov. But the peasant population of the Poltava district, mainly small landowners (or *kurkuls* as they were called then) completely ignored the agronomist's advice, considering it nonsense, just one more *barin's* whim.[9] Our district agronomist confined himself to gathering statistical data. In his own words, apart from some large, exemplary estates where he had nothing to do, his "spiritual retreat" was my estate and two or three others, which operated economically.

To paint a more vivid picture of provincial life and customs in the early 1900s I will elaborate upon some typical characters—inhabitants of this same Lugansk, "the 'sleepers' of the Donets Basin," as Lutugin ironically called them. Within our own zemstvo, I cannot overlook our long-term marshal of the nobility, Sergei Mikhailovich I. He was a remarkable man in his own way. A monarchist and extreme conservative, more by mood than by actual opinion, he was endowed with a very corrosive, almost rude sense of humor. Outspoken and bold, even with his superiors, he was elected from one three-year term to another, in spite of the completely disorganized state of property matters and a great deal of *khokhol*-style laziness in the conduct of his duties. Sergei Mikhailovich impressed the voters not only by the peculiar "brightness" of his unusual kind of intelligence, but also by the cool-headedness, almost cynicism, with which he approached various life circumstances. The way he considered even his own person and his hopelessly complicated personal affairs, indicated a good deal of his self-styled philosophy—he was a real "original," and this was rather uncommon in Russia. Once when he was in Petersburg on business he had something like a stroke. To test whether it was the real thing, he decided to live it up with his friends—he loved to drink. It turned out to be a false alarm—there had been no stroke.

In the first years of the new century, before the Japanese War, as part of my duties as a landowning engineer, I had to receive the governor of Ekaterinoslav Province, Count Keller, who was inspecting the district.[10] The governor had quite a retinue, which included the marshal, the president of the [zemstvo] board, the land captain and various provincial and district officials. After lunch we all went to the village to inspect canton [*volost'*] affairs, and I was invited along as a guest. I remember how, in the presence of canton officials and peasants, there was a discussion about a very inadequate law concerning the peasant ownership of land. The land captain was trying to prove that the law was not applicable. When the governor insisted that the law should be

enforced as it was not yet abrogated, Sergei Mikhailovich loudly re-
marked, "This is a foolish law," to which the governor's answer was
simply a reproachful, "Sergei Mikhailovich!" I remember a district
zemstvo meeting that took place at about the same time in Lugansk.
The chairman was Sergei Mikhailovich, and the agenda was to consider
granting an allowance to a female Jewish medical assistant named Friedman, as far as I can remember. The "opposition" insisted that Friedman's
request be fulfilled. The vote went in her favor. However, when one of
the voters unaware of the outcome asked the chairman what the decision
had been he replied with majestic calm: "The request was granted, of
course—don't worry about it, they always grant Jewish requests." Such
"jokes," which were rooted in the habits of the hinterlands in those
times, did not provoke the reactions they deserved, despite the really
fine people who composed a zemstvo like ours, for example. In the Old
Russian provinces tendencies that appeared altogether incompatible
often showed themselves in the same place or even in the same incident.

Among the other remarkable Lugansk characters was a specimen
who might have been taken from Shchedrin's gallery of odd characters,
the old bureaucrat and district subsurface surveyor, mining engineer,
and state councillor,[11] Grigorii Grigor'evich A. Having lived in Lugansk
for many years, he was a familiar figure, and was known as Gri-Gri.
His duty as state surveyor was to verify all the drafts of mines, which
were invalid without his signature. If a state surveyor found a mistake,
he had the right to do all the surveying over again, at a very high price.
Moreover, with the mine's consent he could do all the mine's mapping
for an extra fee. Because of this opportunity to earn extra money, state
surveyors received a very modest salary, about 1000 rubles a year. In
practice the matter was solved in the following way: all the big mines
had their own surveyors and their drafts were accepted without verifi-
cation by the state surveyor, evidently in exchange for an annual payment—so almost all the mines were "legally" supporters of Gri-Gri.
Consequently he lived in Lugansk in a paradise of idleness, animating
his life with the usual provincial entertainments: slight, but perpetual,
drunkenness; cards, the beloved vint; and a bit of debauchery. Gri-Gri
was not married. His chubby, hairless, rather feminine face, with its
cunning, half-drunk bleary eyes, hinted at his merry good nature. The
Lugansk society being extremely tolerant—because in one way or
another it reflected the very image of Gri-Gri—he was on familiar terms
with almost everybody in his circle, addressing most of the people
informally, and being welcomed everywhere as an agreeable guest.

One time, engineer Krzywicki and I were appointed as jurymen for
a session of the district court in Lugansk. On the evening of our arrival,

while having tea in our hotel room, we had the unpleasant impression that some merrymaking was going on nearby. We could distinguish Gri-Gri's voice, a woman's shrieks, and carryings-on that threatened to keep us awake all night long. Having called on Gri-Gri, we heard an astonishing tale, even for a place like Lugansk. He told us that he was "saving" a young woman, a German governess, who had been fired from a house he knew for having an intrigue with the husband. The governess had moved to the hotel where Gri-Gri was "supporting" her, raising the money for her return home. Her room had become some sort of a "salon," where, of course, drinking was not all that went on. To our indignant reproaches he answered only that everybody knew that a governess did not deserve any more consideration. Seeing that all our interference was useless, we insisted that the "party" should at once be moved to some other place.

Gri-Gri showed up again, this time in the professional arena, during a "strict" inspection. The professor in charge of teaching the technique of surveying at the St. Petersburg Mining Institute was a man known even abroad, a first-class scientist, my classmate from the institute, V. I. Bauman—a trustworthy and honest man, but, alas, addicted to the Russian habit of drinking.[12] Well aware of the surveying practices in the field, and indignant about it, Bauman obtained a mission to the Donets Basin, for a thorough inspection. The inspection began in Lugansk, and there, by God, it ended! First of all, Gri-Gri refused to see Bauman, who was staying with me at the mine, when the inspector summoned him, arguing that because Bauman held a lower rank in the civil service, Gri-Gri was not obliged to come. If Bauman wished to make an inspection, then he could travel to Gri-Gri in Lugansk.

So, Bauman went, indignant to the point of extreme sternness, which was quite unusual for him. When accused by Bauman of never actually going to the mines, of never checking the drafts, of selling his signature for illegal gratuities, Gri- Gri simply replied that he in fact never checked the drafts as he had full confidence in the mine personnel.

The inspection ended in classic Lugansk tones. Spectators were treated to the following scene: Gri-Gri leading the inspector to the train—then the half-drunk Bauman standing at the window of the first-class carriage, while on the platform stood Gri-Gri, bedecked with the obsequious countenance of a butler, holding a tray on which stood a bottle of champagne. With tears in his inebriated eyes, an emotional Gri-Gri was beating his breast with his fists, proclaiming to Bauman: "Although you are a German, I know you are a good man."

Such were then the lives and customs of the Russian provinces, even among the "sleepers" of the Donets Basin.

Of course, not everybody in the provinces, even in Lugansk, was that bad. There were people like the Radakovs and other progressive persons, there were energetic public leaders among the "third" element of the zemstvos—doctors, teachers, agronomists—but they were individual people, and the life-style in a district town like Lugansk at the turn of the century was not fashioned by them.[13]

In Lugansk there was also the administration of our Mining Inspectorate, represented by the so-called "regional engineer." During my stay, the regional engineer was a very respectable old mining engineer, Ivan Avgustovich Stempkovskii. In all fairness, it should be mentioned that regional engineers, in contrast to state surveyors, who everywhere had something in common with Gri-Gri, were typical, good Russian civil servants, almost above reproach (at least in the South.) They fulfilled their duties with neither captiousness nor laxity. Their assignment was very important, as they had to supervise all the mining operations to ensure safety and compliance with laws protecting workers. They upheld their professional authority toward us, toward the foreigners and toward the workers with great dignity; any bribery by the firms was simply out of the question.

At least part of the zemstvo "third element," by which I mean the employees of the public institutions, is worthy of some attention. Among the itinerant teachers, the medical assistants who dealt with the epidemics, the statisticians, various instructors, and office employees of the zemstvo board, all of whom were people somewhat removed from everyday "business," even then were many strong opponents of the government and the established state of affairs. These were the home-grown "socialists," whose entire spiritual substance consisted of raging hatred of the landowner, the industrialist, the district police officer, and the government. They were often capable agitators, in close contact with the peasants or the "conscious" element among the workers.

This lower layer of zemstvo employees, for the most part the idle flotsam of the Russian province and of Russian life in general, restless and spiritually empty, was recruited from various sorts of Russian misfits and played a big part in the creation of the first cadres of Bolshevism. I knew this type of person well among the outstanding examples of this "third element" in our organization, the Association of Southern Coal and Steel Producers. I knew about their treacherous role against its board in the early years of Bolshevism.

Speaking of Viktor Nikolaevich Radakov, I feel unable to proceed without paying homage to his memory. He was not only a close friend, but a very typical figure of this bygone era.

Victor Nikolaevich remained in Russia after the Bolshevik upheaval, and died suddenly in Kharkov, a few years ago. He lived his last years, as did all people belonging in his class, in incredibly painful conditions. Viktor Nikolaevich possessed a respectable estate in the Slavianoserbsk District, which he inherited from his old aristocratic Ekaterinoslav family. But he was not much concerned with its management and dedicated all his time to zemstvo activities. Our zemstvo, whose administration was leftist, or "red" as they used to say, was considered almost a model one, and this was due primarily to Radakov's activities.

On closer inspection of his work, though, I think there was a hint of inner frustration, not only because he found many obstacles on all sides, but also, it seems to me, from some inner source. He was very intelligent, sensitive, gentle with people, a well-educated barrister and a moderate liberal, without any extreme left-wing "inclinations." Eventually he became a distinguished provincial Kadet and an excellent debater, but in spite of all these qualities, the practical results of his public work always showed a curious underachievement. It was as if in the sphere of these familiar and cherished activities he was bound by some inner restraint that prevented him from doing what he thought necessary. The generally leftist mood of the turn of the century, in such sharp opposition to the government's policies, demanded from social leaders of such public concerns as the zemstvos that they not only be efficient but also embrace a leftist position, regardless of its chances for fulfillment or of the truly serious consequences, that might result from such a position. Nobody ever wanted to think about consequences, dismissing such concerns with a shrug of the shoulders.

The zemstvo's educational program called for the feverish creation of a network of schools, even in cases where the teacher shortage limited this to the construction of buildings alone. There were schools but there was no education, there were no schoolmasters, or the schoolmaster's position was occupied now and then by some "pedagogical" rolling stone or a revolutionary agitator. Leftist agitation among the peasants by the third element met no resistance—at the most people looked the other way.

This is why schools continued to lack teachers for lengthy periods, while under the influence of these agitators the "land-hungry" mood of the peasants grew ever stronger, with its unquenchable thirst for the landlords' land.

The clever and practical Radakov could not but notice sinister rifts in the zemstvo he was directing, but he was overpowered by the wave of oppositional feeling. In Radakov's management of the zemstvo there was the "idea" and there was the "policy," but what was lacking was the "management." They were unable to recruit a staff of schoolteachers; they were unable to give them acceptable living conditions or to organize their relationship to the peasants or to the priest. So the schools given to the peasants were under nobody's supervision, and consequently the teacher, unless he were pursuing a revolutionary agenda, usually ran away, as his living conditions at home, in the school, and in the village were very uncomfortable.

I wish to add a few words about some of Radakov's collaborators in this zemstvo activity. Vasil'ev (I do not remember his first name) was a landowner member of the administration, and a pale replica of Radakov himself, whose unselfish devotion to his work seemed to fill his whole life. In his understanding and conduct of zemstvo work he failed to see any gray areas, and Radakov's "doubts" were quite alien to him. This kind of idealist in the realm of practical social activities, more than any other type, could be found among the Russian landed gentry in those days.

Nikolai Frolych Agapov, an agronomist of indeterminate social background, was in many regards just the opposite of Radakov and Vasil'ev. He was a conceited, reserved man: Was he secretly ambitious, meditating on great social concerns, or was he an agitator and revolutionary? People said that he was very close to Radakov, having married one of his relatives, and that he skillfully pulled the strings in order to give Radakov's policies a leftist bent.

I cannot avoid mentioning a man very popular in the district as a delegate, a big landowner of the merchant estate, Ivan Pavlovich Iakovenko, whom I knew well as a coal producer who built a great anthracite business in the Don Military Region as well as a member of our association for many years.[14]

At zemstvo meetings, I. P. Iakovenko was an invariable and ineradicable "liberal," all of his contributions being in support of Radakov's leftist policies and in opposition to local "die-hard right-wingers" of Sergei Mikhailovich I.'s type. Ivan Pavlovich's zemstvo activities were in fact restricted to his role as a delegate; that is, they carried no responsibilities and were a form of relaxation for him. At the Southern Association, where he was a big financial contributor, and even more so in his everyday setting at the mine, he was quite a different man. Then there was no trace of liberalism, and the association leaders often had to oppose his stubborn resistance to industrial policies that he considered too sweeping, especially if they required expenditures. At the mine he was an avaricious master, consistently and stubbornly chasing every kopek—a classic example of the characteristics of his estate. I think that a liberalism akin to the merchant Iakovenko's was rather common in the zemstvo. The opposition to the leftist course in the zemstvo did not come from such people, who in fact were outsiders in the village and in the zemstvo, but rather from the native gentry of a "rightist" persuasion. I almost never met any delegates who were peasants.

Speaking of the general characteristics of zemstvo activity in Russia, the historian of our zemstvo, V. V Veselovskii, underscores how motley it was. This was not so much due to the composition of the delegates as to the lack of proper people to direct the practical side of the zemstvo work. The heterogeneity of zemstvos' activities was striking, starting with the example of our two neighboring industrial districts: the Slavianoserbsk District was actively building schools, while the Bakhmut District built almost none. The chairman of the Bakhmut Zemstvo for many years was old A. A. Karpov, an excellent manager and a hard worker whose main efforts lay in the domain of medical, agronomic, and various economic improvements, leaving schools aside. He discarded all criticism of this posture with the jest, "Believe me, it's easier to live with fools."

I want to take the opportunity to talk about a remarkable zemstvo worker, in fact I think the only example of the kind of zemstvo leaders whom Russia needed so badly. He was the locally well-known former chairman of the Volchansk District Zemstvo in Kharkov Province, Vasilii Grigor'evich Kolokol'tsov. I recount this with much respect, although his activity was outside the range of our interests and outside the scope of my personal observations. I rarely met Kolokol'tsov in those years, as our roads seldom crossed, because we industrialists had nothing to do with the zemstvo in Kharkov Province. I came to know him better much later, in the hard days of 1918 and 1919 when he was the "minister" of agriculture first under the hetman of the Ukraine and then in the government of General Denikin. But even in the early 1900s I knew a good bit about him and his activities.[15]

He was an agronomist by education and a very rich landowner of the Volchansk District. Kolokol'tsov was elected chairman of the district zemstvo in 1901, and he remained in that position until the end with only one interruption, when he was elected for a three-year term to the Kharkov provincial zemstvo. Kolokol'tsov did not remain in Russia after the Bolshevik upheaval; he spent his last years in France, where he celebrated his sixty-fifth birthday in 1933 and died the following year. The data concerning his activities are taken from the material gathered for this "jubilee," which was partially published.[16]

The balance of measures in the sphere of public education realized by the Volchansk Zemstvo during Kolokol'tsov's management stand as follows: at the beginning of the war (about 1914–1915), 168 primary schools already were operating in the district, showing that within twelve years the projected school network within a 2-verst radius had almost been completed. This was the task that Kolokol'tsov had undertaken in 1901. In the meantime, 68 two-class schools were open, as compared to two in 1902. Six higher preparatory schools, which prepared pupils for the gymnasium, had opened in the same period. The school buildings were erected according to the standard type considered one of the best in the empire. Each school possessed a kitchen garden of 1 desiatina for the teachers. The school's appearance was handsome and tidy. Medical assistance for the population was available through fourteen zemstvo hospitals at the war's outbreak, as opposed to six in 1901; this meant that each canton had its own hospital of ten to fifteen beds. Volchansk itself boasted a model zemstvo hospital of 200 beds. Veterinary service likewise was broadly available. And in agronomic assistance the zemstvo was first in the empire in the number of consulting stations, with each canton receiving its own zemstvo agronomist. Unfortunately, I cannot go into other important zemstvo services, such as the exemplary maintenance of roads and the excellent postal and telephone networks, the latter placing second only to St. Petersburg in terms of length of line and amount of equipment. At the outbreak of the war, the Volchansk District was in such a state of cultural development and equipment that it was in a position to shelter about 11,000 wounded and close to 16,000 prisoners of war. Many of the latter were trained professionals who were employed in further economic development.

A local author describes the life of peasants in the small village of Burtsevo in the following terms: "Now in Burtsevo nobody sleeps on the floor on straw, now iron beds are in every house, not to mention the wooden ones. Everybody has a watch, in eighteen houses there are great wall clocks, in the others small plain ones; nineteen houses have cupboards, two have spring armchairs, nine have chests of drawers and wardrobes, in fourteen there are mirrors, in twenty-one sewing machines. The village has its own electricity. People dress almost as they do in towns. There is meat in every home."

All these enormous undertakings, which I just broadly outlined, brought results previously unheard of in a Russian village, and all of these achievements of the Volchansk Zemstvo were made possible because of Kolokol'tsov's enormous energy and selflessness. These qualities enabled him to overcome not only internal opposition, and there was plenty of this, but also to deal with the obstacles raised by provincial and ministerial authorities. It seems that Kolokol'tsov found some way to carry out such irreproachable activities in spite of the government "supervision," which at the time was considered hostile to any substantive zemstvo efforts. In his memoirs, unfortunately unfinished and not published, Kolokol'tsov tells how he

> began his work in an environment where any progressive work was met with great opposition, where the opponents were very powerful, and used whatever means they chose without compunction. Especially in the beginning, their greatest weapons were endless revisions, first by local, then by provincial councillors, then by the governor, then by the gendarmerie, then by the ministry. . . . Utimately, one developed the habits of accuracy, strict observance of the law, never overstepping one's rights, and above all, of keeping perfect records and of separating zemstvo business from all political overtones. In this way it became possible to resist attacks from a number of governors, revisions by the ministry, the army administration and other institutions.

Kolokol'tsov tells how he and the zemstvo were treated by some of the landowning gentry, "who had a very negative opinion of the broadening of the zemstvo's sphere," a feeling shared by a number of Kharkov's governors. The nobles were particularly irritated by the ever-increasing zemstvo taxes and "uninhibited in their methods of struggle." In fact, zemstvo taxes were very high, having risen from 40 kopeks per desiatina in 1901 to the "monstrous sum," as people used to say, of 4½ rubles at the outbreak of the war.

Here I must add a curious note: zemstvo taxes in the industrial districts of Ekaterinoslav Province never exceeded 50 kopeks per desiatina. This modest rate of taxation on land prevailed through the whole period, only because the Slavianoserbsk and Bakhmut zemstvos levied very high taxes on other entities: namely, our industrial enterprises, which were always taxed at the maximum rates. Agriculture was freed from taxation at industry's expense. Had our zemstvos been run by a leader like Kolokol'tsov, they could have raised enormous sums with a relatively modest and not overly painful increase in real estate taxes and could have developed programs comparable to his. Unfortunately, we did not have any leaders as exceptional as Kolokol'tsov, and I think this was the case throughout Russia.

The Volchansk District did not have much industry, and all these exceptionally high zemstvo expenditures were supported by land taxes, so it is little wonder that the landowners were discontented by the astronomical rates. "And therefore," says Kolokol'tsov, "this group [of noblemen] tried to influence [Governor] Tobizen, but he was a clean man, a former barrister, and avoided all illegalities, trying to stay within the law." Kolokol'tsov remembers three other governors he had to deal with: Prince Obolenskii, Gerbel', Vatatsi, and their common vice-governor Azanchevskii. "All three," he recalls, "quickly understood the state of affairs in Volchansk, and within the limits of the law they contributed to the development of the zemstvo. Denunciations met with no success. When the governors were called to Petersburg, which was quite frequently, Azanchevskii, a former district zemstvo chief, was the acting governor; he had the reputation of being an extreme rightist, but he understood zemstvo affairs and accounting perfectly, and quickly realized what sort of man I was. Our progressive work met no opposition from him, and as long as it was in accordance with the law I always had his support."

What, then, was Kolokol'tsov's political orientation among our educated public, this man who had succeeded in organizing and achieving such great social improvements, which proved, according to V. E. Brunst's testimonial letter, "that it was possible for autonomous local administrative units to develop to such a degree"? Brunst himself provides an answer when he says that Kolokol'tsov's principle was to "protect the zemstvo and admit no politics." "Everybody," Kolokol'tsov used to say, "needed the zemstvo, which stood alone, apart from political parties." It should be mentioned that to Kolokol'tsov's credit he always firmly applied this principle to zemstvo work, that the zemstvo was divorced from politics, from top to bottom, including Kolokol'tsov himself. I do not know whether he himself belonged to any political party, but I think that he did not.

Is it possible not to conclude that it was is precisely this impartial attitude that created the fertile ground upon which to achieve a task of unquestionable national importance? Though it is difficult to admit it, it was by strictly applying the very laws that were generally considered a hindrance to zemstvo activity that Kolokol'tsov succeeded in gaining the cooperation even of the government machinery itself. By giving the teachers adequate living conditions and by directing them firmly, he created a permanent staff of excellent teachers and was able to get rid of the politically minded "drifters," who abounded in some other zemstvos. His other activities in the zemstvo followed a similar pattern. Unfortunately, the conclusion one must reach is that Old Russia was unable to produce institutions equal to her real needs, either in the political or social realms. Kolokol'tsov's work and personality were among the few existing exceptions.

Because of Kolokol'tsov's significance as a public figure, I would like to sketch him a bit more closely as a person. What I knew from personal encounters, and what I knew of the character of his work indicated an enormous amount of personal energy that he applied to his efforts, efforts he approached simply and directly. He was the son of a rich landowner and had no financial problems. Living permanently in the village, rooted in the concerns of the village, he had realized even as a young man that the peasants were illiterate, that they had no culture, and were paupers; and this was why they lived so miserably. His exceptional drive impelled him to change this way of life—in essence, his own life—it was something that had to be done. He began his work, his service to the village, in his own home, by creating a model school for handicrafts. When he joined the zemstvo, he pursued the same aim, in the same simple direct manner. But there he had to face the government and the law, which could not be changed and with which one had to cooperate, because without their contribution, it would be impossible to fulfill the primary task. Introducing politics into the process, that is, struggling with the government instead of recognizing it, would only have hampered and complicated things. So it was essential to find a compromise, a means of peaceful coexistence and cooperation with the government. Kolokol'tsov succeeded perfectly in solving this problem, which in fact turned out not to be so difficult. What helped him, apart from his prodigious appetite for work, was his realistic and balanced assessment of forces and his great will to overcome obstacles. During this whole struggle for the zemstvo, Kolokol'tsov was a pragmatist, he stuck to reality, and in this sense he might be compared to a businessman, only his field was that of cultural service to the people— and how incredibly grateful people were to such a leader.

I am not ashamed to say that Kolokol'tsov's approach to his task was similar to our own approach, the approach of the technical intelligentsia of the period, rather than that of the political intelligentsia, who crowded the ranks of the "liberation movement"—he was, in our sense of the term, a true "man of the eighties."

The Internal Life of the Maksimov Mine

I could not avoid digressing from the true theme of my memoirs. Nonetheless, I am not writing memoirs of my private life, I only mention it when it helps me to characterize general conditions. This is why I do not give details about the conditions of my work, about my "management," which, as in every big business, gave me a lot of satisfaction and joy, but of course some grief as well.

The English appeared to be quite correct masters, as they gave me full autonomy, but they were insistent on "pumping" money from the mine, not only to pay the holders of bonds that had been issued shortly after the Englishmen purchased the mine, but also to pay the annual dividends to the shareholders, on a capital investment that was far too big considering the real productivity of the enterprise. The result was that after three or four years the mine was approaching a critical financial situation, which had a direct bearing on the new undertakings that always are essential in coal mining. I could not conduct these undertakings properly and had to prepare for future coal extractions with limited means, a situation that often resulted in damage to the mine. This was quite possible in our case, because the already poor coal deposit was further complicated and marred by major tectonic disruptions. All of this gave me a great deal of anxiety and grief. The fall in fuel prices two years after I joined the company exacerbated the financial situation; selling coal and coke became more and more burdensome, which always happened when we had a "crisis."[17]

As I already mentioned, the Maksimov Mine was very diverse in its economic branches and very scattered because of its multiple shaft system. The technical staff had to be rather numerous and lived in different quarters of the mine. Senior employees, my assistant, the engineer who had to replace me when I was away from the mine, the head miner who was in charge of a number of shafts, the supervisor of railroad shipments, the manager of mine machinery, the doctor—all of these men had individual, furnished houses and a personal complement of horses. The other employees, such as the shaft foremen, the heads of the coke furnaces, and the supervisors of coal washing, lived in two- or three-flat houses and were not given horses. Office employees, the chief accountant, and the bookkeepers lived at the "estate," in the village, in a few multiflat houses.[18] The timekeepers, clerks, and team leaders lived in individual flats at the workers' quarters. The mine had a big school with two teachers and an auditorium for theatrical productions and "balls." The mine's hospital with its twenty-five beds, was located halfway between the mine and the "estate." An individual home for the doctor stood close to the hospital, and there also was lodging for the doctor's assistant and the rest of the hospital personnel. As this description indicates, the Maksimov Mine had quite a large staff, managed by me and my technical assistant. The mine owned over 1000 desiatinas of land, most of which was rented to peasants. We cultivated part of it ourselves, for feeding the horses.

As for the social circle in which my family and I lived at the mine, I must give a brief account of my closest assistants. My first assistant was the mining engineer Pavel Petrovich Kazitsyn, who joined the mine after a short period during which my assistant had been K. F. Detil'e, an old employee of the Maksimovs. Kazitsyn was a colleague and great friend of V. A. Stepanov, my assistant at Verovka, about whom I already have written. The two shared a strange fate. Kazitsyn got married about the same time as Stepanov, and his wife also left him after two or three years of marriage. Poor Kazitsyn painfully resented this family tragedy, which had taken place while he was absent from the mine on his leave; he tried unsuccessfully to shoot himself and returned to the mine quite sick. For a long time he was unable to walk through the underground galleries and had to be carried in a cart.

"Long Kazitsyn," as people used to call him because of his exceptional height, in spite of fine qualities as an engineer and employee, such as efficiency, calm, fair-mindedness, and tact, was not particularly gracious in his manners. He was a rather sullen man, and his mood was often ironical. He and his wife were my family's great friends, especially his wife, Olga Pavlovna. When Kazitsyn first came to our house without his wife, the children fired questions at him about her, where was she, when would she be coming? "Olga Pavlovna?" answered Kazitsyn with a crooked smile. "The dogs ate her up." The wound in his chest would not heal and in fact made him unable to work. Our mine doctor N. A. Geider, an able practioner and a close friend of Kazitsyn, was unable to cure him completely. But sometime later, returning from a furlough in Germany, Kazitsyn, who loved teasing the doctor, triumphantly declared that he had been completely cured in Berlin by the first doctor he met. This doctor, he said, lived somewhere in the suburbs and on his front door the only sign was one that said "At Home." He would just stick a plaster on a wound, and the wound was healed as if by magic. How he was really cured I never learned, but in fact he had completely recovered when he got back. After he left Maksimovka he no longer worked in mines. I later learned that he had become a mathematics teacher in a technical high school in Petersburg.

My long-time assistant at Maksimovka was mining engineer Andrei Andreevich Naranovich, a man of great initiative, an excellent engineer, who directed the mine independently when I moved to Kharkov. He remained at the mine almost to the end; that is, when the mine was sold to the Dneprovsk Company.[19]

After this, as far as I know, Naranovich no longer worked as a mine employee, but managed his own affairs, mainly in the anthracite region where he was partner in a small mine. As a member of our association, Naranovich represented the interests of the anthracite industry. Andrei Andreevich remained in contact with me and we have maintained our friendship ever since we worked together at Maksimovka.

At the Maksimov Mine were two young Englishmen training for the mining business, first Nichol and then Hawtrey. After sufficient training they used to return to England to take their examination for the degree of "mining engineer for coal extraction." Their role during my period was rather insignificant, if only because of their youth and inexperience, and was limited to observing how things were done at the mine. Both were very decent young men. Hawtrey, or "Hawtrey Ivanovich" as the miners called him instead of "Ralph Ivanovich," remained at the mine for some time, learned Russian well, and ultimately became one of my active assistants.

It is with personal feeling that I must mention a long-time employee, in fact the oldest at the Maksimov Mine, who had first been with the Maksimovs and then with me, the foreman Stepan Alekseevich Miokovich, who was officially our head miner but who in fact had much more extensive responsibilities. Miokovich was a native son, the descendent of a ruined noble house of Slavianoserbsk District, the numerous Miokoviches. I do not know for what reasons this gifted man had only the education of a head miner. But once a head miner he learned so much from personal experience that he understood mining technique so well that he executed his tasks perfectly, even in jobs where he had never worked before. He gave me a convincing demonstration of his efficiency when close to the end of my period as director I had to charge him with the very complicated and difficult task of retimbering a deep shaft where there had been a collapse in an area of weak rock.

Miokovich was one of the rare head miners to be known not only in our region but throughout the Basin. His popularity was not only due to his knowledge and experience. He was a very conscientious worker himself, and he knew how to obtain similar work from others; he was rather a modest man by nature, at least without pretense, and he always knew how to behave, how to tackle a given situation. Miokovich was particularly efficient in directing the workers; in fact it is hard to believe what authority he had and how much people liked him. I think that if we had no strikes it was, along with other factors I will mention later, an effect of his influence upon the workers. His word and his decisions were never questioned or criticized by the miners. As he was in charge of several shafts, and was the head of all the team leaders, it sometimes happened that young engineers were under his control, but I do not recall a single case of insult, friction, or insubordination. It goes without saying that Miokovich and his wife were welcomed members of our social group. He faced both superiors and subordinates with a remarkable air of calm and with true dignity. He did not leave Russia, and remained under the Bolsheviks. I do not know what has become of this worthy Russian man, or even if he is still alive, but I am sure that even in that environment he found an altogether righteous way to live.

If I have gone into too much detail about Miokovich, it is because my memory records such a clear image of this positive Russian character. Miokovich, Lutugin's Moses Gorlov, and that brilliant example of a fine

Russian man, Kolokol'tsov, all shared certain qualities that, even though rare, I think of as characteristically Russian: a clear understanding of one's business, the knack of performing it under any conditions, and the notion of service as duty.

Our mine doctor, the kindly Nikolai Aleksandrovich Geider, a German subject of the Russian empire who had graduated from Dorpat University, spoke Russian with a characteristic accent. Although, as was always the case with Germans, his whole outlook, for us Russians, was the subject of jokes, jokes about him were gentle and harmless and everybody liked him as a person. As a doctor he gained general favor, not only among us but throughout the region. He had a good practice even outside the mine. Poor Geider's love for hunting resulted in a painful accident: while boating on a duck-hunting expedition an imprudent companion accidentally fired his shotgun point-blank into Geider's leg. The leg had to be amputated, and Geider walked on a peg after that, preferring it to an artificial limb. He was so used to his peg that he resumed hunting, frightening the game with the sound of it, as Kazitsyn used to attest. The doctor was married to a widow, a mother of two daughters who grew up at the mine and got married there. They had a son, Orest, who was born at the mine. Mariia Grigor'evna Geider was a thin, small woman, who was constantly smoking or rolling a new cigarette. She was a gracious hostess, and everybody liked their home, which was popular among Maksimovka inhabitants as neutral ground, where tedious professional concerns had no place.

It is hard to imagine how important this combination of a skillful doctor and a good man is in such a secluded circle, cut off from cities as mine employees were. A doctor is not only a man who often saves the lives of dear ones, or even your own, but who is also your intimate friend, who gives you bracing advice in many circumstances, concerning your way of life or your health. Sadly, Geider died prematurely of acute tuberculosis after a severe cold he caught in the Caucasus Mountains where he was driven by his passion for hunting. I keep an abiding memory of this excellent man, who more than once saved my wife's health and my children's lives.

The railroad spur was managed by Wladislaw Ivanovich Plenkiewicz, another long-time employee. He was a graduate of the Railroad School, a minor technical school. Plenkiewicz was of Polish origin, a scrupulous and careful worker with a huge family. His wife was a beauty who drove the local youth out of their wits, and they had five daughters, or maybe fewer in those days. Plenkiewicz had tremendous responsibilities, which he undertook almost independently, as we mining engineers had very little competence when it came to railroads. Plenkiewicz had a very amiable and sociable personality and was a gracious host, but he was so involved in his work and his family life that nothing else seemed to matter. He invariably diverted the course of any conversation to the subject of locomotives, which in his words acquired the qualities and the variety of human beings. Kindly Wladislaw Ivanovich died long ago, as did his wife—in 1927 we accidentally ran across his daughters in Poland.

Space does not permit me to recall all the other employees of the mine, the young engineers who often began their career "under Miokovich" in the minor shafts, our numerous foremen, the men who supervised the coke furnaces and the coal washing, often people with no education who made their way up from the ranks of the simple workers and became, at least most of them, skilled craftsmen. I should mention that toward the end, when the number of mining machines increased sharply, I had to hire a specialized mechanical engineer to supervise all the mine machinery (excepting the railroad). For a given period it was engineer Vyrvich, who married the doctor's wife's youngest daughter.

I might also mention a very original character, Feodor Vasil'evich Shiplik, our agent at the Almaznyi Railroad Station. We regularly shipped huge quantities of coal and coke through this station, about forty or fifty cars every twenty-four hours, including the load from the Golubovka Mine, which we serviced as well. Our office at the station had to receive empty cars, and distribute them to the mines keeping a strict account of the scheduling, as every standstill of over eight hours was fined. Many mines were connected to the Almaznyi Station and as there was a permanent shortage of freight cars, Shiplik's task was to keep a close eye on the traffic to prevent the station from making mistakes in the other mines' favor. Among other duties he had to make the fee deductions for the freight, the timber, and so forth that passed through our section of the line. These were complicated tasks, which required a lot of promptness and tact, and Shiplik could perform them most ably, with the help of only a young clerk. We rarely had to pay fines and even these were quite modest, as our relationship with the station master was excellent. True, we paid him a monthly salary, although a very low one, as he received only forty rubles. But such was the custom, everybody did the same; of course, for such a small sum we did not ask for anything illegal, it was just a sort of insurance against potential difficulties or harassment.

After all the long years of service Shiplik developed a most peculiar countenance—a cunning grin never left his face, and his eyes seemed always ready to persuade and contradict. Shiplik was considered an old fox, but this was rather groundless—really he had just developed a professional knack. Among his unofficial duties he had to take or bring to the station the higher mining officials and their families starting with myself. Shiplik did all this most readily. He would always phone us to say precisely when the train was leaving, he would meet us at the station, take care of the luggage and unfailingly entertain us with conversation based, frankly, entirely on station business. When he appeared now and then at the main office, he looked like one who feels out of place and does not know what to do with himself.

I will not dwell on the large staff we had at the main office, but their chief was A. G. Obraztsov, who had come with me from Makeevka and about whom I have already spoken. The office clerks who were poring over account books were not as individualized as the technicians— at least that is how they appeared to me; maybe I just did not know them well enough because at the main office I dealt exclusively with Obraztsov.[20]

I will add a few words about the extent of my responsibilities and my work. Of course I had not only to be informed but personally involved to direct all the work of the mine, especially the preparation of new sections for future coal extraction. I had to keep track of the output level, the cost of the coal, the miners' pay, and so on. "The director of a mine has to know everything that's going on," asserted my predecessor at Maksimov, L. G. Rabinovich, who spent the whole day on the phone. It is true, though, that he would add that the director should also leave the mine now and then, so as to give the employees a rest from his presence. Joking apart, however, the director's duties were quite important and various in the mine, and also out of it, starting with the concern for timely and profitable sales, for generating the necessary funds for the mine, and so forth. But these direct duties were not the only ones, general duties often were closely related to the previous ones—such as the effort to provide the entire industry with sufficient rolling stock, of which there was a permanent shortage. Coal shipping throughout the Basin proceeded under the banner "the struggle for freight cars." In time there would also be the struggle for prices and the struggle for "technical conditions," meaning the quality of coal and coke shipped to the railroads, the fleet, and the factories, our primary consumers. More generally, there was the struggle for the railroads; that is, the construction of new lines in order to enlarge the coal market, the struggle to lower and equalize coal freight rates, the struggle for tariffs on foreign coal, and so on. In other words, issues of industrial policy compelled me to go to Kharkov, to the Southern Association and to the Committee for the Distribution of Freight Cars. So while I lived at the mine, I had to go to Kharkov almost every month. Traveling to

Kharkov for the meetings, sharing the same rail car with representatives from the whole region, we would begin our meeting right there—whenever we or our staffs met all we could talk was business.

My routine at the mine started almost every day with an inspection of the works, down the shaft, conversations with the heads of different sections, and a visit to the mine's office to concentrate on the accounts. In the afternoon I worked at the main office. The most important part was in the evening, at my own desk, where I balanced accounts and drew up future plans. The mine demanded constant attention. This was my daily routine for many years, not the least bit boring, a lively enterprise shared with others engaged in the same challenging work.

I have elaborated purposely on the characteristics of the Maksimov staff, because the other mines of the Basin had comparable personnel. I think that the comparison could stand even for the quality of the people—Old Russia produced excellent human material for the most various tasks, the best of whom often issued from relatively low social levels, as they were healthier, more in control of themselves, and better able to grasp the function of their chosen sphere of activity.

My memories have focused here on the image of my erstwhile colleagues on the staff, just as earlier I focused on the collective image of the miners. Fully convinced of the accuracy of my impressions, it seems to me that in this work I am trying to describe, all of us, from the miner to the general manager, were engaged in a constructive, interlocking cycle of effort vitally important to the country as a whole. In this understanding of everybody's task, there were no exploiters and no exploited. The difference in our positions was dictated by the difference in our qualifications, by the difference in our degrees of responsibility; as a whole, this difference was part of a way of life that grew out of particular historical developments.

But these simple, and one would have thought, indisputable and universal situations were not seen this way by our intellectual vanguard. I have already spoken about the malevolence with which we "industrialists" were viewed by contemporary (or was it only contemporary?) public opinion in Russia. This public opinion had not the slightest understanding of either what we Russian engineers were accomplishing for the economic development of the country nor what an enormous role foreign capital was playing. This foreign capital invested in southern Russian industry played a role that I think is best illustrated by the very modifications in the region's industrial life that I describe here.

I recall one event out of my personal life that illustrates these things very well. My family spent the spring and summer of 1902 in the Crimea. There they lived on the Tokmakovs' estate, Oleiz, near

Alupka, in a cottage called the Grey Barracks. I myself was so busy at the time that I was able to join them only for two or three short spells.

I remember how one afternoon when I was there we had an unexpected visit from Sof'ia Andreevna Tolstoy, who was accompanied by her daughter Aleksandra L'vovna. Lev Nikolaevich Tolstoy,[21] who was recovering from a severe illness, was staying very nearby at Gaspré estate, which belonged to Countess C. V. Panin. We did not know anyone in the Tolstoy family—Sof'ia Andreevna came only because she was looking for a cottage for some relatives and thought we were leaving soon. Having met such interesting guests we asked them to stay for tea. Sof'ia Andreevna was an interesting looking woman, not yet old, whose conversation was kind and unaffected, who made herself at home. Naturally she wished to know who we were and what my occupation was. When she learned what I did she dropped her eyes and uttered the following, straight from the heart, and not meaning anything in particular: "You manage a coal mine! Well, everyone has to earn a living." I refrained from reacting to her astonishing comment—it was not only Tolstoyan, but typical of the period. While she was leaving, Sof'ia Andreevna offered to introduce us to Lev Nikolaevich. This encounter in fact came to pass two days later, when we accidentally met her and Lev Nikolaevich at the seashore.

I well remember the impression which Tolstoy produced upon me, which was for the most part superficial because the encounter lasted only a few minutes. His eyes struck me first—they were small, gray, piercing, full of worried concentration and a strained, almost painful anxiety. One felt sorry for Tolstoy because of the weight of the constant strain of thinking. What next struck me were his voice and his speech, which did not coincide at all with what one would have imagined, for some reason—the voice was too high, the speech too aristocratic and "Great Russian," most unusual for us southerners. Learning that I dealt with workers he literally threw himself on me, hurrying to explain to such an appropriate listener his own ideas about how easy it would be to solve the "labor problem." Tolstoy was writing on this very subject just then. The simplicity of his solution consisted, as far as I remember, in "not doing to workers what you do not wish to be done to yourself." I very much doubt that after such a statement about the question I could find a common language with Tolstoy. In fact we quickly parted, as Lev Nikolaevich was not supposed to tire himself with arguments. To my great regret, I never saw Tolstoy again.

CHAPTER SIX

My Neighbors and Colleagues

My neighbors and colleagues—that is, people who surrounded me during those happy and satisfying years when I was the independent manager of an industrial enterprise—were people with whom I had much in common. Our own busy personal lives, with their periodic unavoidable difficulties and sometimes real troubles, flew by for all of us. But not even the competition for coal sales induced us to clash with each other; over the course of its historical development the coal market was gradually divided up among the mines. Our personal relationships grew during our leisure hours and in the course of addressing common administrative problems, that is, issues we all faced. In the whole time we were neighbors I cannot remember a single instance of misunderstanding, much less a real quarrel. The common character of our individual efforts bound us together, as did the subtle sense of spiritual uplift that comes from real achievement, from creative "business." In those days one really felt that he was serving the common good and opening up wide and various horizons.

My neighbors at the Maksimov Mine were the mining engineer J. R. Krzywicki, for many years the director of the Golubovka Mine, replaced by the French engineer Homard and his Russian assistant P. A. Nikishin around 1903 when the mine was sold to the French; J. M. Dworzanczyk, a technical engineer who was first the director of the Kadievka Mine and later of the new Irmino Mine, which also was in the vicinity of Maksimovka; the mining engineer J. F. Krzyzanowski, my fellow graduate, who replaced Dworzanczyk as director of Kadievka; mining engineer Ia. D. Priadkin, the permanent director of the Krivoi Rog mine; mining engineer G. M. Montlewicz, who managed the Kamenka Mine of the Aleksei Mining Company; mining engineer I. V. Mironov, who managed the Irmino Mine before Dworzanczyk; technical engineer C. R. Bukowski, director of Mar'evka Mine, who joined us although he worked not in the Almaznyi District but in the neighboring Mar'evskii District.[1] In our Almaznyi District there was also mining engineer L. G. Rabinovich, who was the president of the Irmino Coal Company. He lived permanently in Kharkov, but paid frequent visits to the Irmino Mine. He also had served as director of the Maksimov Mine, under the Maksimov brothers, before I arrived. Rabinovich was our elder, and we rightly considered him the senior professional figure in our region. We were all on close and friendly terms with him.

These were my neighbors: of nine names, five were not Russian; four were Polish, one was Jewish. Such was the Russian blend of "tribes and dialects." Polish engineers were very prominent in Russian industry, as they were good technicians and provided many an example of successful organizing and administration. Despite the common conception, and in contrast to what is happening today in many newly restored states, Old Russia was far more tolerant of people of other nationalities. It should be noted that the originality and the considerable broad-mindedness of Russian life successfully "recast" the other nationalities, without any kind of compulsion. As a result both our Poles and our Jews acquired an interesting blend of the two cultures, where the positive characteristics of one nationality combined with the positive traits of the other to produce, for example, those Polish intellectuals who, even now, after becoming Polish citizens, still have much of the Russian in them. This assimilation was particularly conspicuous in the business environment, which kept away from divisive political concerns. A brief account of the lives and characters of my dear Polish neighbors and of L. G. Rabinovich will illustrate this.

Jozef Romual'dovich Krzywicki, a close friend and mate from the Mining Institute, was a man of poetic instincts and an excellent musician. We both found ourselves in the same so-called French Company (the Rutchenko Coal Company), near Iuzovka. As I observed earlier, in those remote times the Basin looked more like a virgin steppe than an industrial center. The services of engineers were scarcely in demand, and before our arrival there had been fewer than ten engineers in the whole

Basin. Our solitude was so complete and the environment so desolate that we would welcome a cricket in our room as a charming musician. After two or three years as a junior engineer at the French Company, Krzywicki was appointed manager of a very big coal mining enterprise, the Golubovka Mine of the Golubovka-Berestovka Company, which was linked to the Almaznyi Region, where he remained for about ten years before the mine was sold to the French Company. There he became my closest neighbor when I joined the Maksimov Mine much later.

Krzywicki fulfilled his duties as manager of a great enterprise in an original and quite unusual way, as a sort of old-fashioned "landlord-engineer." Not without reason did the engineers of the Donbass replace the agrarian landowners who had almost disappeared in our region. Krzywicki had the manner of a generous, elegant, mild *barin*, and at the same time he had a perfect technical and commercial understanding of the business. He was a kind and just superior for his employees and workers, as he was naturally devoid of any harshness in the way he commanded people. Like most Poles, he was endowed with a great and practical intelligence, but his mind was very peaceful, almost lazy. Krzywicki managed the big Golubovka Mine very successfully for many years. When the mine came into French hands he had to leave Golubovka: Krzywicki and the French, or just the West European industrial practices in general, were incompatible. After having directed two big mines (Seleznevka and Kadievka) for a brief period, Krzywicki went into business for himself, and in his last years he and his family never left Kharkov. He and his wife, Evgenia Stanislavovna, were really our closest friends at the mine. We had much in common, from our student days, to our first steps as engineers, . . . even to our large families with children of similar ages. Krzywicki's music was also an attraction, such a lovely diversion from everyday life at the mine.

Krzywicki left a fine legacy, primarily among the workers who greatly appreciated his delicate attitude and kindness in dealing with subordinates. I can picture him in his ungainly little office, when we were beginners and he was in charge of one of the shafts at the French company, trying to solve some of the workers' problems. He met complaints, usually about trifles or drunken quarrels between miners, with cheerful good nature. For instance, one time a miner hammering a nail into a wooden partition woke up his neighbor, who shouted, "Stop knocking or I'll knock you!" The hammering went on and from the other side of the wall came a stunning blow with a log, which sent the plates flying from the shelves onto the floor. Both men wound up in front of the engineer, and while he was trying to understand the situation, it started to pour outside. The office had no ceiling, just a sheet metal roof and the noise was deafening. "Miloslavskii!" called Krzywicki to his assistant for workers' affairs—the surface foreman (traditionally responsible for lodging and for order in the workers' quarters). "Go out and order the rain to stop!"

"As you command," answered Miloslavskii, and he went out. General laughter eased the tension.

Krzywicki, like most of our engineers, was a family man who was above reproach. There were lots of anecdotes about his love for his family. The owner of the Seleznevka Mine, the well-known engineer Mscychowski, who hired Krzywicki to direct the mine after he left Golubovka, used to say that since Krzywicki had five children and a mother-in-law, there was always somebody sick at home, and he loved them so much that he could never leave them to come to the mine. He was just as reluctant to leave his family for a business trip, and Mscychowski claimed laughingly that he always did his best to miss the train. These exaggerations by the "boss" were in keeping with Krzywicki's character. Along with his devotion to his family, he was a very independent person and resented his obligations. He finally went into private business, which he continued in Poland later on.

Krzywicki died in 1933 when he was about sixty-seven years old. His death was quite unexpected, as he had never suffered any illness. Even in the circumstances of his death he involuntarily acted as though he did not want to bother his family with a long disease. In the morning he did not feel well. The doctor, a friend of his, after examining him proclaimed, "Get up! Nothing's ailing you, there's no need to loll around in bed!" That evening Krzywicki died of a heart attack.

Bukowski was quite a different character, although a charming man as well. Casimir Romual'dovich Bukowski was Krzywicki's nearest neighbor, a technical engineer from St. Petersburg who directed the Petro-Mar'evka Mine. He was just like Krzywicki, an exceptionally good-hearted man. Bukowski first appeared in the Donbass in the early 1900s. I was already living at Maksimovka when I heard that the Petro-Mar'evka Mine (of the French Company) had a new manager. I remember quite well the first rumors: "a simple man, very kind, yes, friendly with everybody, shortish, neat, accurate; he goes to the mining balls and dances so touchingly, almost always with his wife, who is also short and a bit plump—such an uncommonly loving couple!"

We got acquainted, as I recall, on the train when a whole delegation of engineers from our area was going to attend a meeting in Kharkov. When we inquired whether anyone else was coming the conductor told us that an "old fellow" from Mar'evka was traveling in the front compartment. The "old fellow" was Bukowski; it is curious that in the whole course of the twenty years that I knew him he always gave this impression. Perhaps it was because not only his face but also his head were carefully shaven, or perhaps it was that his eyes shone with such profound kindness.[2]

Both Krzywicki and Bukowski sincerely loved Russia and everything Russian. "When I read your letters," Bukowski would write years later when he was in Poland and I in exile, "there is an air of something wonderful and now so remote." He had an excellent knowledge of Russian literature and appreciated it, which was not all that common in industrial circles, even among Russians.

Bukowski directed the Petro-Mar'evka Mine almost the whole time he was in the Donbass. When he moved to Kharkov around 1910 he became a member of the board of the newly created [South Russian Mine and Factory] Insurance Company. We did not know each other very well when we lived at the mines, but in Kharkov we became great friends, as the Bukowskis lived in our house for many years. His family, including kindly Elena Germanovna who always was tenderly in love with her Casimir, and their daughters became our close friends. Later, in Poland, Bukowski was a high ranking civil servant as he became the manager of all the country's salt mines. He died the same year as J. R. Krzywicki and in a similar way, from a previously unnoticed heart disease after just three or four days of illness.

Jozef Mikhailovich Dworzanczyk was a graduate of the Kharkov Technological Institute. He started his activity at the service of a famous self-made man, A. K. Alchevskii, who was the founder of two big Donbass firms: the Aleksei Mining Company and the Donets-Iur'ev Metallurgical Company. Alchevskii had a high opinion of Dworzanczyk's abilities as an engineer. Brisk and mercurial, bursting with energy, with nerves strained to the breaking point, Dworzanczyk was an excellent salesman and administrator. He assumed top positions in the Basin as he became executive director of some large coal enterprises, first the Irmino Coal Company and later the Shcherbinovka Company. Dworzanczyk was an indefatigably hard worker, and he loved huge industrial achievement; of all of his colleagues he was the one nearest to the European model of an industrial entrepreneur. "Business" and industry were his passions. His ever-busy mind was always engrossed in "business" and its interests. The quickly expanding industrial activity of the Donets Basin was an environment exceptionally favorable to individual creativity. In this period Russia had neither syndicates nor trusts, so the enterprises were not limited in their activities, and the top managers had full initiative from prospecting the mine to coal sales.

The situation changed sharply in 1907 when the Produgol cartel was created. Produgol now coordinated the coal sales of those firms that joined, as well as regulating their output to a degree.[3] Produgol was established by foreign capital, which sought to improve the rather low profitability of the mines through a marketing organization. I do not intend to describe the functioning of this cartel, which I believe was the first in Russia.[4] Produgol did not receive much sympathy from the public, which was quite natural considering Russian public opinion. I will point out only that this public animosity did not stem from any particular activity of the cartel itself, but rather from the antitrust mood, which was rooted in a lack of understanding of the indispensiblility of such cartels for capitalist industry.

The attitude toward Produgol indicated a certain degree of division among the industrialists of southern Russia, in particular between the Russians and Poles. The Poles acted like Europeans, the majority of them taking key positions in Produgol, a kind of commercial arrangement into which they entered easily. For many Russians, probably the majority of them, it seemed somewhat alien. It was more in the nature of the Russian industrialist to want to control his business from start to finish. J. M. Dworzanczyk in particular was passionately devoted to this notion of uniting the purely commercial aspects of the industry, which interested him much more that any other.[5] Indeed, the oppressive environment of the mine often weighed heavily on him. His attitude toward our Southern Association was restrained, or even a little bit cool.

Dworzanczyk's exceptional talents were later appreciated by Polish industry, as in his last years he was appointed director of the very big mining company, Guichet, in Silesia. I last saw him about two years before his death. His life-style seemed quite luxurious, but this was all for show, because in fact his family life was just as modest as it had been in Russia; he worked in the same feverish way that he had in his youth, but one sensed his overwhelming weariness. He died of a heart attack in 1934 at Vichy, where he had gone for treatment.

We were on very friendly terms with J. M. Dworzanczyk's family, first at the mine and later in Kharkov, where we moved almost simultaneously. My wife and I were very fond of Elena Aleksandrovna. May she forgive me for saying that she was a charming Russian *barina*, of Polish descent.

From 1906 on, after Dworzanczyk's departure, the director of the Kadievka Mine was my fellow graduate Jozef Feliksovich Krzyzanowski. Unfortunately, we moved to Kharkov about a year after he arrived, and I lost the opportunity to become better acquainted with Jozef Feliksovich, whom I seldom met after our graduation. I came to know him better much later; that is, after we emigrated. Of course, I naturally cannot express my personal feelings about living colleagues as I freely as I have done for the deceased—I must limit myself to strictly biographical data. With considerable regret, this is what I shall do in my description of the life of the Almaznyi region, concerning J. F. Krzyzanowski and Ia. D. Priadkin.

Krzyzanowski was responsible not only for Kadievka Mine but also for the two Kadievka blast furnaces. The Annenskii and the Lidiia coal mines, directed by the engineers I. V. Pokrovskii and N. N. Gorletskii, also were under his supervision. This whole industrial complex, the largest in the region, belonged to the South Russian Dnepr Metallurgical Company, whose executive director was the well-known Ignatii Ignat'evich Iasiukovich. He was a brilliant engineer and administrator (a graduate of the Petersburg Technological Institute). Iasiukovich, a man I greatly respected, told me that they had hired Krzyzanowski to solve their main problem, which was to supply their great metallurgical plant, one of the largest in existence, with its own coal and coke. Krzyzanowski fulfilled this great technical and administrative task brilliantly. In his ten years as manager (1906–1916) the coal output rose from 30 million puds to 70 million puds and the production of coke, exceeding all records, rose twelvefold, from 3.3 million puds in 1905 to 36 million puds in 1915. The Kadievka mine became Russia's largest coke producer. It was the first to be equipped with Cowper's new furnaces, which later spread not only in Europe, but also in America. Their popularity in America was due to a 1913 visit to Kadievka by Mr. Gary, owner of the largest coke plant in Pennsylvania.

Speaking of Krzyzanowski, let me describe some of his nonprofessional activities to throw some light on his personal qualities. At the peak of the fighting during the World War, in 1915, Jozef Feliksovich by his own initiative raised enough money to bring presents to the soldiers engaged at the front. Visiting the trenches was a very risky move, which he described in the Polish paper *Swiat [The World]* in its 15 February 1916 edition. The trenches could be reached only on horseback, so he rode with two mounted orderlies. As they crossed the open ground they were subjected to artillery fire from the invisible enemy, whose blows were directed by a German observation balloon that could be seen easily with the naked eye. On their return trip, they had to make their way through a forest almost entirely destroyed by explosions, creeping from tree to tree. "We did not hear the 'hiss' of the ordinary bullets, but the wasplike buzz of the explosive shells we heard very well," he wrote.

After his return from the trenches Krzyzanowski told me that he had received an excellent impression of the Russian soldiers, with their quiet courage—he was especially impressed by the Siberians. In a letter he wrote me later, he told me how difficult it had been to obtain the authorization to visit the trenches; he had been assisted by the Cossack general Madritov, whom he had met before the Russo-Japanese War, when traveling through Manchuria, Korea, and China on a mining expedition organized by A. M. Bezobrazov.[6] Krzyzanowski had a very good opinion of Bezobrazov, and paid tribute to his energy, wisdom, and great insight. During a diplomatic meeting chaired by General Alekseev[7] in Port Arthur, also attended by Russia's ambassadors to China, Japan, and Korea (Lessar, Izvol'skii, and Pavlov, respectively), Bezobrazov made the following observation: "This is Russia's last chance to break down Japan, and if we do not do so at once, in half a century the fate of Asia and Siberia will be decided by Japanese residing in Tokyo and Peking, and in a century the essential decisions concerning Europe will be announced by the Japanese sitting in London, Paris, and Berlin." Judging from recent events at the beginning of 1938, one may wonder whether the sagacious Bezobrazov in fact was not overly optimistic. The world hegemony of Japan (the yellow race), which he predicted and which was not stopped in time, may in fact be realized much earlier.

Krzyzanowski left the Kadievka Mine at the end of 1915, and the Russian government sent him on a mission to the United States regarding problems facing the armaments industry in 1916. He remained there until 1918. Under the Provisional Government, still confident that there would be a favorable end to the war, he started working with his American friends on a project to create a great Russian trust of machine and metallurgical firms, with the participation of American capital. Because he had held a high position in the Putilov Works, he was arrested by Zinov'ev when he returned in 1918 and held in Bolshevik prisons in Petersburg and Moscow for more than two years.[8] Krzyzanowski was first incarcerated in the Petersburg prisons of Gorokhovo and Liteinyi, and later at the Androniev Monastery and at the Lubianka and the Butyrki [prisons] in Moscow. It is a wonder that the Bolsheviks did not "write him off," especially as he made an unsuccessful attempt to escape from the Butyrki. J. F. recorded his impressions of the Bolshevik jails in an interesting pamphlet that I will use when I speak of my own life in Russia under the Bolsheviks.

In 1921 Krzyzanowski was exchanged for a Russian communist, a prisoner taken by the Poles during the 1920 war.[9] After his suffering in Bolshevik jails he started a new life in his restored fatherland. There, in the atmosphere of a great national reawakening, J. F. developed extraordinary energy and initiated a half-private half-state organization, the Central Council of Military Factories, that aimed to establish a defense industry. In 1927 Krzyzanowski left this council to undertake private ventures. Backed by French investment, between 1927 and 1929 he established a great synthetic silk and wool factory in Chorzow,[10] and later a subsidiary plant in Lodz. At present he is the chairman of the board of the great firm he built at Chorzow.

To conclude this bare outline of Krzyzanowski's remarkable industrial achievements and exceptionally eventful life, I must say a word about his touching attitude toward the Russian emigration. He said in one of his letters that no one knew this "wicked stepmother" better than the Poles, who themselves had whole generations of political emigrés. "We Poles," he wrote, "can have no attitude other than heartfelt sympathy and full understanding toward your hard living conditions in emigration since 1918." I cannot deny myself the sincere pleasure of bearing witness here to the assistance that Jozef Feliksovich often bestowed on the Russian emigrés, always unexpectedly and without being asked. In all these actions, he remained the same as always: a grand person who, to put it frankly, seemed amazing and almost inscrutable in the context of the brutalities of our era.

Such were our Polish friends—erstwhile players in the Almaznyi region and my colleagues in the industrial "profession." Did not Russia endow them with many of her own characteristics? I am not only convinced, but I know that now, living in their own beloved Poland, they harbor no bitterness toward and remember sympathetically their life and work in Russia.

Before turning to other engineers of our region, I must mention the eldest member of our community, Lazař Grigor'evich Rabinovich, now deceased. I have already noted that he was the executive director of the Maksimov Mine when it belonged to the Maksimov brothers. After he left them he collaborated with the engineer S. S. Montsiarli in founding the Irmino Mine, which was quite close to ours, and became its executive director. He lived at the mine throughout its construction phase and was a permanent member of our community. He later lived for a long time in Kharkov, where he was involved in industrial policy.

During the period I am describing, Rabinovich's activity had already expanded not only beyond the limits of our region, but beyond those of the Donets Basin. He was popular in many Russian social circles, where he was known as an important figure of the southern mining industry. He was a long-term member of the council of the Association of Southern Coal and Steel Producers, one of our plenipotentiaries entrusted with representing the industry in St. Petersburg. Later the association unanimously voted him an award of merit as tribute to his exceptional services (although he insisted that the balloting be kept secret.) Almost all of the public achievements of the association were due to his initiative and cooperation. In those last years before the war, the association's activities took on a breadth I think was possible only in Russia.

Rabinovich also was not indifferent to political activity. He was elected as a representative of the Kadet Party to the Second State Duma. His own personal commercial and industrial activities were daring and diverse. He deserves the credit for opening up the new western part of the Donets Basin known as the Grishinskii Region. He took the risk of investing considerable sums of his own money in a new and poorly explored area. His hunch, based on scarce and obscure data provided by a small scale surveying operation, turned out to be entirely correct: the region was rich in excellent coal.

Rabinovich was endowed with a rare blend of technical, administrative, and financial talents. He was at the same time an able business manager and a financier gifted in tackling new or rehabilitated enterprises. This rare combination was even rarer among Jews. Nobody can deny that Jews are often very gifted in finance, but the majority of them have limited administrative talents, especially when it comes to actually managing an industrial enterprise. Such work is not well suited to their very lively, even fidgety, character. Besides creating a great mine in the Grishinskii region and earlier establishing the Irmino Mine, Rabinovich took a great part in the financial rehabilitation of the Grushevskii Anthracite Mine, which belonged to the Stakheev trading firm. Unfortunately I cannot elaborate on the details of Rabinovich's activities in the Donbass. He became a really rich and independent man only toward the end of his long industrial career. He always remained quite self-restrained, limiting himself to modest necessities. However, he spent a lot on others, and the scale of his personal humanitarianism was quite large.

My own relationship with Lazar Grigor'evich was very close. I had known him at the institute, from which he graduated when I was in my second year. I remember his quiet wisdom when he benevolently soothed student conflicts. To me and to our mutual friend Krzywicki he always seemed the respected elder. Later we got to know each other even better professionally, both at the Maksimov Mine and at the Southern Association.

After my independent work establishing the Verovka Mine, Rabinovich took it upon himself to recommend me to the English group that had acquired the Maksimov Mine. In Rabinovich's company I took my first steps into the public work of the Southern Association, where he already was a comparatively senior member. When I had to make frequent trips to Petersburg later on, I stopped at his house almost every time, as he lived there permanently then. We worked together in Petersburg representing our industrial interests. So our personal and professional connections were interlocking.

Rabinovich did not leave Russia after the Bolshevik seizure of power in 1917—he could not bring himself to abandon his old mother and his sick sister. At first, during the NEP period and the rehabilitation of the Donbass, he even held an important position in the southern coal organization, the so-called Donugol.[11] However, in 1928 after the Shakhty trial he was jailed and sentenced to ten years of hard labor, where he died, I think in 1933 or 1934.[12] During the trial Rabinovich was remarkably straightforward and courageous. Speaking about him, Krylenko said, "Rabinovich is alien to the whole spirit of the Soviet regime, but the method of defense he adopted could not fail to impress one."[13] Loathe to offer factual refutation of the calumny hurled at him, Rabinovich simply stated, "Mankind needs new life, but what you are bringing is worse than the old."

I cannot remain silent about the first trial of the "wreckers," which was a public trial, highly dramatized by the Bolsheviks, many of the victims of which were my close friends. Even though the accused were defended by highly reputed lawyers from prerevolutionary days, this trial clearly displayed all the traits that were to become the standard at all the other show trials: the prosecutor's impudent lies, the shameless portrayal of imaginary crimes, provocateurs who had either been bribed or scared to death, and finally, "the ultimate penalty," for absolutely innocent people. This was the beginning of a system beyond the scope of human comprehension, designed to destroy the Russian intelligentsia physically and morally, one of the techniques by which the Bolsheviks rule Russia.

I do not intend to give details of the trial, which I have already described in an article I wrote for the paper *Rul'* [*The Helm*].[14] It is sufficient to mention that many of the emigrés who once had had responsible positions in the Donets Basin were incriminated as well. Engineer B. N. Sokolov was accused of giving 600,000 francs in Paris to Soviet engineer Iusevich, in support of wrecking the Donbass. I was accused of being something like the head of a wrecking organization in Poland, although during my whole emigration period I have lived in Czechoslovakia, and visited Poland only once, in 1927. Soviet engineer

Deter, one of my old acquaintances, was sentenced to ten years of hard labor, apparently because he met me accidentally in Warsaw.

Looking back on that trial with disgust and horror I must mention a significant and frightful incident that occurred during one of the sessions. One of the forced "provocateurs" was the engineer Skoruta, a former member of the Southern Association, whom I knew quite well. He was certainly not a bad man, but had a very weak, almost hysterical personality. When he started producing evidences of Rabinovich's guilt, his wife, who was in the audience, could not bear to see her husband's moral degradation, and shouted, "Don't believe him, he's lying!" The wretched Skoruta fainted when he heard his wife's voice. The session was interrupted, but Skoruta came to and confirmed his statements.

Speaking of this trial of wicked memory, it is impossible to omit mining engineer Nikolai Nikolaevich Gorletskii. He was not really one of the engineers of our region, as he managed the Dnepr Company's remote Lidiia Mine, but the director of our Kadievka Mine was his boss. Gorletskii often came to visit us—he was an excellent person and we liked him very much.

Gorletskii surely was not a capitalist, not even a rich man, as the hangman Krylenko accused him of being, contrary to all the evidence. During all those years he had served modestly in companies as a subordinate engineer. Nikolai Nikolaevich was naturally a mild and quiet man, and he was exceptionally frank. His refusal to tell lies was enough to arouse Krylenko's hatred. During the trial Gorletskii stated with great courage that he was not a socialist, that he did not believe in socialist construction, that he did not believe that what was going on in Russia was right. But he added that all this did not prevent him from being loyal to the Soviet regime. "I could never be disloyal," said Gorletskii, "to my country or to the economy of her people for money." His calm and noble attitude was so conspicuous that one could sense it even through the harsh and mocking account of the Soviet papers. From the very beginning of the trial his innocence was obvious, as it also was obvious that he would be condemned. In him the Soviet regime was destroying what it hated most, the dignity and the truthfulness of the human spirit. They mercilessly sentenced Gorletskii to be shot.

To resume my tales of my fellow engineers, it is worth noting that in the Almaznyi region only a few of the engineers who exercised on-site management had the full responsibilities of an executive director. Those who did included only the managers of the Kadievka and the Irmino Mines, Krzyzanowski and Dworzanczyk, respectively, during this period, along with the director of the Orlov-Elenov Mine, Ia. D. Priadkin and the author of this memoir.[15] In our terminology, the engineers Krzywicki, Nikishin, Montlewicz, and Mironov were managers of mines but did not have the full responsibility for overseeing the whole industrial enterprise.

About mining engineer Iakov Dmitrievich Priadkin, who is in perfect health, I must limit myself to strictly biographical data. But may he forgive me, I still wish to write a few personal lines about him.

When Iakov Dmitrievich appeared in the Almaznyi region he was a young man of twenty-seven or twenty-eight, and in spite of his youth he was the director of the Orlov-Elenov Mine. We, who were older (Krzywicki, Bukowski, and I were close to forty, and Rabinovich, who was at that time busy constructing Irmino, was over forty), were quite astonished by his insight and his profound understanding of industrial economics, in many ways better than ours. In a way, our conception of industry was vague, relying strongly on the idea of an individual "owner" [*khoziain*], as a father exercising tutelage over both the business and the workers. In contrast, Iakov Dmitrievich had a very clear view of the industrial enterprise, and he gave priority to big capital and big industry, believing that commercial associations were indispensable. He had similar views of the labor question. Although he was very fair and humane in his attitude toward the workers he believed that our position toward the labor question even at that time should be guided by the concept of class struggle, as long had been the case in West European industry. Compared to the rest of us Iakov Dmitrievich was in fact a new man, he was a true industrialist, having much in common with our Polish colleagues Dworzanczyk and Krzyzanowski. In spite of personal differences they in fact belonged to the same category of industrial leader, as did Rabinovich to a large degree.

From his very youth Priadkin had been shaped by a new environment, both as a student and as an engineer-trainee. While a student, during the first political wave of the late nineties, he was said to have been a leftist, almost a Social Democrat, but of course in a very youthful way. This political education, in conjunction with his first professional experience in a very well-managed enterprise at the height of Witte's industrialization policy, gave him a deeper understanding of the real nature of an industrial economy and its social implications. None of us had a similar background. We had been educated during the period of political silence in Alexander III's times, and took up our first professional positions in the dull backwater of southern industry. Many of Priadkin's contemporaries, incidentally, also belonged to this category of new engineers. For example, among his fellow graduates were many well-known figures in southern industry, such as R. F. Zivert, B. N. Sokolov,[16] A. A. Naranovich, P. S. Sergeev, L. P. Eiler—about whom I shall speak in the second part of my memoir.

His great involvement in public affairs, particularly in industrial affairs, demonstrated the Russian side of Priadkin's character. He became a leading member of our association. After this introduction, for which I hope Iakov Dmitrievich will forgive me, I shall return to his biography.

After graduating from the Petersburg Mining Institute in 1898, Ia. D. Priadkin was engaged by the French Coal and Salt Mining Company, as a manager at one of the biggest mines in the South, the Shcherbinovka. Priadkin worked there for five years, at first having responsibility for one seam and in the end becoming technical manager of the whole mine. In 1902 he moved to our region, where he became the local manager of the Orlov-Elenov Mine, which belonged to the French Krivoi Rog Iron Ore Company, whose main office was in Paris. He remained there until the Bolshevik upheaval and the emigré evacuation. Under his direction a small mine that produced, I think, about 6 or 7 million puds per year became a great coal producer, virtually a whole new enterprise with an output of 34 million puds in 1915.

It was not in Iakov Dmitrievich's nature to limit himself strictly to the interests of the mine. But the dull and sleepy atmosphere of the province did not provide a very favorable background for public activity. In our province, in fact throughout Russia, the requisite awakening appeared only after the [1905] Revolution, during the so-called prewar period. Priadkin readily responded to the new spirit: he became a representative of the Lozovo-Pavlovka Education Society and energetically helped to establish a classical gymnasium in Lozovo-Pavlovka, a large village in our area. He also became the president of the Mutual Credit Society, and from 1912 on he was regularly elected a member of the Slavianoserbsk zemstvo. Unfortunately I could not observe this interesting period of our provincial life, this bright reawakening, personally, because I had already moved to Kharkov by then. I shall speak about this period in the second part of my memoir.

Priadkin started to participate in our association's activity as early as 1903, and in 1904 he was elected a member of the audit commission. At the general assembly of 1904 he raised the question of the need to modify the regulations of the meetings, which he thought no longer corresponded to the new reality of the southern mining industry, developing so rapidly under the influence of large-scale corporate capital. During his whole career in the association, Priadkin defended the interest of big capital—"Herod's slaughter of the innocents," as his work was labeled by the representatives of small firms. On behalf of the association he was the chairman of the Mining Industry Committee for Freight Transport, and later he was the association's delegate in Petersburg, as a spokesman for our industry's interests. Only highly influential and authoritative industrialists were chosen for this position. Still later he became the chairman of the commission that had to spell out the details of the South Russian Mine and Factory Insurance Company. He became the company's president when it began to function. From 1909–1910 on Priadkin became one of the directors of the new coal cartel Produgol. This enumeration gives some idea of Priadkin's intense public activity. His professional work was just as intense. Besides directing the Orlov-Elenov Mine, he was a member of the board of the Tula Blast Furnace Company, and of the Boguraevskii Mining Company. He was also an engineering consultant to the Seleznevka Company.

Under the Provisional Government, minister of trade and industry A. I. Konovalov appointed him to a very responsible position, vital at the time: plenipotentiary for the national fuel supply, a post he occupied from April to August 1917. Both at the mine and later in Kharkov, my family and I were on very friendly terms with Iakov Dmitrievich and his wife, the kindly Jeanne Ernestovna, now, sadly, deceased.

Priadkin was able to resume his industrial activity in exile, on the same grand scale. In 1923 he became the executive director of the Laurium Greek Mining Company. For four years he was also consulting engineer for the French Mining Company. Since 1927 he has been the consulting engineer and director of the Algerian Lead-Silver and Zinc Mining Company. As a representative of this company he participates in the French metallic ores syndicate. Priadkin has not abandoned his public and industrial activities during his emigration. He participated in the Commercial, Industrial and Financial Union and is now a vice-president.[17] Needless to say, our relationship is as friendly as before, but alas, the distance between us is great and our refugee lives have taken different directions.

Another very original character from our coal mining family was Vasilii Sergeevich Sokolov. He was not from our region precisely, but from neighboring Varvaropol'e. He was in a sense the exact opposite of some of the figures I have just described. Sokolov was not a mining engineer, he was a graduate of the Kharkov University School of Law. A lawyer's career did not appeal to him, however, so he turned to mining on his own estate, where there was a good coal deposit. He became a small-scale coal producer. His mine was not a purely old-fashioned, artisanal one, but neither was it exactly industrial. It represented a sort of transition between farming and industry.

I had known Sokolov's parents since my childhood. When I first met him he was a very young man, much younger than I, but already the head of the zemstvo of the neighboring district. He won my sympathy through his open, straightforward, very lively personality from our very first casual encounter, which took place in a railroad car. V. S. Sokolov belonged to the gentry of the Slavianoserbsk district, and according to local lore, we were very distant relatives. I remember how in my childhood I traveled with my father from the Bakhmut district to Slavianoserbsk to visit the Sokolovs. I remember the long journey and the warm reunion in the village. I have a vague recollection of Sokolov's parents, although he himself was not yet born. The family estate was quite near the Varvaropol'e Station, in the midst of the coal region. There were outcroppings of excellent coal on the estate, but Sokolov's parents never noticed them, not even his grandfather who was a mining engineer. From the time he was in his teens, Sokolov grew up in an environment of small coal producers, who were quite numerous in such "centers" as Varvaropol'e.

As a member of the association, Sokolov naturally became the leader of the small coal proprietors.[18] After the foundation of Produgol the contrast between the small and the large coal producers started to become conspicuous. Sokolov was an authoritative spokesman during our sessions, as he had united the numerous and noisy members of the "lesser brotherhood." These people really had great influence on the association, thanks to the "constitution," especially in the selection of the leadership.

V. S. Sokolov was a typical "native son," a steppe landlord inspired by industry; he was a provincial leader, removed from the unrealistic tantrums of our intelligentsia. He was always benevolent toward the people around him, he passionately loved his province, his Russia, and his tsar: he was a monarchist, but untouched by the excesses of the extreme rightists. During the terrible first years of Bolshevism all of his exceptional and practical energy was directed against the Soviet power, in support of the Volunteer movement. He had active connections with General Alekseev, he raised money for him and conveyed it to the army.[19] He tirelessly campaigned for support for the Kharkov front, was in close contact with General Kutepov, and led the struggle against General Mai-Maevskii of ill memory, who was then in the final stages of alcoholism.[20] Sokolov, who understood the Russian *muzhik* perfectly, had a keen appreciation of events, and an intuition about their tragic extent. "Believe me," he once said, "the Russian people won't be able to settle down, won't be able to get back to normal, before the land is once again taken away from them, and this will happen sooner or later." In this, Sokolov proved prophetic.

Sokolov was reliable in friendship and in business. During the hard winter of 1918 I proposed that he accompany me on a trip from Sevastopol to Odessa. Business trips, this one was for the Volunteer Army, were very difficult then, but he immediately accepted, though he was traveling without portfolio and had to bear the expenses himself. When we arrived we were completely exhausted. The ship had been overcrowded and there was no fuel in Odessa, which was almost frozen. We looked so miserable that the Jewish friend who met us, a small businessman who knew us from Kharkov, broke into tears out of nostalgia and sorrow.

Sokolov did not want to flee abroad, he did not want to leave his family, which was stranded in Kharkov. He was caught by the Bolsheviks in the Crimea and shot, without any such foolishness as a trial. Ivan Vasil'evich Mironov, another member of the association, was shot with him. Sokolov and Mironov shared an estate in the suburbs of Sevastopol, where they were executed.

Ivan Vasil'evich Mironov was a mining engineer, a Cossack by descent, and a long-term member of our Almaznyi District community.[21] In spite of his natural kindness, there was something sharp in his character, and his decisions sometimes were unexpectedly bold, like those of a man who suddenly puts into action some long-cherished and daring project. He did this, for example, in certain decisions about his children's education and he took his family boating before he learned how to control the sails. His last such experience came just short of killing his wife and little son. He had taken them for a sail on the river Kalitva during a flood, and their boat turned over. An excellent swimmer, Mironov had to support his swooning wife and little son for an hour until help arrived.

Mironov never reached the topmost positions in the Basin. He usually was responsible for a group of shafts in one of the big mines or was the chief engineer in a given mine, which was his position at Irmino when he was my neighbor. The October Revolution found him directing a small mine in the Don Region. He tried to cope with events by organizing a collective miners' directorate, which made him appear a committed supporter of the new power. However, this experience did not last long, and Mironov had to leave the mine. But his reputation among the Bolsheviks was so good at first that he was able to help save the council of the Southern Association from the firing squad. Its members had been arrested in early 1918, including the author of these lines. Mironov and his workers got us out on bail.

I do not know how or when Mironov got to the Crimea, as I also do not know the details about his and Sokolov's shooting. I think they faced the firing squad at the end of 1920, after General Wrangel's army evacuated the Crimea.[22]

One of the oldest figures in Donets coal mining was mining engineer Albin Mikhailovich Zavadskii, who faced the firing squad at about the same time, also in the Crimea. For years he had been director of the Briansk Mine in our region. Why did such a kind man, incapable of harming anybody, have to face such a horrible death in his sixties? No one can answer this terrible question.

Pavel Andreevich Nikishin, another mining engineer of Cossack descent, was in charge of Golubovka Mine for many years. He arrived there after Krzywicki's departure. He was five or six years younger than I. Pavel Andreevich was an exceptionally calm and modest man. An excellent engineer and hard worker, he in fact directed the Golubovka Mine quite independently for twelve years. His boss, the French engineer Homard, seldom visited the works.

Pavel Andreevich gave me the impression of someone completely devoid of ambition. He never tried to ascend, seemingly quite happy with his work, which in fact was rather interesting—Golubovka was quite a big mine. Public activities did not interest him at all. I knew him very well, met him frequently and discovered how touchingly faithful he was in his feelings. He had lost his wife before coming to Golubovka, being left with a tiny little daughter, Valia, but he never even envisaged another marriage and cherished the memory of his late wife. His whole private life was absorbed with but one aim, the love and care of his daughter. He did not even send her to a gymnasium, as he could not stand being separated from her. Apart from his daughter, his other love was his big country house in his native Cossack village of Uriupinskaia, which he was rehabilitating and hoping to settle into as soon as possible. Destiny was cruel to poor Nikishin. Valia got married and had a son, whom Pavel Andreevich literally adored. But her husband was an artillery officer who was killed in the war just after his son's birth. Pavel Andreevich himself died very soon after his son-in-law, from a painful and rare disease, lung cancer. He was relatively young, scarcely over forty-seven or forty-eight. I saw him in the hospital a day or two before his death—I remember his emaciated face, his barely audible voice. He asked me to take care of his Valia. Alas, I was unable to fulfill his last wishes, as soon afterwards I had to leave Russia with my family and could not find Valia—she was not in Kharkov, at any rate. I remember this man with great sympathy and compassion, for under the unassuming countenance of this hard worker there burned the flame of tender love and faith.

As a general rule, the mine directors had to go to Kharkov once a month to settle different economic problems. I want to mention an industrial figure, not directly involved in mining, but one who acted as a link between our association and its council in Kharkov.

Nikolai Feodorovich von Ditmar was my fellow graduate from the Mining Institute, where we became fast friends in our higher courses. After the [1905] Revolution when I moved to Kharkov, I became Ditmar's close collaborator at the head of the association from 1907 on, when he was elected president and I his deputy. I will treat Ditmar's election and his activities in the second part of my memoir.

At the beginning of the 1900s Ditmar was in charge of the statistical department of the association and lived permanently in Kharkov. He owned a small metal working shop in the suburbs, on Petinskaia Street, where his apartment also was located. Ditmar never wanted to be "employed," preferring to live on an income from his own business, however modest. He wished to leave neither Kharkov nor his activities at the association. I often stopped at his house when on trips to Kharkov. He visited us a number of times when we lived at the mines, first at Verovka and later at Maksimovka. I knew Nikolai Feodorovich very well, and I always liked him. I must say that in spite of his German name N. F. von Ditmar was a pure Russian, by his very nature, by his tendencies, and his sympathies. His mother, née Sokolov, was a daughter of the northern provincial nobility, and his father was a thoroughly russified German. Nikolai Feodorovich was first educated in one of the cadet corps of Moscow and then in the Petersburg Mining Institute from which he graduated in 1889.

Some remarkable qualities in Nikolai Feodorovich's personality explain how this man, who was not an industrialist, who never worked in mines or metallurgical plants became such a successful and long-term chairman of an organization in whose direct interests he was not involved. During N. S. Avdakov's presidency,[23] Nikolai Feodorovich was in charge of the statistical department of the association, which was entirely his own creation. This enabled him to study the southern mining industry as a whole, and understand it better than any of us. His extraordinary ability to grasp the essentials of every situation made him an invaluable expert in synthesizing the needs of this industry. His very lack of "direct" involvement in business imparted to him an aura of impartiality. Nikolai Feodorovich also had the rather uncommon ability to listen carefully to every business opinion and to take all of them into account in the final decisions. His detractors as well as his collaborators never had the impression that their opinions were being neglected, as is so often the case with our leaders. In fact, when I said that he was not involved in industry, this is not entirely correct, because later his shop became a small plant producing farm implements and various mechanical products, especially mining safety lamps.

I still can remember him clearly in his student days. Nikolai Feodorovich never drank or smoked. His reclusive life was almost that of an ascetic, a very rare attitude among students in those days. Nikolai Feodorovich had an exceptional capacity for work and was very tenacious, but at the same time he was quite good natured and very cheerful. Who could ever forget the way he laughed to the point of crying. In later years he became a first-class debater. In his various public activities his clarity of thought and facility in understanding people were a great asset. His many-sided talents and natural disposition toward people enabled him to become a close associate, almost a friend, to people in different positions. One time he had to pay a business visit to the bishop. After a few minutes he was singing some new-fangled canon he had heard at the last service, the bishop singing along with him. He soon was elected a member of the State Council, representing industry. There he sometimes brought forth heretical views never before heard in this solemn company, but always astonishing in their novelty and acuteness, even in fields quite new to him.[24] As a member of the Kharkov Municipal Duma, agitating on behalf of some new economic measure, he once assailed the councilors with the observation that they could be roused from their sleepiness only by a German bugler playing in the streets of Kharkov. In those years before the war this was only a bit of eloquence, but Kharkov society had reason to recall it in 1918 when the German bugler did indeed blow his horn in the streets of their town.

All of these qualities of his richly endowed personality not only contributed to his election, but also made Nikolai Feodorovich an excellent president for our association. He was particularly able during that prewar period of frantic activity and bold initiatives. He never hesitated to undertake some completely new approach if it seemed called for or if it might increase the luster and influence of the organization he represented.

What were Ditmar's political opinions, what was his attitude toward the political events of the early 1900s? When I pose these questions I anticipate that as a long-time resident of such a great city Ditmar could be expected to have more definite political views. But I am quite embarrassed at the difficulty of defining the political orientation of most of my friends or even my own views, during that first revolution. Like all of us, of course, Ditmar violently opposed the Revolution. He was also a convinced opponent of every form of socialism, which he considered an aberration and an evil. I think he was a monarchist, as we all were, and did not consider the autocracy merely a harmful holdover from the past that needed to be eradicated completely and immediately. We knew the foundations of Russia too well not to appreciate how vigorously our tsars had served the state and with what good will. But, like most Russians, we were embarrassed by the government's weakness and by its bad luck, especially military. We were tormented by the apparent impossibility of finding a solution to the whole Russian dilemma. The stereotypical political parties that were then coming into existence did not seem very convincing. And the conspicuous dearth of real leaders at the head of the "liberation movement," as well as the rampant unruliness of the popular masses threw us into despair.[25]

I do not remember precisely when Nikolai Feodorovich got married—on Petinskaia Street he was still a bachelor. He got married in Kharkov to the beautiful, kind, and quiet Iraida Ivanovna Ivanova. After we moved to Kharkov we were on very friendly terms with Nikolai Feodorovich's family. The events that occurred in Kharkov the year before we left are deeply imprinted in my memory. Iraida Ivanovna, Mariia Pavlovna Sokolova (the wife of engineer B. N. Sokolov), and my wife displayed heroic courage when we, their husbands, were arrested by the Bolsheviks, and they had to defend us from these brutal and arrogant authorities.[26] Every day they came to the station (we were incarcerated in a railroad car), brought us food, and when the guards did not let them in, remained for a long time at the car's windows. I remember their sad, worried faces and tearful eyes as though I were seeing them today.

Nikolai Feodorovich and Iraida Ivanovna died long ago. Nikolai Feodorovich died in the summer of 1919, in the senseless way the majority of [sic] people died in Russia in those chaotic days. He caught typhus when we were traveling with Bazkevich and Skoruta from Rostov to Kharkov, which was then occupied by the Volunteer Army.[27] I do not know what was the fate of their three daughters. Here I end my account of this great man, who did so much to develop the economy of Old Russia.

Here I have reconstructed a small group of people who had something in common, a small piece of Old Russia. Most of my friends and brothers in arms are no longer alive, many met a tragic end, and some of those who survived are now enduring the hard life of emigrés. But before I leave the company of these dear people, my lifelong companions, I wish to point out what was really new about us, what was coming to be, in those days, a new class in Russia.

In a certain sense we were actually new people in Russian society.

We were not professional industrialists by heritage, but instead represented various strata of the Russian intelligentsia. In the historical development of this intelligentsia we were probably the first to feel real enthusiasm for constructive economic work. We forsook the Old Russian illusions, the "thrilling deceptions," and preferred the "mundane truth" of ordinary tasks, a rather uncommon attitude in the still very idle Russia of those days. In this sense we were the characters Chekhov had been dreaming about, when he celebrated, like no one before him, the "significance of work as the foundation of culture." As Gorki put it in his memoirs, "Chekhov loved the building of houses, the growing of gardens, the embellishing of the earth; he felt the poetry of labor."[28]

Here is the actual balance sheet of what we achieved. Without having any established educational background, as the foreigners did, and without any special preparation, we were able to replace the foreigners at the helm of their own enterprises. We achieved this without any outside pressure, simply on the basis of our merits. We established, or in fact we created, new relationships with the workers as well as with all of our subordinates. We were even able to reap the first rewards of this— was not the relative peace in the mining enterprises, in the midst of the first Russian Revolution, a result of our policy? Both the time and the environment were favorable, as they enabled us to demonstrate such positive Russian qualities as simplicity, good nature, benevolence to others, and great capacity for work when accomplishing a task. We were inspired by our mission, and we can state assertively that personal wealth was not our aim. In spite of what public opinion held at the time, we knew perfectly well that our efforts were the basis for culture, that they were gradually educating new people from our workers to ourselves, and that this undertaking was laying the foundations of a better life for the Russian people and for the Russian state. The very nature of our work, the complexities of its production and the marketing of this essential fuel, put us into contact with various components of the national economy. Our horizons, our conceptions of life, gradually broadened.

I will end my recollections about the figures of the Almaznyi region with a bit more detail about Leonid Ivanovich Lutugin. Leonid Ivanovich was a frequent guest in the area while he was producing the map of the Donets Basin for the Geological Committee. He usually stayed at Rabinovich's house and later at mine. If I speak of Lutugin, it is not to show the contrast between him and us, but to show how this former schoolmate of ours formed a living link between us and a very different world.

Lutugin had an incredibly strange and complicated personality—he could be two quite different men. Many people considered him some sort of refugee from an unfinished Dostoevsky novel. Some were convinced that this public atheist was bowing to icons at home. This was an exaggeration, of course, but without a doubt this double personality was not an act. If circumstances "compelled" him to appear an activist in the "liberation movement," he did so, appearing unrecognizable and even hostile to those who had been his friends the day before, those who had nothing to do with that movement, which was most of us. Yesterday's witty and agreeable companion, who had apparently shared our opinions, or more precisely our lack of opinions, would shoot fiery glances at us and shake with unprovoked wrath during oppositional meetings or during any opportunity for defiance against the hated "reactionary," the director of the Mining Institute, Professor Konovalov (as a lecturer Lutugin was a member of the institute's board.) During their frequent trips to Petersburg, Lutugin's friends, such as Rabinovich, Krzywicki, myself, and others from the South, would call on him. He lived with his mother, his brother Viktor Ivanovich, and the Bauman family, as his sister was married to Professor Bauman, another of my fellow graduates. At home with his family, Lutugin was as charming as he was in the Donets Basin. He came from a merchant background, as his father had owned an ancient jewelry establishment, and his family maintained many old-fashioned merchant traditions. Mammy, his mother Olga Artamovnovna [sic], was a very devout old woman, with very lively black eyes. She never missed a service at church and had a full iconostasis[29] in her room, in front of which an oil lamp was always burning.

Leonid, as they called him at home, was her pride and joy, but to be fair, this complete devotion had not spoiled him in the least: he was a respectful and tender son and a very loving brother. In Petersburg, Lutugin was "one of us," and obviously considered his southern friends as an elite, in contrast to his Petersburg associates. He always underscored the pleasure he felt at meeting us, whether it was Krzywicki, Rabinovich, or my wife and me. He always referred to Rabinovich as his erstwhile "provider." After having spent long periods at Rabinovich's house, he immortalized Rabinovich, himself, and his immutable Moses in a big photograph inscribed, "from the foster-children to their provider." Characteristically, Moses was standing respectfully beside the garden-sofa where Rabinovich and Lutugin were seated. Leonid was such an authority in his own home that when the childless Baumans, who were longing for a child, found a newborn boy abandoned at their doorstep, they hesitated to adopt him, fearful of what "Leonid will say." Leonid was then in the Donets Basin, but on his return he put everybody at ease, saying simply, "What strange people, they are offered a son with no trouble and still they hesitate."

Lutugin was a very gifted man and an excellent, learned geologist. But he was not granted a scientist's status although he lectured at the institute for a long time. When we would approach him about his neglect of his situation and his laziness, he would inevitably answer that he took much more pleasure in thinking about a thesis than in writing one. So, he never wrote it. I do not know whether or not he hated the Russian government and the whole regime as much as he appeared to when he spoke in public. I rather think that he was a prisoner of old student attitudes and the Petersburg political environment. We, his colleagues and friends, with whom he shared many opinions, were free from such political bonds, primarily because of our politically neutral student years and later because of our positive work in the down-to-earth industrial world. But in Lutugin's mind the political "maximalism" of the Russian leftist intelligentsia was never quenched and would often burst into bright, "heroic" flames if circumstances were right. Such is my memory of this doubtlessly talented man, who lacked inner consistency. My memory only retains the good side of our mutual friend Leonid Ivanovich, a very interesting Russian personality, a guest we were always willing to welcome to our bear's dens.[30]

Poor Leonid Ivanovich died unexpectedly in a foolish way during the World War, I think in the summer of 1916. He was prospecting the Kuznetsk Basin in Siberia, where he fell sick with an acute form of dysentery. His lengthy illness culminated in a pronounced decrease in his mental faculties, almost to the point of insanity. I was told that before his death he would walk restlessly from one corner of his room to another. Strangely enough, the last words he spoke were about the South.

CHAPTER SEVEN

Echoes of
Political Struggles
at the Mines

*T*he years that preceded the 1905 Revolution are famous for the labor strikes, especially those in the factories of Petersburg. This strike movement reached the Donets Basin, but in our mine there was never a strike, either before or during that Revolution. This was because our mine was unusual, as I shall show.

I remember a lengthy and irksome strike that occurred in 1903 or 1904 at the neighboring Kadievka Mine, which had already become the property of the South Russian Dnepr Metallurgical Company and which was directed by engineer Dworzanczyk. In fact, the workers had no particular reason to strike, especially in such an aggressive way. Their mood was irritated by the political tension that agitators insistently nourished. The workers of any mine could readily find reasons for discontent and for strikes. First there was the wage issue, the "alpha and omega" of any strike. Wages were more or less identical from one mine to another and regulated by long-term practice rather than "economic" reasons and calculations, but from the workers' point of view the pay could and should be increased. Strikers sometimes complained about housing conditions, which were nowhere really satisfactory. Although everybody knew perfectly well that these could not be changed, it was a good subject for protest. A new issue pertaining to the political moment was the demand for the eight-hour day. Even in the workers' view, however, this demand was rather "academic," and they never insisted, simply because all skilled workers, including those posted at tiresome tasks, already worked no more than eight hours, and often even less.

I already have spoken about the living conditions of our workers. I have to add a few words about their budgets. The lowest income of an unskilled worker was at least 20 to 25 rubles per month. The wages of skilled miners such as hewers or tunnelers was much higher. Food was very cheap. The mine's administration contracted with a special foreman to provide meat and bread. Meat cost around 8 kopeks and white bread around 3 or 4 kopeks a pound (miners did not eat black bread). With these prices the monthly expenditure for food for a single worker (cooking was usually collective) amounted to around 6 rubles. Taking into account that lodging and heating were free of charge, even on a minimal salary a regular worker who was not a drunk had quite a bit of money left over to satisfy his other needs and for sending "to the country."[1] This aspect of the workers' life was not a source of discontent in those days. As I said, lodging was not always satisfactory, but our workers were not demanding.

Kadievka Mine, where the strike developed, had a peculiar characteristic that was exceptional in the region. In addition to the scattered minor shafts was one enormous central shaft that concentrated a great mass of workers in one working and living space. This circumstance greatly facilitated agitation and gave rise to a belligerent state of mind. Agitators fanned this aggressiveness, but it stemmed from the quick and often quite destructive volatility of our Russian crowds.

It is remarkable that at the Maksimov Mine, where many of the workers' living conditions were worse, there were no strikes at all, nor could there be in that environment. Our mine extracted coal from six, sometimes seven, small shafts, each employing a limited number of workers; and the shafts were relatively remote from one another. The fact that the shafts were scattered, that they had only 100 or 200 workers each, as well as the lack of bonds between workers of different shafts and the fact that it was difficult to agree on one gathering place, all help to explain the absence of strikes at our mine. Coal miners mostly were young peasants who had not severed their links with the village. They were inclined to feel that taking part in a strike was a kind of "rebellion" [*bunt*], like something not exactly punishable, but full of rakish protest. These motives often were more important than the direct reasons for the strike. The prerevolutionary and revolutionary periods brought something new in the workers' mood, which became generally excited. Now and then we met downright arrogance, something inconceivable before. A new type of simpler agitator appeared among the miners. In some of the mines engineers received anonymous threatening letters. I myself received such a letter, written by an illiterate, which threatened to kill me if I did not increase the wages of the office watchmen. The author was found to be the watchman Ivan Buts, a youth from our village, who was betrayed by his handwriting, which he did not even think to disguise. During the inquiry Buts kept grinning stupidly, obviously seeing nothing unusual in his letter—this kind of thing was common.

Clashes with the workers, although rare, were the most unpleasant aspect of managing a mine and the most morally stressful—especially those that took the form of a general strike. It is never pleasant to deal with an excited crowd, but when you are the focus of its aggressions, it is worse, even dangerous. Clashes became more acute and more harsh, and we felt that the old "patriarchal" era in the Donets Basin was now over. I remember how in 1891 during a strike at the Karpov Mine the very appearance of authority, of a single police officer, had an immediately soothing effect. No armed force was even needed, for it was not fear but the power of resolute authority that restored calm. In all fairness, it is worth mentioning that our local police had demonstrated the right tone of authority with resorting to "active measures." I already spoke of the peculiar strikes at the Makeevka Mine, but there the strikers were the *khokhols*, the seasonal workers, not professionals.

During the revolutionary years the whole atmosphere changed sharply. There was a new air and the old authority was strongly shaken, if not wholly shattered. Workers started perceiving us as direct enemies. But we ourselves were sometimes subject to a sort of political contamination, brought to us by the air of approaching revolution. All of this complicated the already painful atmosphere of a mining strike even further. In fact, the director of the stricken Kadievka Mine, Dworzanczyk, came to the verge of a nervous breakdown; and we, his neighbors, had to take an active part in resolving the strike.

Observing our mining strikes, I always felt that there was something deeper and more important than the apparent causes—an inner protest against an unlucky fate, an unquenchable longing for a different life. Our workers, mostly those who did not make it in this new life—that is, the unskilled workers who in fact were the majority—did not adjust well to mining. The transition from *muzhik* to miner was painful, and the organized, mechanized, directed work was oppressive. Workers were nostalgic for their creative "toil" [*trud*] on the land and could not easily submit to "work" [*rabota*] in an industrial enterprise. It was not without reason that the mines suffered a shortage of labor, sometimes an acute one, not only during the harvest, but in fact throughout the summer.

As I mentioned earlier, in our region as in the Donets Basin as a whole, we managing engineers always tried to coordinate our methods of operating and administering the mines. It is understandable that when strikes occurred in the region such consensus was particularly needed and quite a moral boost to the management of a stricken mine. I remember that the question of the eight-hour day attracted much attention—the majority of us considered its adoption untimely and irresponsible in view of our equipment and unnecessary, as I said before. This issue was raised with unexpected results at the Irmino Mine after 1905—as far as I remember it must have been by the middle of 1906, before the elections for the Second State Duma. This bold reform was undertaken by the director of the Irmino Mine, L. G. Rabinovich, of whom I spoke earlier. Rabinovich introduced the eight-hour day in his mine after long and fruitless discussions with the rest of us. We failed to convince him and, alas, acquired the impression that, besides his personal conviction that the measure was economically feasible, Rabinovich also was motivated by his efforts to win election to the State Duma. This reform had one immediate consequence that was unforeseen and remarkable: the governor of Kharkov, General Peshkov, a petty tyrant not much inclined to respect the law, threw Rabinovich into jail for "introducing on his own volition a measure contrary to public safety." This decision had a direct impact on Rabinovich's election—he won a seat in the Second Duma as a representative of the Kadet Party. Lazař Grigor'evich's imprisonment lasted a month or two and did not much resemble a genuine incarceration. He had an individual cell, furnished with his own furniture including his bed, his meals were brought from his home by the maid, and visitors were admitted almost anytime. At that time, there was so much liberality inside the prisons that prisoners held meetings in the corridors or in the bigger cells, a nuisance Rabinovich complained about. This "penal" regime was not unique to Kharkov, I think, and even Peshkov had no power to change it—such were the times.

It is noteworthy that the introduction of the eight-hour day at Irmino had no effect on the workers' mood, either in our region or in the Basin, because workers, as I have said, attached little importance to the eight-hour day.

Our Political Outlook

How did our personal lives proceed in those years preceding the general troubles of 1905–1906, and what posture did the mining intelligentsia take toward those events that now were ablaze? I think I am not wrong when I say that the period around 1905, which was one of turmoil in Russian society, a period replete with meetings, and antigovernment proclamations, was exceptionally quiet in the mines and villages as well as in our small towns. Workers' strikes were not generalized and, when they happened, rarely gave rise to excesses. The impression was that somewhere far away in the capitals a part of the intelligentsia was rebeling, mainly the people of the northern zemstvos. Incomprehensible acts of terrorism were going on there: almost indiscriminate assassinations of ministers and high officials. It seemed strange that the government was unable to handle events that seemed so localized. But even this strange aspect of Russian politics, as I remember it, did not worry us much. Trying to analyze the indifference of the wide circle of Russians who took no part in these events, I realize that our indifference was not devoid of a hint of sympathy toward the "struggle" against the government, known as the *liberation movement.* As we were virtually deprived of any contact and lived in solitude, this sympathy was nourished mainly by the press, newspapers and "thick journals." Almost all of the familiar Russian papers were then sharply oppositional, even in many respects *Novoe vremia [New Times]*, which I think had the widest circulation of all. Besides the generally oppositional tone of the press (neither Meshcherskii's *Grazhdanin [Citizen]* nor *Moskovskie vedomosti [Moscow News]* nor *Russkii vestnik [Russian Herald]* ever reached our area) our critical mood was bolstered by sporadic encounters with our local revolutionary vanguard.[2] This included the Lugansk zemstvo leaders, the academic circles in Kharkov, the advanced industrial circles in Petersburg, or whatever public or private meetings we had the chance to attend when we were away from the mines. It was practically impossible to support the government, even in words, in the excited atmosphere of the urban intellectual circles that I more or less frequented.

There is no point in hiding the blame—in many ways the government itself was responsible for this atmosphere. For instance, our police understood politics very poorly and displayed complete incompetence in their struggle with the terrorists, whose daring attacks were met with indignation by the moderate circles to which we belonged. On the other hand, the police took excessive measures where it was completely unnecessary; for example, trailing, in arresting, and deporting people simply because their "ways of thinking" were suspicious, to use the terminology familiar at that time. Our police were capable of suspecting the "ways of thinking" of quite unexpected persons, whose loyalty was above reproach. Everybody resented this threat of being so easily caught up in such unpleasant complications, and this raised hostility toward the police.

I remember two instances when I had to deal with the authorities.

The first was at the turn of the century, when I was already more or less a prominent figure in our province, being the director of a mine. I do not remember precisely if it was at the end of the 1890s or in the first years of the 1900s that I was called up for six weeks of summer training as a reserve ensign. I was sent to Sevastopol, as I requested, though I do not remember precisely to what infantry regiment. Having received from my commander permission to live in town, I felt myself to be completely at rest, because there in fact was no training at all. The tsar was to inspect the troops at the end of August, and the only issue was the preparation of a solemn parade. Soldiers used to say that all this was to "teach the generals how to command." Brigade and division commanders were quite elderly, and their incapacity to command was obvious even to the soldiers. In Sevastopol I met a very old friend from my student days, the "philosopher" Popovitskii. He lived in his parents' house; and we met very often, usually at my place as I did not know his family. I have to admit that the "student" spirit we once had in common had vanished after all those years. But Popovitskii had not changed in his poetic, aimless way of life, and it was with a pleasure tinged with sadness that I loved to evoke our "jolly, care-free youth" while chatting with him.

In mid-August, as I remember it, there was a two-day holiday, which we decided to spend at the southern shore, at Alupka. We were both passionate devotees of both nature and the Crimea. My commander gave me permission to leave, adding, "Say, put on your civilian clothes, or else people will say that our lieutenants are wandering around with nothing to do." We returned from Alupka in the morning and had tea at my place, I still attired in civilian clothes. Unfortunately for me the police were just then visiting houses to check, as we later learned, personal documents, especially those of newcomers, in connection with the tsar's upcoming visit. Only those brought up under the Old Regime could understand how ticklish my situation was. "Who are you?" they asked, "Why are you dressed in civilian clothes, where have you been, why Alupka, where did you spend the night there, why did you choose Sevastopol for your service?" These insistent and suspicious attacks were terrifying. The upshot of it: "I will have to report all this to the regimental commander." It is necessary to add that wearing civilian clothes was strictly forbidden to any of the military, that we met nobody in Alupka and so had gone there "simply for a trip with no particular aim," that for "unknown reasons" I had chosen Sevastopol rather that Ekaterinoslav or Kharkov, which were nearer—all this looked very strange in the eyes of our police. In addition to all this, I was a mining engineer, a man dealing with dynamite every day. My case became very suspicious, as the inventive police officer explained to me, because he also suspected Popovitskii not to be a "safe person." It was clear that my situation was becoming truly embarrassing, and I started feeling guilty—a feeling well known to anyone who has for some reason fallen into the hands of the police, but I believe the feeling was even more acute if it were the Russian police of those years.

It was essential to find a way out. Our regiment was commanded by Count Shuvalov, who according to the officers was strict to the point of insanity. My problems must not reach his ears or I risked a court martial. The situation grew even more complicated when my company's commander, after hearing my story, told me sharply that I must understand that once I was "stuck" I was not to drag him into any trouble. I had to forget that he himself had advised me to wear civilian clothes. "Sooner or later you'll get out of trouble, and this, my friend, is no reason for me to ruin my career," he added, rather sensibly. But nevertheless he gave me a good piece of advice: "Go and see the battalion commander—the regimental commander despises him and the battalion commander would never want all this trouble to get to him." This was exactly what happened. After loudly chastising me for my imprudence and thoughtlessness, the battalion commander went to see the police officer and arranged everything. For punishment I was transferred from town to camp, and had a week's house arrest; that is, I had no liberty to leave the camp or to carry my weapon. In addition, because I was unknown in Sevastopol I had to provide the battalion commander with telegraphed information about me from various local officials. Only after this was all suspicion about me lifted and I returned to the military preparations for the tsar's inspection.

This "incident" left a painful impression. I really had felt the mighty tentacles of power. The very fact that my superiors took this "misunderstanding" so seriously, even though the cause was just a trifle, was far more significant testimony to the fatally complicated and dangerous state of Russia's internal affairs than to any underlying fault of individual people. After my stint was over I went to the police officer with indignant reproaches. His attitude was halfway apologetic, but he told me that they always had considered Alupka a nest of revolutionaries, and the way I had visited it was at first glance necessarily suspicious.

I remember how I found myself in another very unpleasant situation on a different occasion, for an even more absurd reason. One of my old friends, the landowner N. F. Pleshcheev, had come to visit us and, noticing some of Tolstoy's forbidden works, asked to borrow the books. He took them with him, but left them by accident in the first-class waiting room at the Almaznyi Station. I remember the amazement with which our station master Shiplik told me on the telephone that the gentleman who had just left my house had forgotten forbidden books, that the books had been found by the station gendarme, who was planning according to the regulations to send them on to the gendarme administration. What could be done? I must underscore that possessing forbidden foreign editions could be construed as an antigovernment offense, and at least would be considered evidence of a "dangerous way of thinking," quite unsuitable for the director of a mine. After some worried brooding I suddenly realized that the head of the gendarmerie in Lugansk was a certain Colonel Norberg, Pleshcheev's brother-in-law. I told Shiplik not to interfere with what the gendarme was going to do and immediately wrote to Pleshcheev.

Close contact with the higher administrative authorities or local governors did not always enhance the government's prestige. I remember a visit the representatives of the Southern Association had to pay in 1906 to the governor of Kharkov, General Peshkov, on behalf of the association. Peshkov regularly used to gather the representatives of various social organizations, such as zemstvos, industry, towns, and so forth, and loved to give them political admonitions, always recommending the organization of "Unions of the Russian People."[3] In spite of his general's rank, Peshkov made a rather poor impression.

In all fairness I must say that most of the governors I met personally were sensible people, often quite good administrators, capable of upholding the government's prestige even in troubled times. Such were the military governors of Ekaterinoslav, Count Keller, of whom I have already spoken, and Prince Sviatopolk-Mirskii, who later became minister of the interior. I met the prince when he was visiting the factory of the Russian-Belgian Company at the end of the nineties, when he was the governor of Ekaterinoslav. Because the factory's management was mainly Belgian, I was asked, along with some other senior Russian officials, to show the company to the governor. After this I had one or two other occasions to meet Sviatopolk-Mirskii in Ekaterinoslav. He was evidently a cultured and benevolent man, but what most struck one about him, even in such brief and infrequent encounters, was a conspicuous, almost pathological, weakness. He would often break off speaking, with a thoughtful countenance, as if exhausted. People who knew him well were quite amazed to learn of the great expectations that accompanied his nomination to the Ministry of the Interior at the end of 1904. In spite of his good intentions, his brief administration, as everyone knows, was most unsuccessful: there was the absurd granting of permission to Gapon's demonstration on 9 January 1905 [O.S.], which culminated in shooting, and similar senseless decisions that led the pitiful prince to declare, "Oh God! What have I done?"[4]

I also remember the governor of Kharkov, Prince Ivan Mikhailovich Obolenskii, who presided over the rather famous repression of the peasant "rebellion" in Kharkov and Poltava provinces. In fact this "rebellion" consisted of plundering the landowners' farmsteads in response to the tsar's "golden warrant," an anonymous document skillfully employed by political agitators.[5] Groups of villages used to make joint raids on the landowners' property, taking away spoils, mainly wheat, and now and then burning the place. I do not know by whose orders the "pacification" of the participants in the rebellion included physical punishment, applied publicly. I already owned a small estate in Poltava, but I had not yet started farming, so there was nothing to be taken and therefore I had no rebellion at my place. Neighboring peasants "rebelled" in the area of such rich estates as Durnovo, Babanin, and others. When I went there soon after the events I was shocked to learn that my neighbor, a peasant named Gustodym who owned a fairly big piece of land, had been flogged, obviously by mistake. In fact, Gustodym had been accused of being an agitator and an instigator by his neighbors, most likely by those in the village who were his enemies because he was a rich peasant. Gustodym was unable to prove that he took no part in the rebellion, and the blindly zealous authorities, as often was the case in our country, took no time to understand the situation and the unfortunate Gustodym was flogged. I was told that when he stood up he just said, "Some law . . . [*otse zakon*]"—such was the law. Gustodym never complained and did not seek rehabilitation; he was more angry at the *muzhiks* who had denounced him.

I remember how Kharkov's public organizations, including we industrialists, gave a farewell party for Prince Obolenskii, who was appointed governor-general of Finland. I remember that one of the minor industrialists, the rather well-known S. S. Kgaevskii, a die-hard member of the Black Hundreds, a man of great arrogance and little culture, the *"enfant terrible"* of our meetings, took it upon himself to give a speech praising Obolenskii for his brilliant repression of the peasant rebellions of 1902. His speech made a painful impression on the whole audience and above all on Obolenskii himself. Obolenskii was obliged to answer, and he did it with considerable dignity, saying that the life of the lower classes often undergoes ugly convulsions that produce corresponding reactions from the authorities. These, he said, like severe illnesses, were better forgotten.

Among the governors of this period I also remember S. N. Gerbel, General Starynkevich, and Azanchevskii, who was vice-governor for a long time, under many a governor. He directed the business part of the provincial administration almost independently, a very able but rather dry person. He was an extreme rightist but very respectful of the law.

Public opinion and our vanguard press never stopped insisting that the government apparatus, through its governors, was more interested in spying than in upholding the law. Personally, living at the mines I had little to do with governors, but I was familiar with the general character of their administration, as I was well acquainted with many of the social figures of Kharkov and Ekaterinoslav, where I often went. Apart from General Peshkov, a rather unsavory person who really had a poor understanding of the meaning of the word *law* and little inclination to respect it, in fact given more to words than to action, most of the governors I knew were quite respectable people, their freedom of action limited by a well-established administrative apparatus. They governed us within the limits of the law. V. G. Kolokol'tsov, the long-time, active president of the Volchansk district zemstvo and sometime president of the Kharkov provincial zemstvo of whom I spoke earlier, had similar opinions about the same people.

CHAPTER EIGHT

The Revolution Approaches

Although the big towns and some of the northern provinces were under the revolutionary thunderstorm during the years 1903–1904, there was almost perfect calm at our mines and villages, as I have said, and the strikes there were not general.[1] There was no violence and hardly any politics. But in the big towns the picture was sharply different. When we visited Kharkov, Moscow, or Petersburg my colleagues and I were confronted with a state of mind more revolutionary than oppositional at various public gatherings and meetings. In Moscow, I once found myself at a crowded noisy meeting at the end of either 1904 or 1905, I do not remember precisely. What struck me was the volatile, unrestrained speeches of most of the spokesmen, demanding a national consultative organ on the model of the Assembly of the Land [*Zemskii sobor* of medieval Muscovy], full general amnesty, and a constitution—almost a republic.[2] True, one participant, obviously out of his wits, made most of the interjections that the meeting's organizers were unable to curb. I also remember attending the meeting of the Ekaterinoslav Assembly of the Nobility in 1904,[3] the purpose of which was to address the sovereign with a proposal stating that it was indispensable to create some national legislative body along the lines of the zemstvo councils—at that time the noblemen did not yet dream of anything else. I remember the perplexed countenance of most of the noblemen—among others, the puzzled expression of M. V. Rodzianko, who was then president of the provincial zemstvo board—his hesitant, almost frightened speech. Nevertheless, the proposal was unanimously accepted.[4]

One of the manifestations of the "liberation movement" was student unrest. For almost six years, until the end of 1906, no regular courses could be taught at the universities. This phenomenon reflected the impact of the public mood on the students. The students' attitude became a sort of barometer of social opinion, something almost unknown in Western Europe, which clearly indicated the immaturity of the whole Russian society. As the famous Pirogov put it, such a thing would not be possible "where the political strivings and passions have penetrated deeply enough through all the social strata. When," he adds, "these passions randomly reach a society which is not used to gradual or radical transformations, society's mood is strongly reflected in the universities."[5] Even when I became an emigré I was able to observe the same phenomenon in 1920–1922 in, of all places, Egypt, during the acute political movement of the rather small, politically primitive Egyptian intelligentsia. There, too, the students were the main protagonists of the movement.

If the main activists of the coming revolution were the students, the main weapon of the revolution was terrorism, individually directed against the highest government authorities. And of course our unfortunate students received the first blows of the government's resistance to the revolution. Gatherings were broken up by Cossacks; students were arrested and deported en masse. It was mostly students who provided the active fighters for the terrorist center of the Socialist Revolutionary party, which directed the terror in Russia from Switzerland, where the leaders went for safety.[6] From such students were recruited the assassins of ministers. Karpovich killed Bogolepov, Bolmashev assassinated Sipiagin, and Sazonov murdered Pleve.[7] These murders were accomplished in 1901, 1902, and 1904. The dry enumeration of the murders and attempts, mainly directed from Switzerland and accomplished by morally intoxicated Russian students, paints only a partial picture. Those who were murdered include ministers Bogolepov, Sipiagin, Pleve, Grand Duke Sergei Aleksandrovich, governor of Kiev General Kleigels, the head military procurator Pavlov, and General Min.[8] Attempts were made against the lives of the following men; that is, planned murders that failed by accident: Governor-General Dubasov, minister of the interior Durnovo, Admiral Chukhin, minister of the interior Stolypin, and General Launits.[9] Most of these assaults occurred within a period of three or four years. How corrosive this massive assault must have been for the peace-loving population, accomplished as it was by invisible, elusive hangmen, against the highest bastions of authority. And so hypnotic was the effect of this revolutionary epidemic, which lay in wait for everyone, everywhere, that nobody cared really to think about the reality of the events going on. The public attitude toward most of the victims, at best, was cool indifference.

All of this turmoil in Russian life in the early years of the twentieth century did not much affect the main strata of provincial society, including the mining population. Among us, the most affected by the political events were the engineers, mainly those having opportunities to encounter broader social circles in the provincial towns or the capitals. All those who remained at the mines permanently and who knew about these events only from the papers or from conversations were much calmer and dedicated to their work in the mine, which went on without interruption. During conversations concerning these events, members of our staff reacted mainly according to their personal temperaments. Obraztsov was aggressively oppositional, Miokovich and most of the junior staff members were almost conservative, Kazitsyn, as usual, was skeptical, ironical, and in fact, indifferent. Doctor Geider, following his inbred German sense of order, did not entirely support the growing opposition, probably because of its lack of organization and its pointless disruption of business. But as a doctor, brought up in a zemstvo environment, he did not side with the Russian government; he did not like it; and I remember that he returned from a meeting of the Pirogov Medical Society in quite a revolutionary mood.[10] Even then he considered us, the senior engineers, "exploiters" and lackeys of capitalism. In fact this mood of his quickly faded away in the healthy atmosphere of everyday work. In the neighboring mines people reacted with the same variety of temperament and the same uniformity of action.

But what was our mood, the mood of the engineers who directed the mines and who had much more to do with the outside world? Frankly, it is quite difficult to answer this question. I do not think that there was any precise orientation or willingness to join actively with the "militants of the liberation movement," especially at the beginning of the revolution when it was just starting to heat up. We were too realistic, the events were too remote from us, and most of all we were too worried about the situation at the mines, where "events" might occur at any time. But certainly we were politically aroused and rather intuitively inclined toward the opposition. Of course, attitudes varied among individuals. Our Poles were apparently the most worried by the possibility of industrial conflict and tactfully avoided speaking about politics even in private conversations. Priadkin, whom I knew very little at that time, kept a worried silence and was on the alert, awaiting events. Mironov swung his arms about, made a lot of noise and was obviously ready to enter the fray. Nikishin just shrugged his shoulders in perplexity and busied himself more than ever with the mine. I do not remember what Sokolov did. In reality, Rabinovich and I were the closest to events—he was living in Kharkov and I traveled very often to Kharkov or Petersburg. Some of the incidents of that time became deeply imprinted on my memory.

In mid-December of 1904, Rabinovich and I had to travel from Petersburg to Kharkov. We found in our hands newspapers announcing the "Proclamation to the Senate" and the "Government Communication" of 14 December 1904 [O.S.].[11] We were both exhausted by the frantic public activity we had found in Petersburg. There was the foundation of the "Union of Unions" and of all sorts of unions including the Engineers' Union, where Lutugin, who had lost weight, was exerting himself, more revolutionary than ever. Petersburg was shaken by the Resolution of the Zemstvo Congress demanding a "constitution."[12] The universally hated interior minister Pleve had been replaced by the liberal Sviatopolk-Mirskii, whom we knew well—in fact, for this reason he did not inspire our confidence in him. His nomination ushered in a "spring," and the proclamation of 12 December [O.S.] that we had in hand was a clear indication of government concessions. To us practical-minded provincials the sinister turn of events was only too obvious. We both had the same impressions of confusion and uneasiness, of tiresome and often exaggerated political bustle, of the crackle of identical resolutions issued at different meetings. The restaurants were jammed in spite of the events, and a whole flood of drinking and debauchery was sweeping over part of Russian society. In addition to all this were the ominous setbacks of the war with all the inappropriate ceremonies at which the tsar saw off the troops, while the icons received their usual blessings. To me all of this seemed repulsive and more than a little unsettling.[13]

I remember the ominous impressions I had of 1905. It seemed that a whirlwind of appalling events was roaring down upon us from outside, as from a horn of plenty. But at the mines, by some incomprehensible paradox, we lived and worked in perfect peace. After Gapon's actions and the shootings of 9 January, there followed the thorough defeat at Mukden, the severe defeat of Rozhdestvenskii's fleet at Tsushima, the wave of agrarian unrest, and the mutiny of the Battleship Potemkin. It is not surprising that this storm of stunning blows, always accompanied by revolutionary speeches on the part of the capital's political elites, disturbed our province as well.[14]

I remember a summer day in 1905, presumably mid-July or August, when I was on a business trip to Kharkov. A small group of us was having lunch in the garden restaurant of the Commercial Club. Among us were N. F. von Ditmar and L. G. Rabinovich, and others I do not remember. We were talking about the tsar's recent reception of a delegation from the Zemstvo Congress conducted by the very popular Prince S. N. Trubetskoi.[15] I remember our impressions both of the reception and of the reactions of public opinion in the capital. In Petersburg, Trubetskoi was much criticized for his address to the tsar, which was seen as being too kind, for keeping too much distance between himself and the revolution, and for getting soft and trusting the tsar.

In fact, our reactions were different. We were not favorably impressed by all the inconsiderate and, in our view, frivolous noise that the leaders of the Petersburg intelligentsia were making about this reception, especially as the general atmosphere was already very tense. We felt that the zemstvo people had not made sufficient use of their organization, which in itself was quite exceptional for Russia, nor had they appreciated their authority as the "voice of the people," which many thought they possessed. Our skeptical view of the zemstvo's influence was due in part to the fact that we knew from direct observation that the zemstvos were very different from what the Petersburg and Moscow intelligentsia, and to some extent the government, had imagined. We did not overestimate their significance in public and political life.

Trubetskoi's address did not seem to us so unforgivably moderate. At any rate, Trubetskoi seemed far more acceptable to us than many of the frantic zemstvo leaders; for example, N. N. Kovalevskii of Kharkov, who was also in the delegation. It was said that after the reception of this delegation in Petersburg, Kovalevskii went to Peterhof and rudely demanded that some of the tsar's original expressions be restored to the minutes, which allegedly were inaccurate. We felt abashed and concerned by this derogatory treatment of the tsar, by the way his image was being sullied before the people's eyes. As far as I can remember, the general atmosphere in Kharkov was far more moderate than in the capital—at least, it was not so revolutionary. Even the students, who were in many regards the vanguard and the makers of the revolution, were far more moderate there.

I remember another aspect of my impressions of this time. Two social principles suddenly appeared to be in complete opposition, the tsar and our progressive public opinion, which was supposed to represent the people. What happened was that neither the tsar's image nor his behavior at that moment aroused any hostility among us. Instead we felt compassion for this benevolent and mild man, who was perhaps becoming flustered in the face of the events and of these "new" people—a rather different kind of man, belonging to a realm that was difficult to understand, and bearing enormous, almost frightful, responsibilities. To these feelings of ours, one must add the "mystical" sense that in those days contaminated every Russian. This "mystical" feeling made me feel, when I saluted the tsar with my sabre as an officer at that Sevastopol parade, the exceptional emotion that Tolstoy described so masterfully in *War and Peace*.

We had the general impression that something was radically wrong in the attitude of our leaders. We had the vague perception that they did not have the proper feel for the historical dimension of the events and of the person. This impression was enhanced by our meetings with such progressive political figures as this very N. N. Kovalevskii. His pronounced leftism, his instinctive hatred of the regime and of the tsar, his stubbornness and straightforwardness, all had an irritating effect on us. Generally speaking we were in a mood of continuous and vague unease, a state of mind affecting the whole Russian population, which was quite removed from politics.

These spontaneous impressions were later reinforced by a hint of tragedy, when we learned of the unexpected death of Prince Trubetskoi, a hapless victim of the student autonomy that he himself had worked so hard to obtain.[16]

I also remember how one of the most active members of our newly formed Union of Engineers, I. I. Feodorovich, after staying in Petersburg for a while just before the strike, returned almost cured of his political activism.

The Formation of the Union of Engineers in the Donbass; the Congress in Kharkov; I Become a Kadet

I do not remember precisely when and by whose initiative the Donets Basin branch of the Union of Engineers was founded.[17] I think that its office was somewhere in our region. During meetings we also started taking resolutions and sending telegrams to Witte to express our political demands. Moreover, we organized a general assembly of engineers in Kharkov, in August or September of 1905, I believe. This was the extent of our political activity, of which my record book is the only surviving legacy. In it the clerk copied our correspondence with the government—a completely one-sided conversation. Only a year later, scanning this chronicle that I had come across accidentally, I was abashed and even frightened by the general tone of our requests. They followed the stereotypical pattern of days which were already long gone.

The political congress of engineers and representatives of industry that we organized took place in Kharkov in the autumn of 1905. The congress decided to express the political demands of southern industry to the government. I do not remember the precise text. The chairman of the association was the well-known mining engineer N. S. Avdakov, a man much older than the rest of us. He also was the chairman of the political meeting. Avdakov was considered a rightist, but in fact he was politically indifferent. Through his public and industrial activities he came into close contact with certain government circles. In his professional life he was very cautious and in public activities he was very cunning. Avdakov did not openly contradict our unanimous and enthusiastic overtures, but expressed our "demands" in a loyally worded telegram—for which he later received imperial thanks. We learned about this much later, when passions had been soothed and the storm was over. Knowing Avdakov quite well, we met this conclusion to our political efforts with good-natured laughter.

Later I shall describe the way elections to the First State Duma were carried out in Lugansk. I was chosen to be an elector on behalf of the Kadet Party.[18] Why did I choose this party? I do not remember by exactly what procedure I came to join, or if I was ever officially enlisted. I probably was, but only on the provincial level. As far as I remember, I never had the opportunity to move in the party's national or even regional circles. Generally speaking, my whole political activity was limited to my nomination as elector.

Why did I remain in this party nominally? There are a few reasons, both external and internal. In actuality, there was no other party in our region—I do not remember a single Octobrist and of course there was no such thing as a party of "peaceful renovation" or "democratic reform."[19] I cannot recall whether there were any rightist parties, but these would not have attracted my attention anyway, nor would the leftist ones, beginning with the so-called Trudoviki, whose program was ill-defined but sharply oppositional and socialistic.[20] Indeed, at that time as well as later I felt keenly the lack of a truly "centrist" party to which I could belong. There was no such party, and no such party could have existed among the Russian intelligentsia of those days. There was neither the program nor especially the personnel for such a party. Beginning with the Third Duma the "Octobrists" filled the gap, but only partially, since the party was still too much under the control of the gentry and too agrarian, with all the corresponding defects. Rightist parties, especially in those days, were ultra-monarchistic, and only extremely conservative people could join them, people who did not want to accept even the changes that had occurred in one way or another.

Did I fully accept the Kadet program? Of course not. For example, the demand for universal suffrage appeared to me absolutely unacceptable, as I knew the Russian peasantry well. But strangely enough, the question of the party's political platform attracted very little attention from those who joined the party. This was not only due to the political illiteracy of most intellectuals, including myself, but to the programs themselves. According to one politically competent witness, our parties' programs "were exceedingly doctrinaire in their basic positions." They "were nothing but brief summaries of constitutional law, to which were added a series of laws concerning the economy, agriculture and social problems. These summaries bore no visible relation to the urgent needs of the Russian people and state" (V. E. Slonimskii, December 1906). This analysis held true even for a "sensible" party such as the Kadet and was self-explanatory. Because these programs lacked any kind of practical significance they were almost unnecessary, especially for the provincial industrialists or businessmen who were far more practical people than the intellectuals from the capital who had written the programs. They were not taken seriously, because they were obviously impossible to put into action and at best applied to a very remote future. Finally, the programs of the parties that were acceptable to me, from the Kadets to the Octobrists, differed little from one another. In fact, for me as well as the majority of people who were then involved in politics, personal relationships were a very important factor in the ultimate choice of a party. Radakov, Vasil'ev, Rabinovich, and myself, who shared many views, all joined the Kadets.

I had no "political luck." I fell seriously ill upon my arrival in Ekaterinoslav and was unable to attend a single electors' meeting. Fate spared me the ordeal of witnessing the first encounter between the Russian government and the Russian parliament. The former arrived with ludicrous laws about remodeling the launderies and the latter answered with the heavy artillery not only of the Kadet platform but of the Kadet tactics as well: demands for a general amnesty, responsible ministries, and universal suffrage. Their program, exaggeratedly abstract and doctrinaire, triumphed. The First Duma ended in apotheosis, with the politically futile "Vyborg Appeal" (i.e. the appeal issued at Vyborg, Finland).[21]

I thus was cured of all attraction to politics, as L. G. Rabinovich was later on, after going through the Second Duma.

The Mining Life in 1905

I noted earlier that this year passed peacefully at our mines—there were no labor troubles and scarcely any strikes.[22] In the broad sense this was true, but there were a few events more typical of the times. In the spring of 1905 a strike began at the neighboring Golubovka Mine. After this had been going on for three weeks some "outsiders" arrived and began gathering the workers at political meetings where they made fiery speeches. The workers were agitated but there was no violence, and the police did not intervene. On paper the mine's director was a Frenchman, but in fact the mine was managed by the mining engineer P. A. Nikishin.

Both the mine's management and the striking workers decided to appeal to a court of arbitration. We neighbors were chosen as judges, with the workers electing the "outsiders"—guest agitators—to speak for them. The session took place at the mine's school, brimming with workers. The agitators spoke out and we spoke out as well. The whole scene was quite novel, the speeches were new—bold, not always fair or restrained—but the workers remained quite calm. The court made its decision and the strike ended. There was also an attempt to organize a strike at our Maksimov Mine. The main agitator turned out to be our timekeeper, Chumichev, a young man of about twenty, who was the son of our police guard. He was seized with the "movement" to the point of utter intoxication. Our workers were not inclined to strike. I called Chumichev and suggested to him that he leave the mine at once, threatening to inform the police if he refused. Chumichev did leave the mine, and I heard no more about him until 1927, when I received a proposal from a "leading communist" to return to work in Russia. This invitation was transmitted through an engineer I knew who was working in the U.S.S.R. The leading communist turned out to be Chumichev. I came across articles he wrote about the Donets Basin in the Soviet press.

Here is another episode from life at the Maksimov Mine in the same period. In the summer of 1905 I was on leave in the Crimea and met a well-known opposition writer there, Bogoraz-Tan, who was planning to visit the Donets Basin.[23] He asked me (as the mine director) for permission to give a lecture to the miners about the peasant movement on the Volga and about how they had organized a peasant union. I accepted. Such permission was rather unusual, but quite in keeping with the spirit of the times, which was rather frivolous. Back at the mine I learned that the lecture was delivered but that our mine's policeman had written a report about it, which he was planning to send to his superiors. All this threatened to bring about unnecessary complications. The report started out this way: "Mine Director A. I. Fenin sent Mr. Tan from the Crimea to deliver to the workers of the Maksimov Mine a lecture about peasant rebellion on the Volga." When I went through it, I was shocked to see that the policeman said nothing about the lecture itself, which he did not understand or maybe did not even attend. Instead the report was full of confused, misplaced denunciations of a student who was being trained at the mine and whom the policeman hated for some personal reason. The student presumably had said something after Tan's lecture. When, in bewilderment, I asked the policeman if he were at the lecture, he told me that engineer A. A. Naranovich (my assistant) forbade him to come, "but, pardon me, it was my duty to attend, so I went in disguise and sat behind the cupboard." The workers understood the lecture even less than the policeman had. Our workers, like our *muzhik*-peasants, did not much understand intellectualism, especially if it were delivered at some length. Even theater was perceived in a very peculiar way. We sometimes had a play at our school, the local employees having organized quite a good amateur company. I remember how once they presented a drama that had nothing comical in it. The workers who had filled the place were in a very good mood and laughed heartily, I think mostly at the saddest moments. As we later learned, they considered that people went to the theater only to have a good time, it was inconceivable not to have fun, and even more inconceivable to cry. Besides, it was really amusing to see Vasilii Ivanovich Kravtsov (one of the pit foremen), who had no reason to mourn, there on his knees, weeping and beating his chest. Surely he was only doing it "for the fun of it," just to play the fool.

Generally speaking, in those days the easiest way to excite workers to a frenzy was to make aggressive interjections at political rallies, shouting out short declarations. It was not so much the meaning of what was said, but the urging of the orator, that produced this effect.

During the general strike the mines were cut off from Kharkov and consequently had no cash.[24] Our region organized a trip to Kharkov, using our own transportation—our own locomotive and three specially adapted freight cars. The passengers were the mine managers with a guard of ten hand-picked miners. The local railroad committee granted us permission and provided the railroad personnel, because the issue was a very important one. We left Almaznyi Station in the morning and by noon arrived at Debal'tsevo, the region's major railroad junction. The passengers' lounge was almost devoid of furniture, the buffet had been removed, and there was a large crowd of people armed with the most incredible weapons—home-made pikes, shotguns, even scythes, which

gave the gathering the appearance of one of Pugachev's bands.[25] A
political rally was in progress, after which the "people in arms" planned
to go to Gorlovka Station where rumor held that there was fighting
between workers and soldiers.[26] We were quite amazed to notice the
station gendarme sergeant, in full uniform pacing up and down in the
midst of the crowd completely unarmed, as he laughingly explained to
us, so as "to keep order." Our arrival went unnoticed. We had to stay
at Debal'tsevo for about three hours, until the end of the rally, because
the driver and the workers were earnestly listening to the orators. It
was the first time they had attended such a rally.

I cannot remember precisely the atmosphere we found in Kharkov.
At least there was no unrest among the people, there were no noisy
demonstrations, and nobody heard of any violence. Life was almost
normal, shops and banks were open, and we got our money without
any problems. In the streets I remember there were a few more idlers
than usual, and now and then small crowds gathered to listen to orators.
Tramcars seemed not to be working and no policemen were in the
streets. But everything was calm, and I remember feeling that it was
like a holiday.

In fact, we had already observed this generally calm mood on our
trip to Kharkov. Stationmasters were particularly solemn, giving the
impression that they were the masters of the strike. There were no
passengers at the stations, but sometimes there were groups of young
peasants in their best dress, standing on the platform cracking sunflower
seeds. They had only a lazy, curious glance for the now unusual scene
of an approaching train, and a most extraordinary train at that. I remember that one peasant asked us to give him a lift and that we took
him in the car. He was a man of indeterminant age, traveling with
virtually no luggage and creating a very strange impression. He spoke
half in riddles and half in jokes and maintained the countenance of
someone who had just learned a very important secret. His speech was
amazingly devoid of any clear thought and quite removed from reality.
Our passenger's unbalanced condition was so striking that our guards,
chosen from calm and serious workers, began to examine him quite
suspiciously. No doubt he was a product of the revolution that had
penetrated some godforsaken Russian village far from the beaten path
[*medvezhii ugol'*]. I met similar characters among the peasants, especially
during the second revolution [in 1917].

We left Kharkov by the same train in the evening, loaded with quite
a sum of money. Again we accepted some passengers who were peasants
stuck in Kharkov. Among them was a fat, elderly grandmother, apparently a merchant, a sharp politician-in-a-petticoat, who immediately

started a lively conversation with our escorts. "A few of them at the station," she said, told her that we should "do like they did in France, where there ain't no more tsars." She could not conceive of such a thing and she did not approve of it, indignantly seeking support from the others. Of course the slogan in those days was, "Leave the tsar alone." The workers tried to soothe her, and we fell asleep listening to the conversation. The first words I heard upon waking the next morning were the woman's reply to one of the workers, "Just let me get my hands on one of those *'pans'* and I'll cut his throat!" We felt lucky to be "engineer-managers," as the workers called us and not *pans* (a term reserved for landowners living on their estates).[27] We belonged to a category of people who still had some use.

One more memory; an episode that could have had sad consequences for my family occurred in May or June of 1905. By the light of a beautiful moon my wife and I were taking the doctor's family back to the hospital. Five of us were walking along, the only two men being our accountant and myself. My wife was walking slowly and with difficulty, as she was in her last month of pregnancy. We walked by the workers' barracks, in front of which stood a group of workers. After we were a little way past them we noticed that two men had left the group and were following us, yelling insults. Then they started throwing stones. We asked the ladies to go on as quickly as they could, and we stayed behind them, walking very slowly. After throwing a few more stones the workers gave up, perhaps worried by the fact that we did not run away. The next day, during my routine morning visit to the mine, I stopped at the barracks and told the workers who were there about the last night's events. Giving details of what had happened, I casually asked them if they knew who the hooligans were. The last thing I expected was a confession, but after a brief silence one of the men stepped out and fell on his knees, asking me to forgive him as he had been drunk and did not know who the passersby had been. I knew this worker as he had worked at the mine for years. He was a quiet man, but like the overwhelming majority, inclined to heavy drinking. I had the feeling that he was not telling the truth and that he did know who the strollers were, or else his hooliganism would have made no sense. Intoxication had loosened his hidden hatred and fierce jealousy of the more wealthy man, the alpha and omega of every revolution. At the mine, who better than I represented that "different world?" Presumably repentance had come when he sobered up, as this worker certainly was not a real troublemaker. I did not inflict any punishment on him—he seemed shaken enough by what had happened.

I will add a few words about the impact of the revolutionary movements of 1905–1906 on our provincial life in Lugansk. I went there often,
to attend preliminary meetings for the Duma election, so I was able to
observe events. The movement amounted primarily to a series of political
demonstrations and campaign rallies. The agitators and orators gave
speeches that were rather primitive, aggressive, and rude, directed as
they were toward a rather undiscriminating audience. These rallies were
in fact not very frequent and the orators were outsiders. Preelection
meetings, where the "locals" turned up, were more interesting. Here
one found such categories of people as the extreme left-socialist
Mikhailichenko (a Trudovik delegate from our region to the First Duma).
They were often former workers with their own political history, frequently including imprisonment or even deportation. They were well-
trained to speak at meetings and had assimilated a dull rehash of inflam-
matory statements, the rudiments of Russian socialist propaganda. The
speeches of the other speakers, even the Kadets, reflected a good deal
of political confusion as a result of ill-considered political exaltation and
involvement with the "liberation movement," which was reaching
epidemic proportions. I do not remember exactly what was the tone of
the preelectoral meetings in Lugansk. I think that they were reminiscent
of the political rallies in the big towns, but in a simpler and ruder form.
Identical "revolutionary speeches" were given by local residents. In fact
these speeches were irresponsible and sterile, an outgrowth of the personal lives and personal activities of the "political activists." Everybody
was in the throes of a Khlestakov-like "unusual frivolity of thought."[28]
The people directly involved in zemstvo activities were in a different
position. Their activity was inherently political, because of its public
nature and its proximity to the people. In those places where the zemstvo
electorate was liberal and its "third element" overly leftist, there was
conscious and well-designed propaganda work at the grassroots level
and a direct connection to the "movement." Where the zemstvo leaders
were moderate liberals with sound, practical views, such as Radakov,
the situation often was really painful and produced dramatic clashes—
which we privately employed Donbass engineers escaped, with a bit
of political hypocrisy.

As I already mentioned, we made our own contribution to the general
mood, but we steadfastly protected our own sphere of activity from
any political intervention. It never occurred to us to use our own workers
to support "the movement," as one of the leftist slogans went at the
time. Our attitude toward our businesses was the same as that of

Turgenev's character Solomin in his novel *Virgin Soil*, although that is where the resemblance ended: "Agitate as you wish, but keep your hands off my factory!" In truth, did not the majority of our liberal intellectuals share a similar attitude? I remember how one such wealthy liberal, a newly minted "activist" who had a good situation in Petersburg, opened his luxurious apartment for political gatherings. As he later told us, on one occasion he was terrified to see a stranger, a shaggy Armenian socialist, show up with a whole load of weapons for the armed rebellion. The "activist" immediately closed his apartment and these political meetings came to an end.

Of course at that time the liberal zemstvo figures, generally Kadets, seemed to have the greatest political competence. It should be noted that the zemstvo "nonliberals," that is the rightists and even the Octobrists, took little part in the electoral campaign—at least I never heard them give any speeches. Indeed, they would have sounded too discordant a note in the unanimous storm of opposition. Even the speeches of many of our Kadets, who were more restrained in temperament, might have seemed almost conservative to the motley crowd of political activists, the masters of the political debauchery that prevailed at that time. This is why zemstvo people such as Radakov and his colleagues usually limited their speeches to outlining and elaborating on their party's platform.

During one of the sessions convened under the chairmanship of V. N. Radakov to choose electors to the State Duma, I was chosen to be one of the seven electors from Slavianoserbsk. I do not remember precisely what I said, but my main point was that we must have a representative from the coal industry of our district in the State Duma. From there I went to the provincial electoral assembly in Ekaterinoslav, but as I have said, I caught a severe illness, could not attend the meeting, and was not elected to the Duma. This is probably just as well.

I recall one of the preelection meetings in Lugansk, which if not quite characteristic, was at least not altogether unusual. One of our big industrialists, the founder and owner of the great Seleznevka Mine, engineer K. L. Mscychowski, took a fancy to the idea of being elected from his district to the Duma.[29] He was a most original character, cultured as were most of the Poles, but with a rather poor understanding of Russia and what was going on at that time, in spite of the fact that he had been educated in Petersburg at the Institute of Transport and had always worked and lived in Russia.

Mscychowski was a very generous man in his own way, and did a lot for "his" peasants in the village of Seleznevka. He respected and appreciated Russia greatly, as a large, mighty state that represented the monarchistic ideal, and proudly thought of himself as a member of the Russian gentry. He considered the contemporary political movement to be inconsequential, the work of a tiny handful of troublemakers and not extending to the Russian people as a whole. He thought political parties unimportant and unnecessary to the country and, consequently, did not join any of them. He naively believed that his election to the State Duma could be taken for granted because he had been somewhat active as an energetic public figure and philanthropist. He was steadfast in the pro-state orientation of his views.

Mscychowski was to be bitterly disappointed. He organized a meeting and made a speech that was original but conservative and even national-istic, delivered with his thick Polish accent. From the very beginning his speech struck the wrong tone, the motley assemblage did not appre-ciate it at all. Near the end, while praising the Russian *muzhik* with awkward expressions, Mscychowski commented on the *muzhik's* ability to increase the population under any circumstances. This was too much for the audience, and I remember that one man, apparently a worker, interrupted Mscychowski by shouting hysterically, "You keep your hands off the Russian people!" and adding a few other major insults.

This meeting thus came to an end, and poor Mscychowski returned home offended and disappointed in his best feelings. And so politics seethed in our god-forsaken province, which did not altogether grasp the true meaning of what was going on in Russia.

Vyborg in the Summer of 1906

I was not elected to the Duma, but in Vyborg I was able to witness how it ended. My family had decided to spend that summer in Finland, at Vyborg, where I was able to join them for a month. Quite unexpec-tedly, my stay coincided with the Vyborg session of the dissolved First Duma.

I remember a few of the impressions that this event left in my mind. When I learned that the Duma had been dissolved, and that most of the deputies had arrived for a session in Vyborg I started that very morning to look for Duma members whom I knew. The first one I met was a Duma member [*deputat*] from Kharkov, Professor N. A. Gredes-kul, who gave me a brief account of the events. Later, I think just before the assembly, I ran into my Lugansk friends V. N. Radakov and S. M. Ryzhkov near the Belvedere Hotel. Ryzhkov was the headmaster of the school at the Lugansk locomotive factory and had been elected as a Trudovik deputy. I remember that we stood talking at the entrance to the Belvedere's hall, where I could watch the delegates who were beginning to take their seats, among them the imposing figure of Muromtsev.[30] Delegates passed us in a steady stream, some of them stopping to have a few words with Radakov and Ryzhkov.

I remember that we talked mainly about the reasons for what was later to be called the "Vyborg Appeal," which was to be approved and signed by the Duma members at this Vyborg session.

I did not understand the practical aims of this appeal, as I knew perfectly well that a call for withholding taxes and military service was just wishful thinking that would meet no response from the population. The only result of such an appeal, I said, would be the inevitable repression of those Duma members who would sign it.

Both Radakov and Ryzhkov were obviously disturbed, and Radakov even seemed depressed about what was going on; I knew him well enough to sense that he shared my apprehensions completely. I think that he and Ryzhkov were inexorably caught up in a collective political activity of which they did not approve. I do not remember them objecting to what I said; but I remember quite well how a delegate whom I had never before met, a young man who looked like a worker, interrupted our conversation. He reacted to my words with animation, saying that if they did not do this "the people would tear them to pieces." I was later told that he was Deputy Onipko, a worker or a peasant and a Trudovik. He was later to be shot by the Bolsheviks in 1918, under what circumstances I do not know.

This is how the First Duma ended, the one that was to become known as the Duma of the People's Anger. It was only much later, after the dissolution of the Second Duma, when we were living in Kharkov and peace was gradually being restored, that I could better appreciate the terrible events that had occurred, sometimes right before my eyes.[31] The first Revolution had passed, like some kind of psychosis or disease, its end being greeted, I think, with a general sigh of relief.

Before ending the first part of my memoirs with the revolutionary period, I must add a few words about the destiny of V. N. Radakov, this archetypical liberal-aristocrat of zemstvo Russia, albeit in its most provincial manifestation. Having been deprived of some of his civil rights for signing the Vyborg Appeal, Radakov was unable to preside over the elections in the zemstvo. Upon leaving the chairmanship of the Slavianoserbsk Zemstvo, he did not seek another position, and having no financial problems, he lived in elegant idleness. He gave the impression of being a man inwardly satisfied by the necessity of abandoning his beloved public activities—it was a kind of passive political protest. Radakov spent the next few years traveling abroad and after his remarriage (he had lost his first wife) to a handsome and interesting woman, niece of the Poltava landowner Lizogub, he moved to the Crimea. As far as I remember he lived there in the charming villa he had built near Alupka on the southern coast of the Crimea, until the second revolution broke out. We paid them a visit in 1912 or 1913. Radakov divided his time between reading—he had an excellent library—walks, and gracefully looking after his wife, Anna Il'inichna, and their two children. He was a perfectly happy man.

He was never attracted to any other way of life or to any other "business." At precisely that time Russia was experiencing a general economic boom. Dear Viktor Nikolaevich never noticed it.

Reminiscing about Radakov, I cannot help but think of Kolokol'tsov, a zemstvo leader of another type, of whom I spoke earlier, praising him for his extraordinary creative energy. This was his ultimate fate: he was not in the Duma, so his zemstvo work went on uninterrupted until the second revolution. Then he was forced to abandon his tireless activity and leave Russia for the twilight of emigration. At the end of his life he wound up in Paris working as a night watchman in some factory. I do not know how he was able to live, or who took care of this sixty-five-year-old man. I know only that he fell ill, and fearing that he might lose even this job, Kolokol'tsov, already exhausted and mortally ill, committed suicide by turning on the gas. Is it possible to imagine a greater discrepancy between a man's life and his death?

My recollections of this remarkable period of Russian history, as it was reflected in the lives of the people I knew well, seems to end by casting some blame on the memory of a dear friend and excellent man, V. N. Radakov. But unfortunately it is quite true that he lived long years in idleness, that he took no interest in any new activity once he had been torn away from the one that had occupied him, which was perhaps the only thing he could do. His understanding of his duty toward life and toward Russia was limited to just one idea: serving the zemstvo cause, often in the spirit of political opposition.

He could have devoted himself to his hereditary vocation, that is to his land, which would have been at least an indirect way to improve the life of the peasants. He could have tried to improve the economy of his estate, an urgent cultural task in Russia, but he did not want to because this kind of thing did not interest him. And all of this idleness was accompanied by such great potential wealth: not only did Radakov own a great hereditary estate (although it generated no income, so primitive were its farming techniques), but he also received enormous sums of money for the long-term rental of his coal-bearing land by the

Aleksei Mining Company. But Radakov was by no means an exception. I believe that among the rich landowning gentry many would have behaved in just the same way.

"We are lazy and not very curious," Pushkin once said, but even in the many years since Pushkin's time we never learned to regard life as "hard toil," or as "fulfilling one's duty." For us life was, in many regards, a "delight," in the best cases the delight of serving a beautiful idea.[32]

I think that what Pushkin meant by *laziness* was avoiding the creative work that in the end, when finally achieved, almost always brings happiness to man on earth.

And this lack of a lofty, burning "curiosity" among us Russians, of the curiosity that illuminates human life with a hunger for knowledge and an eagerness to understand things correctly, is that not what was responsible for the tragic oblivion of a man like Kolokol'tsov? The last years of Radakov's life and Kolokol'tsov's terrible death were echoed by the final, tragic chords in the life of Russia itself.

*A*uthor's note: Having now completed what was initially planned to be the first part of my memoir, I feel compelled to give the honorable reader a few explanations.

The second part of this memoir covering the period from 1907 to my emigration is almost written. But its publication remains hypothetical for material reasons. Therefore my memoir can be considered as having been completed with this book, which gives a full account of a given period of my life. For this reason I take the liberty of not calling this *Part One* of my memoir.

A Brief Survey of Russia's Economic Situation at the Turn of the Century and of Alexander III's Reforms

Destiny decided that I should take my degrees from an advanced technical school as a mining engineer. This sort of work was neither my own inclination nor a family tradition. It was my father's decision to send me, a youth of eighteen, to the Mining Institute, which made an engineer out of me. As a result of this happenstance, I spent my whole life working in the Russian mining industry. Most of my colleagues had similar fates.

Naturally I wish to append to my memoirs some data, if only summary, about the role played by the heavy industry of the South in Russia's economy, and about how this industry developed.

I worked in the coal industry, but kept a close eye on the iron and railroad industries—so I was familiar with the bases of Russian industrial life. In order to assess correctly the significance of heavy industry for the Russia of those times, as well as the importance of the railroads that served it, and to understand our work in these sectors, one must have some understanding of the country's general economic situation at the end of the nineteenth century and the beginning of the twentieth. I will begin with the conditions imposed by nature and history.

Natural Conditions:
Coal and Iron Resources

Glancing at a map, one is amazed by Russia's enormous expanse, by her extensive landmass and inaccessible coasts, as well as by her almost complete lack of natural boundaries. Russia is a difficult place to defend and a difficult place to supply at low cost. Both Russia and Siberia display a uniformly flat expanse, in contrast to the mosaic of Western Europe. The soil and climatic conditions of Russia vary gradually from North to South over the great distance of about 4000 to 5000 versts. The poor soil of the North and the Center gives way to the rich earth of the South, but this improvement is offset by unfavorable climatic conditions, exposing the rich soils of the South to drought, which is far more difficult to deal with than the overly wet conditions in Western Europe.

The very immensity of Russia in itself greatly inhibits the development of domestic trade and the country's productive forces. The distance from the seas and the almost complete lack of ports, which are the principal factors of international trade, complicate Russia's foreign relations. Several unfavorable conditions of soil and climate are aggravated by the paucity and poor distribution of mineral wealth—coal and iron ore, the essential components of economic development. Compared to the size and population of European Russia, the country's coal and iron reserves are rather insignificant and suffer from a disadvantageous geographical distribution. That is a brief summary of the mineral reserves of European Russia.

Of the three coal basins, the Moscow, the Urals, and the Donets, only the last contains coke, which is indispensable to the smelting of iron. The Moscow Basin, despite its favorable proximity to Moscow, has almost no industrial importance because of the extremely poor quality of its coal. The Urals Basin boasts better coal, but lacking coke-producing coal and located at the edge of European Russia, it also has little significance for general industrial development. Moreover, both basins have few seams and small coal reserves.

European Russia, in fact, possesses only one basin of national importance—the Donets Basin. The Donbass covers an enormous territory in the provinces of Ekaterinoslav and Kharkov and the Don Military Region, totaling about 25,000 square versts. It contains various types of coal, most of excellent quality. Nevertheless, even this unique basin has some substantial failings: the seams are not very numerous and thin (thirty to forty coal seams with a cumulative thickness of 25 to 28 meters). The whole carboniferous formation is about 10,000 meters thick.

As to the quality of the coal beds, the Donbass is ten times poorer than the German Ruhr Basin, three times poorer than the Silesian Basin, and four times poorer than our own Kuznetsk Basin in Siberia. This results in relatively high equipment costs, as much as two and a half times greater than those of the Ruhr. Moreover, because of the sparse population of southern Russia, the Donbass mines had to build housing for all of its workers and also pay royalties to the landowners—conditions not existing in Germany. The huge reserves of the Basin are linked to its enormous expanse—they amount to nearly 57 trillion tons and up to three-quarters are high-quality anthracite. However, because anthracite is not a coke-producing coal, the reserves of coking coal are relatively small. Finally the Donbass is unfavorably located, far from Russia's industrial and cultural centers (about 700–800 versts from Moscow, 1100–1200 versts from Petersburg) and extremely remote from the Urals, the primary source of iron ore (about 1500 versts away).

In fact, European Russia has only three iron-ore basins. The Ural Basin boasts great reserves of various types of excellent ores; but due to the lack of coking coal in the vicinity, the old iron industry of the Urals operated only with charcoal. The remoteness of the Donbass prohibited the Urals iron industry from using Donets coke, so the Urals industry was unable to develop successfully, even later on. Before World War I the Urals produced no more than 20 percent of all of Russia's cast iron. I do not mention here Siberian coal and iron, as they played almost no role in Old Russia's industrial development. Thus, it is pointless to discuss the possibility of smelting iron ore from the Urals with coke from the Kuznetsk Basin in Siberia.

The Krivoi Rog Iron Basin, located in Kherson province, supplies ore to Russia's most important metallurgical industry, that of southern Russia. This basin contains deposits of excellent iron ores (hematite). Only the proximity of Krivoi Rog iron to the coal fields of the Donbass (about 400 versts away) ensured the rapid and impressive development of the southern steel industry.

An enormous deposit of bog-iron ore is also located in the South, in the southern part of the Kerch Peninsula. Although this iron can be mined cheaply and easily, it is of only limited use in southern metallurgy because of its high arsenic content, which is very harmful.

These three basins constitute European Russia's entire iron supply. Central Russia is said to have huge reserves of poor-quality bog-iron, but they have no industrial importance as they are limited to one irregular narrow seam that extends over an enormous area. All of this suggests the rather unfavorable economic conditions of European Russia.

Historic Conditions and Economic Problems of the Present; Railroad Building and the Industrialization of Russia

I can only touch on the general historic reasons for Russia's slow economic growth and her well-known backwardness. Starting with the nineteenth century, that is, a period when the main countries of Europe began moving along the path of intensive development, we not only failed to match the economic development of Western Europe, but began to lag behind. The primary obstacles to our economic growth were insufficient population–land ratio, lack of roads, the weakness of towns and the outdated and wretched system of serfdom—industry could not grow with unfree labor. Our scattered and underpopulated towns were primarily administrative centers—they were not concentrations of craftsmen as were towns in the West. Nascent industry therefore was found in isolated villages, with their natural economies [*natural'nym zamknutym khoziaistvom*]. The intensive development of towns in Western Europe played a paramount role in her economic growth, and her population growth had begun much earlier than Russia's. The tempo of life in Western Europe was much livelier, the population more enterprising and better educated—all of these being great assets for extensive and rapid industrial progress. This difference in attitude toward "economic expansion" became obvious when conditions conducive to a more intensive industrialization appeared: the use of such inventions as the steam engine and iron ore smelting with coke instead of charcoal all required an educational environment that existed in the West but not in Old Russia. "Town air makes one free," medieval people used to say. But as the Russian economist Tugan-Baranovskii wrote, "The air of the industrial city did not stir in Russia. Russia never knew the well-ordered, polished organization of small manufacturers, from which emanated all the civilization and culture of the West."[1]

Rather, the vulnerability of her borders and the difficulty of protecting such an enormous and naturally defenseless territory made Russia a military state. Witte notes in his memoirs that, "The Russian Empire was essentially a military empire; it had few other characteristics in the eyes of foreigners." Is it any wonder then that because of these peculiar historical conditions, "forced labor set down unusually strong roots in Russia," as Tugan-Baranovskii put it? Serfdom not only penetrated every aspect of the economy and way of life of Old Russia, but it also acquired the traits of genuine slavery, plaguing the whole of Russian life for many long years. Even now we have not fully assessed the destructiveness of this extremely painful fact of our history, which has been only recently abolished.

To complete this brief account of the setting in which the Russian state and the outlook of the Russian people, especially the peasants, took shape, we must mention a phenomenon very typical of the Russians: the spontaneous and eternal craving to move to new lands, which created a continuous internal colonization. "Russia," says Kliuchevskii, "is a country of ongoing colonization." According to Oganovskii, "By the end of the sixteenth century her population, which had been concentrated in Muscovy, started gradually to move to the southeast and the east, and to scatter through the limitless steppes of the black-earth belt."[2] The colonization of the northern Caucasus, Siberia, and the steppe region began in the second half of the nineteenth century. This urge to move, which was embedded in the very nature of the emerging Russian state, can be explained by one crucial factor: the ability of the population to grow quickly and the resulting "agrarian overpopulation" of the Russian village. Based upon the unproductive institutions of serfdom and communal land tenure, the peasant economy remained primitive. Until very recently, the peasants made poor use of the soil, relied almost exclusively on grain crops, and labored in an extensive and essentially noncommerical agriculture. This primitive agriculture was furthered by the restricted size of the urban population and the consequent weakness of the domestic market, by the underdevelopment of industry and by the lack of adequate roads. The result was agrarian overpopulation, long observed in Russia, but especially acute by the end of the nineteenth century. The rural population had always been prone to rapid growth but in the last forty years of the nineteenth century it expanded much faster than the urban population. Consequently, between 1860 and 1900, the urban population rose by 8.2 million souls whereas the population of the villages increased by 34.6 million. Only about 10 percent of this excess village population was absorbed by towns and industry, the rest remaining in the country. The inadequacy of the country's transportation system, manifested in recent times in the very limited railroad network, strongly hindered internal migration. All of this produced an economically disadvantageous and a politically dangerous situation: a teeming rural population, which the primitively cultivated land could not support. Oganovskii points out that, "such a phenomenon never occurred in Western Europe or America; but the agrarian overpopulation and crisis in Russia led to an eruption unparalleled in world history."

Such was the shape of Russia's economy at the end of the nineteenth century: an underdeveloped industry, a poor railroad network, a primitive agriculture, and a menacing overpopulation of the villages.

What was the correct way out of this terrible economic situation, which resulted in Russia's per capita income holding last place compared to Western European countries? It was essential to give people the opportunity to work productively, bearing in mind that our peasants occupied a low level of economic development and their skills were largely agricultural. It was essential to relieve the rural overpopulation, to open up new territories to cultivation; that is, to address the never-ending problem of the Russian people: colonizing the country's unused lands. By the late nineteenth century this colonization depended upon agricultural productivity, which in turn depended upon automated farming. In the end, all of this depended upon extensive railroad building, which "had been the axis of Russia's economic development for many years," according to Grinevetskii.[3]

Equally important for the Russian people was the creation of a mighty industry, especially heavy industry such as coal and iron, those fundamentals of national growth. We needed to be able to produce expensive products ourselves and to use skilled labor more productively than was possible in agriculture. S. Iu. Witte, the primary initiator and creator of the plan to construct railroads and heavy industry in the late nineteenth century on a more ambitious scale than ever before, wrote in his memoirs (vol. I, p. 451), that "To create a way of utilizing labor, it was more than advisable to develop our industry. Emperor Alexander III was personally committed to this goal. I made every effort to expand our industry. This was required not only by the interests of our people individually, but of the state as well." In 1898 Witte wrote to the sovereign (vol. I, p. 468):

> Your Majesty has 130 million subjects, of whom barely half live decently, while the others vegetate. Our budget before the Emancipation was 350 million rubles; the Emancipation gave us the possibility of raising it to 1.4 billion rubles. But now the burden of taxation is being felt. Meanwhile the budget of France, with its 38 million inhabitants, is equivalent to 1.26 billion rubles, while that of Austria, with a population of 43 million, is equivalent to 1.1 billion rubles. If the wealth of our taxpayers equalled that of France's, our budget could reach 4.2 billion rubles.[4]

It stands to reason that a burgeoning industry would drain off a good bit of the excess village population, and thus help to alleviate the agrarian overpopulation. Two tasks, railroad construction and industrialization, were closely linked. Let me remind the reader that very little heavy industry existed at the end of the nineteenth century: in 1890 the coal extracted from the Donbass reached about 183 million puds (3 million tons), which represented about 85 percent of the country's total coal production; in the same year Russia produced 59 million puds (about 1 million tons) of cast iron, of which only 13 million puds came from the South. This meant that most of Russia's cast iron was smelted by the old-fashioned charcoal method, in the Urals. Southern Russia boasted only four small iron and steel plants: Iuzovka, Briansk (in Ekaterinoslav), Kamenskoe, and the Pastukhov Plant, which used anthracite.

To understand our backwardness in relation to Western Europe, consider that in 1860 Germany and Russia produced nearly the same amount of cast iron (30 million puds and 20 million puds respectively), but that by 1892 the German production reached 300 million puds, exceeding the Russian output (63 million puds) by five times.

Economic Construction—
The Economic Initiatives of Alexander III: Finances, Protectionism, Railroad Reform, Construction of the Great Siberian Railroad, and the Liquor Monopoly

As we have seen, Russia's economy in the 1890s was in dire need of a dramatic improvement in the railroad, as well as the coal and iron, industries. It was obvious that the Donets Basin was the only region in European Russia in which to situate such an industry. It was also clear that it would be more profitable to furnish the new railroads with domestically produced rails. The foreign contractors whom Witte attracted (I shall deal with this question in more detail later) were guaranteed state orders for rails for many years to come. Consequently, they began to construct steel mills with rail rolling sections, as well as the supporting coal mines and coke furnaces. The scale of this construction was so grand that starting in 1895, in a five to seven year span, about eight to ten new metallurgical plants had been built in southern Russia, equipped with about thirty to forty huge blast furnaces. Russia's production of cast iron increased as follows: in 1890 she produced 55 million puds; in 1895, 86.3 million; and in 1900, 176.8 million. The corresponding figures for southern Russia are 13 million puds, 33 million puds, and 91 million puds. In other words, the "tsar's five-year plan" between 1895 and 1900 produced an overall increase of 170 percent for the South, or an average annual increase of 35 percent—a rate of growth never achieved in a single industrial sector by the Soviets' notorious Five Year Plans. Coal production expanded as follows: in 1890, 367 million puds; and in 1900, 986 million puds. This represents a total growth of 172 percent, or a 17 percent increase each year.[5] It is noteworthy that the number of workers rose more slowly than the total output. In particular, in metallurgy output rose annually by 20 percent over ten years, but the number of workers increased only 7 percent annually. This demonstrates a healthy expansion of industry and a corresponding rise in labor productivity.[6] It is well known that the development of Soviet industry presents quite a different picture.

The data concerning capital investment in this industrial construction are interesting. It is commonly assumed that this whole expansion was financed by foreign capital. However, this was simply not so, and an indirect proof of this is found in the increasing capital of the Russian banks, which grew from 119 million in 1895 to 280 million in 1900. But it is difficult to give a precise account of the contribution of Russian capital to this industrial development. Foreign participation reached a figure of 778 million rubles in 1900, invested in joint stock companies in all sectors of industry. One must bear in mind that about 40 percent of all of Russia's industrial enterprises started during those ten years, 1890 to 1900. The total basic capital of all Russia's share-holding firms, both old and new, increased by 1.5 billion rubles during those ten years, whereas basic capital had increased only by 919 million rubles during the preceding thirty-eight years (1854–1892).[7]

At the same time, railroad construction proceeded at an exceptional rate, nearly doubling over the same period. This building was based not only on state financing, but on private investment as well. The total treasury outlay for railroad construction reached 1.7 billion rubles, of which only 495 million were covered by loans—the rest was drawn from state reserves. The private investment has been estimated at about 1.3 billion rubles, consisting of foreign loans as well as domestic capital. The operating network, including the Asian lines, increased from 29,100 versts in 1893 to 52,700 versts in 1902—an expansion of about 25,000 versts, half of which was built privately. Rolling stock, of course, increased to a similar degree. These figures shed some light on the essence and the extent of the economic growth of this remarkable period.

The exceptional industrialization of the last years of Alexander III and the first years of Nicholas II, unprecedented even by European standards, sprang directly from the great preparatory work that had been carried out in every part of the national economy earlier in Alexander III's reign, during the political "lull," for which that period is best known.

The chief economic concern of Alexander III's reign was to normalize state finances. Russia had always been a classic example of a country with a paper currency. Although the value of the state's bank notes was guaranteed by law, the unregulated issuance of paper currency under a haphazard monetary policy caused the value of the ruble to vacillate constantly on the international market and sometimes to fall to half its nominal value. This in turn led to an inevitable instability of domestic prices and often to an increase in the cost of living. Alexander III's finance ministers Bunge and Vyshnegradskii began to take measures to stabilize the exchange rate and prepare for the introduction of the gold standard.[8] In order to achieve this, "they accumulated a gold stock from foreign loans, which was deposited in the basement of the State Bank." This wise policy enabled Witte to introduce the gold standard early in the reign of Nicholas II. As is well known, this currency reform was a brilliant success.

The second important reform of Alexander III's reign was the preparation and application of a new protectionist tariff in 1891, which had been drawn up by our famous scientist D. I. Mendeleev. The public greeted this sharply protectionist tariff with malevolence at the time, but it played a vital and positive role in the success of our subsequent economic development. It is significant that from the middle of the eighteenth century to the end of the nineteenth, an era of intense worldwide industrialization, our tariff policy had been characterized by continuous shifts from protective or even prohibitive tariffs to extreme liberalism, bordering on an "open door" policy. Each time the tariffs were liberalized, the consequences were the same: a flood of foreign imports, the stagnation of our own industry, a negative balance of trade and the plummeting of the ruble. Usually this last consequence compelled a return to stronger tariff barriers. At first this detrimental policy was due largely to the conflicts of interest between the agrarian gentry and the industrialists; later it owed much to the influence of "populism" on public opinion.

Professor Grinevetskii observed that, "Tariff defense of our production by means of increased duties on raw materials, semi-finished and finished goods was the primary aim of our economic policy in the nineties. . . . Along with the railroad construction, the tariff of 1891 permitted a notable expansion of our metallurgical, mining and metal-fabricating industries." The following figures demonstrate the soundness of this policy: between 1892 and 1912 the import of metal implements increased from 75 to 395 million rubles, or 400 percent; at the same time the import of semi-finished goods and raw materials rose 240 to 536 million rubles; that is only 120 percent. Thus the goal of the tariff was achieved: the supply of our industry with domestic raw materials, the encouragement and protection of our own extractive industries, and the supply of both domestic and imported capital goods to our own market.

The great and pressing reform of the railroad system was carried out with equal success. Eventually we established an efficient, and in some cases a model, railroad network: goods could be transported directly, freight cars were used reciprocally so that cargo did not need to be unloaded, and the fares and regulations were generally reformed. Ultimately, the entire Russian railroad system was governed by uniform principles and statutes. Establishing a uniform system of rates proved a complicated task, but ultimately an efficient schedule of inexpensive fees came into existence, which served the opposing interests of both the consumer and the producer rather well.

It is well known that the old railroad administration, which dated back to the great construction boom of the 1870s, in the reign of Alexander II, had produced extremely negative results and needed to be fundamentally overhauled. The old system had concentrated nearly the whole railroad business in the hands of a few independent private companies, inadequately supported by public funds, which had a ruinous effect on the state treasury. The result was that in 1878 89 percent of the basic capital of the railroads was either guaranteed or issued by the state. According to Professor Migulin (in "Our Recent Railroad Policy") "the annual supplements paid by the treasury reached 50 million rubles," and "the entire state budget deficit from 1857 to 1877 resulted from the support of private railroad companies."[9]

The notion that such a vital segment of the national economy as the railroads ought to be, if not entirely concentrated, at least strongly united in the government's hands, finally was understood and realized by the administration of Alexander III. A special piece of railroad legislation announced that, "the ultimate authority in all railroad affairs must be the government." Meanwhile, the treasury purchased private lines extensively: in 1882 the state owned only 4.1 percent of the network; in 1890 it already had more that 30 percent, and in 1895 the treasury owned 60 percent of the network.

Everybody knows what unsavory speculation and "money grubbing" accompanied the great railroad building of the seventies. This speculation stemmed from several causes, chief of which was that the state guaranteed concessions to railroad builders. The financial condition of Russian society also played a part, especially the enormous sums paid for the purchase of land (nearly 400 million rubles) and the accelerating decline of the landowning class. All of this created an unhealthy atmosphere and encouraged speculation. This kind of thing, vividly portrayed in our literature, inevitably created an unfavorable impression and a negative public attitude toward railroads, as well as any kind of entrepreneurship in companies, industry, banking, and other enterprises—

all of which, in any case, was quite rare in patriarchal Russia. Shchedrin wrote at the time, "Russian society had recently produced something on the order of a 'bourgeoisie', that is, a new cultural stratum composed of bar-keepers, percentage-mongers, railroaders, wheeler-dealers, and similar embezzlers and destroyers of the peasant commune."

The new railroad construction of Alexander III's time was quite different. It was funded primarily by the treasury, on a rational and sound economic footing. After 1890 finance minister Vyshnegradskii reorganized private railroad building, which remained important. Railroad expert Professor Martens described the system this way: "The government created large groups of private railroad companies which were granted both a delay in the state take-over of their lines, and a commission to construct new lines in accordance with strict financial and organizational guidelines."[10]

A far grander, unprecedented railroad project was the "Great Siberian Railroad," which was begun under Alexander III in 1891. This enormous state project in fact amounted to the linking of Siberia to European Russia, and the beginning of her genuine cultural conquest.

The necessity of constructing the Siberian Railroad was raised long ago and was thoroughly studied, not only in government but also in public circles; as early as 1875 a southerly orientation was agreed to, but later discarded for various reasons. In 1884, three northerly routes were proposed. One of these was finally adopted: a line from the Mias Station to Cheliabinsk. The act issued by Alexander III on the nameday of the heir, 17 March 1891, ended years of vacillation. Construction of the Siberian Railroad began from both ends, at Cheliabinsk and Vladivostok. At the outset its length was estimated to be approximately 7,112 versts and the cost about 350 million rubles. The project was expected to take twelve years, beginning 1893. It is now acknowledged, however, that the actual cost of the railroad, with its offshoots and numerous related undertakings such as shipping on the adjacent waterways, the organization of towns such as Dalnyi and Port Arthur, the organization of resettlement and so forth, reached 1 billion rubles.

In view of the grandiosity of the undertaking, which went on in various and often unfavorable and novel conditions of both topography and climate, some of the technology was not only modified but simplified, without weakening the construction. The goal was "eventually to complete and to supplement as necessary, but never to rebuild the railroad." The difficulty of the construction was exacerbated by the underpopulation, especially in Eastern Siberia, where almost all the labor had to be imported from European Russia; the rails, and the rolling stock and metal castings for bridges were sent by sea through Vladivostok.

Despite all this the Siberian Railroad was constructed in time; in September 1904, the very difficult railroad around the southern shore of Lake Baikal was hastily completed at considerable extra expense because of the threatening Far Eastern situation. With this link, the Atlantic and Pacific Oceans were connected by one continuous route. Contemporaries did not adequately appreciate the magnitude of the Great Siberian Railroad project, which had been organized by Alexander III's government and realized by Russian engineers. Written histories scarcely noticed the significance of this national accomplishment. Part of the explanation for this historical oblivion lies in the unfortunate combination of circumstances whereby the anticipated deficiencies of the railroad, particularly its limited carrying capacity, played a certain, but greatly exaggerated, role in our defeat in the Russo-Japanese War. In any case, it is doubtful whether a railroad equal to the technical and economic demands of the Russo-Japanese War could have been constructed before the outbreak of the war, which no one had predicted.

The reign of Alexander III saw another socially and economically important reform—the liquor monopoly; that is, the selling of vodka exclusively in state liquor stores. The government took over the selling of vodka, but left its production in private hands. In his book, *The Russian Economy*, M. M. Kovalevskii has noted that both reforms—the liquor monopoly and the currency reform—had the character of genuine world-class events.[11] Before the monopoly, vodka had been taxed and sold in "drinking houses," or taverns, whose ruinous moral influence is well known. In introducing the monopoly the government was counting on lower individual consumption but more regular and predictable general sales, and most importantly, on suppressing the existing tendency of the taverns to make drunkards out of the weaker village elements. The presumption was that this policy would raise the quality of vodka, lower its price, and increase government income. The measure was applied gradually, starting in 1895, first in four eastern provinces and the next year in nine southern provinces. The Finance Ministry's summary published in 1897 demonstrated the brilliant success of the measure: the income from "drinking" not only did not drop but in fact increased; but "alcoholism, as everybody has testified, had diminished" (Kovalevskii). This same Kovalevskii correctly observed in the conclusion to his chapter about Russia's main economic trends that, "Because of the number and nature of the questions she poses, Russia is currently the most interesting of all the European countries for the sociologist."

Characteristics of Industrial and Railroad
Construction under Alexander III; the Dramatic
Improvement of the Economic Atmosphere

I have already given some general figures about the intensity of the development of the Donets Basin, almost exclusively by foreign capital, mainly by Belgian and French, in "our period." Alexander III's financial and economic measures, along with Russia's excellent international position, created an atmosphere of complete confidence and great commercial interest for foreign investors. Adding to this was the fact that in the late seventies and early eighties the importance of Krivoi Rog [iron] mining became clear, thus completely altering the potential of the Donets Basin. Mendeleev wrote in *A Systematic Tariff* in 1892 that "Russian industry would only compete successfully with European industry if it were firmly established on the bank of the Donets. . . . Nowhere else in European Russia could one find a set of conditions more favorable to the development of industry."[12] Is it any wonder that foreigners were drawn to southern Russia as to gold fields? This rush for profits was very ably exploited by Witte. The contracts he granted them, permitting them to construct factories that would supply state railroads, were not especially favorable to foreigners thanks to the generally low level of the Russian economy, as became clear even by 1900–1901. The great railroad construction, which had been the primary bait for foreign capital, was almost completed by then, so there no longer was an urgent demand for rails, and the new southern factories now came face to face with the local demand for iron. This was quite low, representing barely one-third of the total of the small industrial demand, as well as the railroad, naval, and urban requirements. The shock of declining iron consumption was so substantial that in 1901 twenty-six other southern blast furnaces (of a total of sixty-three) had to close, and the production of cast iron that year amounted to only 91 million puds, against a southern capacity of 161 million puds. Annual investments in the southern iron industry illustrate the situation (in millions of rubles):

1895	27.87	1900	11.42
1896	27.75	1901	5.5
1897	11.35	1902	0.83
1898	23.49	1904	0.48
1899	28.82		

The industrial crisis in the South, which started in 1900, coincided with the general European crisis of the same years, but lasted much longer, as activity resumed only in 1911. During a thirteen year period (1900–1913), Russia increased cast iron production by only 60 percent whereas Germany's grew by 156 percent and that of the United States by 121 percent. Needless to say, the southern factories suffered great losses during this period.

The story of the first great southern iron factory, the well-known Hughes Factory, illustrates even more clearly the distinctions between the building eras of the seventies and the nineties. Long-time assistant minister of transport under Alexander II, A. I. Del'vig, writes in his memoirs that the British citizen John Hughes contracted with the Ministry of Finance and the Ministry of Transport in 1868 to construct "a blast furnace and iron factory near the Kharkov-Azov Railroad on land provided free of charge by the Treasury, which was to pay him 10 kopeks per pud for cast iron and 50 kopeks per pud for rail produced by this factory for a ten-year period."[13]

In addition to this, says Del'vig, Hughes made big money on the construction of a spur line to the Azov line, building it almost twice the necessary length, extending it "unnecessarily along the Kharkov-Azov Road." Moreover, Hughes declared that he would be "unable to construct the railroad unless he were given 500,000 rubles," and Del'vig maintains that Minister Bobrinskii gave Hughes the entire sum, over Del'vig's objections. I shall not dwell upon Del'vig's account of the reasons and conditions under which Bobrinskii provided all of this money; they are characteristic of the period and explain the "ease with which Bobrinskii wasted enormous sums belonging to the state."

This tale about Hughes' concession clearly indicates how within a twenty or twenty-five year period the atmosphere surrounding Russia's ruling circles changed sharply and grew more healthy, and how they gained exceptional prestige. It goes without saying that in the contracts that Witte signed with foreign enterprises there were no obligations other than the purchase of rails by the state at set prices and quantities, which, as we saw, were cautiously limited.

All of this clearly indicates, I think, the dimensions and the efficiency of the economic reforms and projects of Emperor Alexander III, performed in the calm and stable atmosphere of an uninterrupted social and economic expansion. His reforms, indeed, his entire reign, if evaluated impartially, achieved an almost exceptional grandeur. The economic results of his reforms could be reckoned only much later, as is often the case with great undertakings; they established the basis for and gave shape to the economic boom of the "prewar period," of which I shall speak in due course (in the second part of my memoirs).

The reign of Alexander III met with grateful appreciation and approval, as is well known, only among the "reactionary" circles of Russia's political society and the industrialists, who were traditionally grateful to the state for protectionist tariffs. Accepted wisdom made it compulsory to believe, instead, that "Belgians, Frenchmen, and Englishmen made tremendous profits on their modern factories, while the Russian peasant could not afford to buy an expensive iron plough," and so on. The very possibility of a lengthy crisis in metallurgy from 1900 to 1910, which I have described, stands in complete contradiction to such nonsensical reasoning. Yet another reference to this period appears in a book published under Bolshevik rule in 1923 by the Ukrainian Economic Council, *Industry of the Ukraine,* a source not even remotely friendly to the tsarist era. The author indicates that, "Between 1904 and 1909 the southern factories produced only 38 percent of their capacity of sheet iron and 47 percent of their capacity of rails. The selling price of cast iron was determined by the conditions of the international market and in this period was extremely low—41–44 kopeks per pud." Later he indicates that from 1900 to 1912, twenty-seven enterprises, with a total capital of 87.5 million rubles, were liquidated (in the Ukraine). Dividends (in the iron industry) fell from 7.7 percent to 2.68 percent" (p. 89).

So history is created, and in the heat of political passion wrong impressions arise about the economic development of an important historical period. Is not the political significance of Alexander III's epoch likewise wrongly painted in black? Maybe it is time to abandon the notion that only the inflexible evil will of Alexander III, Pobedonostsev, and their crowd created the reactionary political atmosphere, violating the popular will and sabotaging the interests of the people. Maybe, once the political assessments are done with, a proper appreciation can be extended to the continuous creativity of this period, which had its roots in the great national development of which I spoke earlier.

The Political "Lull" as an Important Factor for Economic Progress; Concrete Economic Work as a School for Political Judgment

A sound patriotism and restraint from the political storms of the preceding, and, sadly, of the following epochs, promoted the emergence of the genuinely creative economic talents of those "heroes of small deeds," as we men of the eighties were later scornfully nicknamed by the leftist intelligentsia. I have already noted that the "politics of reaction" scarcely touched us—we did not notice them, even in our most perceptive student years. Entering directly into the difficulties of work and life in the provinces and villages of those days, almost from the time of our adolescence, and coming into contact with the lower classes of the real Russia, we came gradually to understand in our mature years that prereform spirituality, which prevented any quick and radical change in the political and social order, that was the perennial dream of our intellectual "vanguard." We came to see the political restraint of Alexander III's reign in a new light. Thanks to this perception of the situation, we saw that it would be impossible to transform this great mass of humanity, yesterday's slaves and slave owners, into free, equal, and cultured citizens of their country overnight.

From the very beginning of the nineties we were close to the peasants, still tightly bound to their villages, who were in the process of becoming workers. We came to appreciate the bitter dead-end of the peasants' economic and legal status; we realized that the obsolete system of communal land ownership, with the often total dependence of the individual peasant on the *mir*, functioned as a tremendous brake on the cultural development of the village. But we also understood the impossibility of sudden changes in the form of land ownership, as well as in the cultural and legal structures of the countryside. Apart from the centuries-old historical origins of the village, contemporary conditions also justified its existence. The great mass of millions of uneducated peasants, of limited perspective, knowing nothing but primitive agriculture, needed in the Russia of those times a permanent, inviolable home where they always could find refuge from ever threatening misfortune or failure. The peasant who had severed his ties to the village had "nowhere to go" in case of misfortune—and such cases were seen every day. Demand for peasant labor outside the village was narrow and insecure: the poorly populated towns, the negligible industry, the weak railroad network all limited the number of permanent jobs.

To be rescued by the village was not the best material solution, but it prevented misery for many. It is noteworthy that the itinerant peasantry, scattered all over the Russian land, valued its links to its native villages so dearly that peasants seldom resigned from their community and continued to pay taxes for years without using their allotments. The possibility of refuge in the village, the right always to be a full and equal member of the village, existed only within the constraining structure of village life, which was limiting both economically and in terms of individual rights. This was a very bad arrangement, inevitably producing a primitive economy; it was the unavoidable heritage of Russia's historic cultural poverty and the necessary shape of the emancipation legislation. It was essential to destroy that order, but this destruction needed to be preceded by an improvement in labor conditions and therefore by an improvement in the life of the Russian people; that is, by the creation of industry, the development of towns, the increase in railroad construction. All of this indispensable preparatory work to transform and improve the life of the people in fact was the chief undertaking of Alexander III's reign.

I will not linger on another painful aspect of our village life, which we all know too well, the shortage of land in the peasant economy and the measures taken against this by Alexander III's government.

Our provincial society also was deeply concerned by all these problems of rural disorder. I belonged to the land-owning gentry, and thanks to my parents, I had not severed my ties to the land. So I clearly remember arguments about the commune [*obshchina*], about the advantages of private property, about the necessity of finding new forms of land ownership and use, about communal tilling, and so on. These questions, which then seemed inescapable, could not be solved at that time. The most basic Russian problem—the inadequacies of the peasant economy, especially the land shortages, could be redressed only through ongoing measures such as the establishment of the Peasant's Land Bank, which made available generous and favorable credit to peasant land purchasers, as well as the easing of restrictions on resettlement and organizing its potential.[14] Alexander III's government occupied itself with such questions; and it is well established that these measures had a great influence on the extension of peasant landownership.

I also must point out that the idea of solving the peasant land problem by fiat at the expense of either private or state land simply never arose—it was inconceivable in those days, in both the public and the government. I cannot expand further on the peasant legislation of Alexander III, as this is beyond my area of expertise. I think this side of his economic legislation always was rather unpopular. Thanks to the harsh reality of Russia's economy, of which I have spoken, he had to limit himself to simply preliminary, or preparatory, measures.

I will at present say nothing about the political aspects of his reign— our own "new class" was growing and prospering in many ways under the influence of his "political reaction." However, I shall reserve the privilege of giving my own appreciation of the political aspect of this unjustly denigrated regime at the end of my memoirs.

Notes

Fenin and His Memoirs

1. There is considerable literature available in English concerning the gentry in late Imperial Russia and the problem of social identities. See, for example, Roberta T. Manning, *The Crisis of the Old Order in Russia* (Princeton, N. J., 1982) and Seymour Becker, *Nobility and Privilege in Late Imperial Russia* (DeKalb, Illinois, 1985).

See also Gregory L. Freeze, "The Soslovie [Estate] Paradigm and Russian Social History," *American Historical Review* 91 (February, 1986): 11–36.

2. See, for example, Theodore H. Friedgut, *Iuzovka and Revolution: Society and Politics in the Donbass, 1869–924. Vol. I: Society and Labor in the Donbass* (Princeton, forthcoming).

3. On this subject see Susan P. McCaffray, "The Association of Southern Coal and Steel Producers and the Problems of Industrial Progress in Tsarist Russia," *Slavic Review* 47,2 (Fall, 1988): 464–482.

4. See, for example, Terence Emmons and Wayne S. Vucinich, eds., *The Zemstvo in Russia* (New York, 1982).

5. A clear and helpful discussion of the intricacies of being a "merchant" in Imperial Russia is found in Thomas C. Owen, *Capitalism and Politics in Russia* (New York, 1981).

6. See Gleb Struve, *Russkaia literatura v izgnanie* [Russian Literature in Exile] 2nd ed. (Paris, 1984), pp. 384–385.

Preface

1. All of these provinces and regions were administrative units of late Imperial Russia. In the Soviet period they are all part of the Ukrainian Soviet Socialist Republic. The coal fields of the Donbass encompass 10,000 square miles and include many types of coal. The iron ore deposits of the Krivoi Rog lie 150 to 200 miles away. These resources supported the industrialization of southern Russia. The Donets Basin began to attract sizeable foreign investment in the 1880s and especially in the 1890s. Donbass coal output increased 500 percent between 1887 and 1900, far surpassing the output of the older Moscow Basin. The Donbass surpassed the Urals in pig iron production in 1895 and in steel production in 1896. See P. A. Khromov, *Ekonomicheskoe razvitie Rossii v XIX–XXvv* (Moscow, 1950), pp. 456–458.

2. Count Sergei Witte was minister of finance under the last two tsars from 1892 to 1903, and prime minister under Nicholas II from 1905 to 1906. He was a great promoter of industrialization. His strategies included sales taxes, a state liquor monopoly and a protective tariff, to fill government coffers; and the achievement of trade and budget balances, as well as the gold standard (1897), in order to attract foreign investment in basic industries. His policies usually are credited with generating the great industrial boom of the 1890s, of which the rapid growth of the Donbass coal and steel industry was a significant part.

3. Bakhmut lies in the eastern part of Ekaterinoslav Province and is the heart of the Donbass coal country. The technical high schools (which Russians called "real schools" after the German *Realschule*) had been established as a result of a fundamental reform of the country's secondary education system in 1864. At that time the secondary schools, called *gymnasia*, were officially opened to people of all classes and their number was greatly increased. Three kinds of gymnasia came into existence: two kinds were classical, with educations rooted in Greek and Latin, and a third type was modeled on the German *Realschule*, in which there were no classical languages. There was a simultaneous effort to produce outstanding textbooks in the natural sciences. Fenin attended the Kharkov Real School.

The St. Petersburg Mining Institute opened in 1774, during the reign of Catherine the Great. In the early 1800s the school was known briefly as the Institute of the Cadet Mining Corps and in the 1830s Tsar Nicholas I gave the school a military type of organization. It assumed the specialized academic character that it had in Fenin's day after 1866 and came under the supervision of the Ministry of Government Properties in 1874. By 1891 there were 27 instructors of all ranks and 270 students. An old source on the Institute is S. Loranskii, *Istoricheskii ocherk Gornogo instituta* (St. Petersburg, 1873). Today the school is known as the Leningrad Institute of Mines.

4. See the editor's introduction for a description of this organization.

5. The state council was a group of men from various spheres who advised the tsar. When a new constitutional framework was announced in 1906 this council became the upper house of the legislature, as a conservative counterweight to the popularly elected Duma. Half of its members were appointed by the tsar and the other half chosen by various public bodies. Industry was lightly represented in this council; there were six seats for representatives of commerce (chosen from exchange committees) and six for representatives of industry (chosen from associations like the Association of Southern Coal and Steel Producers). Organizations in which the nonindustrial gentry predominated were much better represented in this council.

6. Fenin abbreviates Donets Basin here as *Don. Bas.* We render this by the traditional English translation *Donbass.* For the sake of style we have used this term interchangeably with *Donets Basin,* irrespective of whether Fenin used the abbreviation in a particular case.

7. Fenin uses the word *Russian* to describe subjects of the tsar; that is, to distinguish natives from foreigners. Strictly speaking, however, a very significant proportion of these Russian subjects were in fact Poles, Ukrainians, Jews, and descendants of Germans, as he himself makes clear later.

8. Here Fenin is presumably referring to the reforms introduced by P. A. Stolypin in 1907, which encouraged peasants to acquire private ownership of and to consolidate the scattered strips of land they long had farmed collectively as part of the village commune or *mir.* Although much land was converted to private holdings, very little of it actually was consolidated, and because of the specific provisions of the legislation, it is not possible to determine whether the bulk of peasants who converted to private ownership really desired to do so.

Chapter One.
Student Days

1. For *educated youth* Fenin uses here the word *intelligenty,* usually rendered "intelligentsia" in English. This is a Russian term first used widely in the late 1860s. It was a self-descriptive term connoting what the literary critic Pisarev called the *thinking proletariat,* and what another social thinker, Lavrov, called *critically thinking personalities.* Although there was little agreement among them as to how progress might come to Russia, the people who used this term to describe themselves, whether political activists or technically trained people like Fenin, exuded confidence that they were at the vanguard of those who were leading Russia forward. See the discussion of this word in James Billington, *The Icon and the Axe* (New York, Vintage Books, 1970), p. 390. As he puts it, "They thought of themselves as practical rather than 'superfluous' people: students of science and servants of history." For

a thorough discussion of the complicated historical implications of the word *intelligenty* (singular, *intelligent*), see Richard Pipes, ed., *The Russian Intelligentsia* (New York, 1961).

2. Saurmogila most likely refers to burial mounds of the prehistoric Saurmatians or Sarmatians, as they were known after the third century B.C. This was a nomadic people related to the Scythians, possibly matriarchal. Zuevka was the country estate of the wealthy and colorful aristocratic-mining family Ilovaiskii, about which Fenin speaks at more length in chapters 2 and 3. Khartsyzsk was a railroad station town on the steppe. Both Zuevka and Khartsyzsk were named for mythical figures. Today there are towns in the Donetsk Oblast of the Ukrainian Soviet Socialist Republic named Zuevka and Khartsyzsk.

3. See Fenin's Introduction, note 3, for a description of the type of gymnasia known as the "real schools." Under Alexander III (1881–1894), in the general spirit of reaction, officials moved to restrict gymnasia to the uppermost classes, including the nobility and the upper reaches of the merchantry, through administrative restrictions and increased fees. A series of reforms associated with Count D. A. Tolstoi, minister of the interior, was launched in 1887. The science curriculum of the gymnasia was not greatly affected by these measures, although the classical content was gradually reduced and there was an accompanying effort to concentrate on religious education.

4. Fenin refers here to the most famous of Russia's nineteenth century writers: I. S. Turgenev (1818–1883); N. V. Gogol (1809–1852); F. M. Dostoevsky (1821–1881); L. N. Tolstoy (1828–1910). Friedrich Spielhagen (1829–1911) was a German naturalistic writer of many novels, novellas, and stories, but who clearly would not be listed in the same category as these other novelists today.

5. This passage refers to conversations and debates between the hero, Onegin, and his friend Lenskii about law, science, and custom. It appears in chapter 2, Section 16 of Aleksandr Pushkin's (1799–1837) masterful "novel in verse," *Evgenii Onegin* (written between 1823 and 1831).

Here Fenin refers to the assessment of Pushkin by the 1860s critic Dmitrii Pisarev (1840–1868). Pisarev, associated with "nihilism," rejected art for art's sake and asserted that all literature must serve a social purpose. Pisarev's critique of Pushkin, Russia's premier poet, in some ways constitutes the coming of age of a new generation with a new literary agenda, and a rejection of the personal questions that had characterized what Fenin later calls *gentry culture*, in favor of social questions. Fenin is describing himself as typical of students of this era, who were influenced strongly by these literary disputes and who were becoming critical of purely introspective literature.

6. Onegin and Tatiana are the leading characters of *Evgenii Onegin*. Onegin, an empty-headed dandy, rejects the love of the pure-hearted Tatiana in order to live a dissipated life. Too late he realizes what he has given up. In this passage Pisarev is making fun of what he considers

the petty concerns of these more or less insignificant gentlefolk. It was rather typical that Fenin should have come to appreciate Pushkin more in later years, as the makers of Russian literary opinion established the "cult of Pushkin" only in the 1880s

7. Bazarov is the hero of Turgenev's 1862 novel *Fathers and Sons,* the rather sympathetically drawn young "nihilist," who rejects conventional values, challenges everything, and undertakes the study of medicine, mostly haphazardly. Rudin is the young hero of a novel of the same name from 1856, which challenges the idealistic older generation for being inefficient and ineffective.

8. Alexander Herzen (1812–1870) was an early Russian socialist who published a very influential Russian newspaper from abroad, *Kolokol,* or *The Bell.* In 1861 he answered young Russians seeking a solution to their country's problems with the proposal that they go "into the people," to teach them, provide technical assistance, and above all, to educate them in preparation for their coming revolution. The most direct response to this plea came in the summer of 1874 when over 2000 young people poured out of the cities into the countryside. The results of this movement were most disappointing for the participants, many of whom were arrested, having been denounced by the peasants themselves.

Here Fenin places a note quoting Spielhagen to the effect that "One cannot be a soldier alone." This idea that one is nothing as an individual, but only as a member of the whole, is the central theme of Spielhagen's 1866 novel, *In Rank and File,* the hero of which is Leo Gutman, to whom Fenin refers here. *Tuski* is probably a russified version of the name *Cziska,* a gypsy in Spielhagen's 1860–1861 novel, *Problematic Characters,* which deals with the problems of the life of the nobility of Pomerania and the inability of some people ever to be satisfied.

9. On March 1, 1881 the "Tsar Liberator," Alexander II, was assassinated by populist-terrorists from the People's Will party. Upon the ascension to the throne of his son, Alexander III, reaction set in in most areas of public life. The government cracked down on students as well as ethnic and religious minorities.

10. Populist, or *narodnik,* was a title given to a wide group of radicals from the 1860s on. Populists were bound by a faith in the Russian peasant as unique, innately communalistic, and capable of achieving revolution. Early in the history of populism (*narodnichestvo*), however, there arose a fundamental disagreement over tactics. The question was whether peasants could achieve their revolutionary potential and mission with the help of *intelligenty,* who would offer them education and propaganda, or whether the role of the *intelligenty,* should be to destroy the state through terroristic violence, after which the peasants could then proceed to make their own revolution. After the failure of the "to the people" movement, populists formed two separate parties representing these alternatives. The People's Will pursued terrorism, which culminated in the assassination of Alexander II. The Black Repartition disdained

this kind of violence, considering it an acknowledgment that the populist faith in the peasants' potential for revolution was unjustified. See Philip Pomper, *The Russian Revolutionary Intelligentsia* (New York, 1970).

11. The Congress of Berlin followed the Russo-Turkish War of 1877–1878, which the Russians won, and the Treaty of San Stefano, which Russia originally imposed on Turkey after the victory. The terms of San Stefano, which included the creation of a "Greater Bulgaria" and complete autonomy for the Serbian-populated former Ottoman provinces of Bosnia and Herzegovina, were deemed by other European powers to be too threatening to the existing balance of power in southeastern Europe, which is to say, too favorable to Russia. Consequently, the other powers forced Russia to submit to a second peace conference, this one mediated by Prince Bismarck, the German chancellor, in Berlin. The resulting Treaty of Berlin rewarded Russia for her victory much more modestly, created only a small independent Bulgaria and left Bosnia-Herzegovina in a legal limbo. Russia's allies in southeastern Europe, as well as Pan-Slavs at home, viewed this episode as most humiliating. There is some truth to Fenin's suggestion that Alexander II was not entirely to blame for the affair, in that he had been quite reluctant to embark on war with Turkey in the first place.

Viscount Eugene-Melchior de Vogüé (b. 1849) was a secretary of the French embassy in St. Petersburg for a period after 1871 and married the sister of a Russian general. He was the author of many works about Russia and other subjects and became a member of the Academie Française in 1888.

12. Author's note: *Journal du vicomte E. M. de Vogüé, Paris–St. Petersburg, 1877–1883.*

13. Author's note: Eronim I. Iasinskii (1850–1930), *The Story of My Life*, (Moscow-Leningrad, 1926).

14. Lizogub was a very wealthy landowner who donated his fortune to the terrorist cause, although he did not take an active part in the assassinations. His trial and that of others before military tribunals were a novelty in the prosecution of these acts, a practice first begun in the South.

15. M. T. Loris-Melikov was minister of the interior under Alexander II. In the last years of Alexander II's reign the minister had persuaded the tsar to approve a project for a consultative assembly, as a means of placating public opinion. Loris-Melikov and other liberal ministers resigned early in Alexander III's reign, when the direction toward reaction became clear.

A. S. Suvorin (1834–1912) was a liberal businessman, owner of a large book publishing company in St. Petersburg, and publisher of the very influential liberal paper *Novoe Vermia (New Times)* from 1876 on.

16. Here and many other places Fenin signals peasant speech by using the colloquialisms and particles which characterized their spoken language. Here the original is *"A chi Vy chuli, kazhut' tsaria vbyto."* We

have tried to find an American idiom which may suggest something of the same class distinctions, although this is at best an approximation. In this case, the peasant speaking is also a Ukrainian, whose language was distinct from Russian in many ways.

17. N. I. Rysakov (1861–1881) was a member of the populist-terrorist group The People's Will from the fall of 1879, while a student at the St. Petersburg Mining Institute. He hurled the first bomb at Alexander II on 1 March 1881, and although this was not the bomb that killed the tsar, Rysakov was arrested, implicated the others in the plot, and was hanged.

18. *Ruslan and Liudmila* is an opera by M. Glinka and *Evgenii Onegin* is an opera by P. I. Tchaikovsky. Each is based upon narrative poems by Pushkin. In the second half of the nineteenth century there was a considerable stir in Russian music as a group of musical nationalists, which included M. Musorgskii, M. Balakirev, A. Borodin, and N. A. Rimskii-Korsakov challenged foreign models as shallow and purely stylistic. Italian opera received much of their scorn. They sought to create a Russian national music that would evoke native themes and melodies as well as offer its own, less formal, style.

19. *Virgin Soil* was published in 1877. The Russian literary historian D. S. Mirsky concurs with Fenin's assessment when he notes that in *Virgin Soil*, "Turgenev's presentation of the revolutionaries of the seventies is like an account of a foreign country by one who had never seen it" (*A History of Russian Literature*, New York, 1958, p. 204).

20. These are all Dostoevsky novels. *Crime and Punishment* was written in 1865–1866; *The Idiot* in 1868; *The Adolsescent* in 1875.

21. *The Possessed*, written in 1871–1872, concerns a terroristic conspiracy of the sixties, based on an actual incident in which conspirators murdered one of their fellows in cold blood. Dostoevsky was exploring what he considered the moral bankruptcy of the revolutionary movement.

22. Tolstoy wrote *War and Peace* between 1865 and 1869 and *Anna Karenina* between 1873 and 1877.

23. "Master and Man" was written in 1895, "The Kreutzer Sonata" in 1889, "The Death of Ivan Il'ich" in 1886, and "A Confession" at the beginning of Tolstoy's new period, in 1880–1882. Tolstoy experienced a religious reawakening in mid-career, after which he believed that he should give up his grand novels for a simpler, parablelike style, which was better suited to expressing Christian truth.

24. V. M. Garshin (1855–1888), was a writer of gentry background who Mirsky characterizes as the "most representative of the novelists of the eighties," but "hardly a great writer." (Mirsky, *A History of Russian Literature*, pp. 349–350.)

25. Garshin dealt with prostitution in two other stories, "An Incident" (1878) and "Nadezhda Nikolaevna" (1885). "The Artists" appeared in 1879.

26. A. P. Chekhov (1860–1904) was a great playwright and short-story writer.

27. N. N. Zlatovratskii (1845–1902) was a "populist novelist" of the seventies who stressed the virtues of the peasant commune rather than those of individuals. Gleb Uspenskii (1843–1902), whose most important works also date from the seventies and early eighties, displayed rather more disillusionment with the populist vision of the peasant.

28. *The Memoirs of Private Ivanov* was published in 1883.

29. Antosha Chekhont is the name under which Chekhov's first stories were published while he was still living in the South, where he was born.

30. These stories date from 1886–1888.

31. "Ivanov" was first produced in Moscow in December 1887 and in St. Petersburg a year later.

32. N. K. Mikhailovskii (1842–1904) was the recognized leader of the populist movement during the seventies, along with P. Lavrov. N. Shchedrin was the pseudonym of M. E. Saltykov (1826–1889), a satirical novelist of radical sympathies.

Thick journals were those that addressed social and literary questions, and that often published oppositional writers. Shchedrin edited two of them in his day: *Sovremennik [The Contemporary]* and *Otechestvennye zapiski [Annals of the Fatherland]*. Mikhailovskii was closely associated with the journal *Otechestvennye zapiski* and later edited *Russkoe bogatstvo [Russian Wealth]*.

33. Marshals of the nobility were elected by noblemen in each province as spokesmen who had limited privileges of addressing the tsar. Fenin is suggesting that Fortunato was remarkably ingratiating if he were able to be elected to this honorable local position after having spent so little time in the province. The position of marshal of the nobility also was one firmly rooted in the old-fashioned world of noble privilege, a world from which Fenin repeatedly asserts engineers were irrevocably separated.

34. A. K. Glazunov (1865–1936) was a prolific composer of the generation after Tchaikovsky, who was trained by Rimskii-Korsakov.

35. A. G. Rubinstein (1829–1894) was a composer and one of the greatest of the nineteenth century pianists. After studying abroad he returned to Russia where he founded the Russian Music Society in 1859 and the Imperial Conservatory in St. Petersburg, of which he became the director. He would later briefly direct the Vienna Philharmonic Orchestra and tour the United States. His brother Nicholas founded the Moscow Conservatory. The Rubinsteins were considered musical conservatives, following the classical German style.

36. This probably is the Andante Cantabile, the second movement of Tchaikovsky's String Quartet No. 1 in D major.

37. Arthur Schopenhauer (1788–1860) was a German philosopher who developed the metaphysical doctrine of the will in opposition to Hegelian idealism, influencing later existential and Freudian philosophy. Eduard von Hartmann (1842–1906) likewise was a German philosopher

who tried to reconcile two conflicting schools, the rationalist and ir-rationalist, by developing a philosophy of the unconscious. Both, but particularly Schopenhauer, were "pessimistic" about the state of contemporary civilization.

38. Georges Bizet (1838–1875) was the French composer best remembered for his opera *Carmen*.

39. Stavrogin is the chief character of Dostoevsky's *The Possessed*, who commits suicide.

40. *Zakuski* are more or less hors d'oeuvres, although rather more substantial, and include a variety of treats, possibly including herring, cold vegetables, or caviar.

41. L. I. Lutugin (1864–1915) became a famous geologist, founder of the scientific school of coal geology. He was one of the first to study the coal-bearing basins of Russia. He studied the Donbass for over twenty years, as well as the Kuznets Basin and others.

42. The Shcherbinovka Mine belonged to the French-owned Coal and Salt Mining Company.

43. The Black Hundreds were right-wing extremists, ultranationalists, and anti-Semites, associated with vicious attacks on Jews, especially in 1905 and thereafter.

44. Slavianoserbsk, along with Bakhmut, was the premier coal producing region of Ekaterinoslav Province.

45. The reference is to Turgenev's novel, *A Nest of Gentlefolk*, published in 1859.

46. I. N. Potapenko (1856–1929) was a naturalistic writer of populist views who wrote tales of Ukrainian life, novels, and plays.

47. I. A. Time (1838–1920) was a famous scientist and mining engineer who worked in the Donbass from 1866 to 1870, served on and off as a professor at the St. Petersburg Mining Institute between 1870 and 1915, and as a member of the Committee of Mining Scientists from 1873 to 1917. He was the author of several technical books including the basic text *The Mechanics of Mining and Metallurgy* (1879) and a pioneer in developing the theory and rules for design of steam hammers, iron-rolling machines, and hydraulic turbines.

48. The "romance" is a poem sung in a very romantic tempo, with piano accompaniment. It was particularly fashionable among the Russian intelligentsia.

49. Ekaterinburg is a town in the Urals Mountains, today known as Sverdlovsk.

50. By "second revolution" Fenin refers to 1917, although it is not technically clear whether he means the Revolution which occurred on 15 March 1917 against the tsar or the Revolution of 7 November 1917 in which the Bolsheviks seized power. Either could be construed as Russia's "second revolution," depending upon whether the Revolution of 1905, in which the tsar was forced to grant constitutional concessions, is counted as the first.

51. It seems more likely that Temnikov and his son were murdered in 1918, by which time the violent Civil War had begun. The war saw brutality on many sides, but the Bolsheviks who held Ekaterinburg in 1918 retain a special reputation as the murderers of the imperial family, which was imprisoned there, in July 1918. It is not possible to verify that the same people killed both Fenin's friends and the tsar, however.

52. The Neva River winds through St. Petersburg (now Leningrad) on its way to the Gulf of Finland, cutting the city up into islands and quarters that can be reached only via one of the city's many beautiful bridges. Vasil'evskii Island, in northwestern Petersburg (Leningrad), was the home of St. Petersburg University as well as other academic institutions.

53. The old Russian grading system ran from 0 to 4 with minuses and plusses, the maximum being a "4 + +." The minimum passing grade was a 3 with a double minus, or "3 = ".

54. Here Fenin uses the word *malorusskii* or "Little Russian" to describe Lysenko's brother. This was a term used by Great Russians, the country's dominant and majority ethnic group, to describe Ukrainians, inhabitants of southern and southwestern Russia. There is certainly some implied condescension in the term, although it was used so widely that we can imagine that Great Russians were not sensitive to this at all. There are those today who maintain that, although the old-fashioned term originally may have been used exclusively to describe ethnic Ukrainians (whose language, religion, and social structure differed from that of Great Russians), by the nineteenth century the term also was applied to those living in the Ukraine, even if they were of Great Russian stock.

55. In fact there is no way to distinguish the names of Russian noblemen from those of more humble folk. The name *Romanov,* for instance, the name of the ruling dynasty, is quite common.

56. Prince A. D. Kantemir (1708–1744) was a Russian classical poet of Moldavian descent who was a pioneering realist and satirist.

57. I. V. Mushketov (1850–1902) was the author of the first description of the geological structure of Central Asia as well as an explorer of the Urals and the Caucasus. Turkestan is a region of Central Asia around Lake Balkash. It was conquered by Russian forces between 1864 and 1885 and remains part of the Soviet Union today.

58. Of the scientists listed here two are quite noteworthy. A. P. Karpinskii (1847–1936) was "the father of Russian geology," son of a mining engineer, graduate of and professor at the St. Petersburg Mining Institute from 1866 to 1896. He helped organize the Geological Committee in 1882, pioneered the study of geology in Russia, and was the first elected president of the Academy of Sciences in 1917. He remained active in the Soviet period and is buried in Red Square.

N. A. Iossa (1845–1917) was the son of a Russian pioneer of the Bessemer smelting process, a graduate of and professor at the Mining Institute after 1882. He served as head of the Mining Department of the government from 1900 to 1907 and also was chairman of the Mining Council and the Russian Metallurgical Society.

59. These are famous Russian composers: P. I. Tchaikovsky (1840–1893); N. A. Rimskii-Korsakov (1844–1908); A. Borodin (1833–1887); and M. Glinka (1804–1857).

60. In this list of opera singers one with another claim to fame is F. I. Stravinskii, who was the father of the famous composer Igor Stravinski and for many years a leading bass singer at the Imperial Opera. A recent monograph on the subject is by Richard Taruskin, *Opera and Drama in Russia as Preached and Practiced in the 1860s* (Ann Arbor, Mich., 1981).

61. Ilia Repin (1844–1930) was the most famous of the nineteenth century Russian painters, a representative of a new school of nationalistic and populistic painters known as the "wanderers." His most famous painting was "The Volga Boatmen," painted between 1870 and 1873.

62. Michael Nestorov (1862–1942) was a painter of religious themes. Isaac Levitan (1860–1900) was perhaps Russia's greatest landscape painter, in whose paintings people seldom appeared. Ivan Aivazovskii (1817–1900) painted over 5000 pictures, almost all of them seascapes.

63. *Snegurochka,* or *The Snow Maiden,* Rimskii-Korsakov's third opera, is a pantheistic fairy tale replete with Russian folk tunes and bird calls. It was written in 1880.

64. Glinka's opera *Ruslan and Liudmila* premiered in 1842 and was at that time a total failure. Based on Pushkin's first important poem, it is basically a fairy tale love story in which the hero, Ruslan, endures numerous hardships in order to win his beloved, Liudmila. This opera is now considered a source of the distinctly Russian musical idiom and Glinka's greatest work. Largely through the work of his indefatigable sister, this opera was finally revived at the Mariinskii Theater in St. Petersburg in 1872, after which time, as Fenin notes, *Ruslan and Liudmila* was appreciated as a national treasure. Franz Lizst was so struck with part of this opera, "Chernomor's March," that he transcribed it for the piano.

65. *Rognede,* written by the minor composer Aleksandr Serov in 1865, dealt with the period of Russia's conversion to Christianity in the tenth century; he also wrote *The Power of Evil* in 1871. *The Enchantress* is an 1887 opera by Tchaikovsky.

66. The Fatherland War was the war against Napoleon after his invasion of Russia in 1812. Today this is called the *First Fatherland War,* the second being World War II.

67. The Nicholas for whom this railroad was named and to whose "times" Fenin refers here is Tsar Nicholas I (1825–1855), under whom Russia's first railroads were constructed.

68. Fenin often employs the colloquial expression *khokhol,* used in prerevolutionary times to describe Ukrainian peasants. The word derives from the forelock of hair which Ukrainian men wore in earlier times, and it suggests a very humble, country person.

69. I. A. Bunin (1870–1953) was a realistic novelist, and the novel referred to here is *The Life of Arsen'ev: The Well of Days* (first published in Paris in 1930). I. S. Nikitin (1824–1861) was a realistic poet who was most famous for evoking the miserable life of poor folk.

70. Author's note: This speech was delivered at the Moscow Historical Society of Moscow University on 28 October 1894.

Editor's note: V. O. Kliuchevskii (1841–1911) was one of Russia's greatest historians. Becoming professor of history at Moscow University in 1879, Kliuchevskii was a renowned scholar and lecturer who abandoned the philosophical context in which so much Russian history had been written, favoring a social and economic analysis of different classes and of various trends.

71. Author's note: This is an excerpt from a student compilation edited in emigration.

72. A. N. Pleshcheev (1825–1893) was a writer, critic, and literary editor of *The Northern Herald*, where "The Steppe" was to appear.

73. Nezhdanov, the hero of Turgenev's *Virgin Soil*, is a tutor to the peasants who understands them very little.

74. A. S. Suvorin is the editor described earlier, in note 15, and the one who encouraged Chekhov to make writing his career. Chekhov did not share Suvorin's politics, although he trusted him in literary matters, and many of Chekhov's stories appeared first in Suvorin's paper, *New Times*.

This letter was dated 25 November 1892. Chekhov was preoccupied that entire summer and fall by the terrible cholera epidemic that gripped the country, especially the South, where he was living. As a physician, Chekhov assumed the role that summer of head doctor of a zemstvo district and spent many months fighting the epidemic. Excerpts from some of Chekhov's letters have been translated by Avrahm Yarmolinsky in his *Letters of Anton Chekhov* (New York, 1973).

75. This letter was dated 30 December 1888. L. A. Tikhomirov (1850–1923) was a spokesman for those who had assassinated Tsar Alexander II. However, he repented and addressed Alexander III with an apologetic and humble petition, begging to be allowed to return to Russia. He ended up as a bastion of the autocracy.

On Mikhailovskii, see note 32.

The zemstvos were established in 1874 as local governing bodies charged with levying property taxes and supplying health, educational, and agronomic assistance to the local population, especially to the peasants. Although the zemstvos were elected by universal male suffrage, the voting was weighted so that the landowning nobility dominated these assemblies, at the expense of the peasants and the industrialists.

76. Nizhnii Novgorod is a city east of Moscow on the Volga, today renamed Gorky. Here Chekhov refers to the same cholera epidemic mentioned previously. This quotation comes from a letter of 16 August 1892.

77. The war Fenin refers to here is the Russo-Turkish War of 1877–1878.

78. Serfdom was a legal system that bound Russian peasants to the estate on which they were born. Gentry landowners technically were not allowed to sell serfs apart from the land to which they were attached, but by the late eighteenth century even this stipulation had fallen into abeyance. Gentry landowners held enormous powers over their serfs. Besides being able to compel the serfs to perform some type of labor service or payment to the master, landowners had judicial and fiscal powers over peasants, as well as the right, eventually, to exile them to Siberia for misbehavior without trial. This system existed legally from 1648 until 1861, when it was abolished by Tsar Alexander II. At the time of Emancipation roughly half of the peasants were serfs on the land of private landowners, while the other half enjoyed somewhat better conditions being bound to state land. The Emancipation meant that gentry landowners either had to hire paid workers to farm their estates or to rent parcels to land-short peasants. The literature on Russian agriculture in the post-Emancipation period is vast. A sensible, short introduction to this literature is Peter Gatrell, *The Tsarist Economy 1850–1917* (New York, 1986), especially Chapters 4 and 6.

79. Russian cereal prices had in fact risen through the 1860s and early 1870s in response to the growing size of rural and urban populations. However, a precipitous decline set in, more serious in rye than in wheat, by the early 1880s. Although grain exports did grow from about 6 percent of total harvest to 20 percent between 1860 and 1879, contemporary economic historians would point less to Russia's dependence on foreign markets than to the world-wide trend in grain prices. The main development was the opening up of the U.S. plains through railroads and steamships, which challenged all European grain producers. The decline continued until about 1900, except for the years of harvest failure in 1883 and 1891. See Gatrell, ibid., pp. 130–134.

80. Kulaks were relatively well-to-do peasants who hired laborers, rented out surplus land, and lent money to their fellows at exhorbitant interest rates. The word is a peasant expression from the word for "fist." This suggests much about how peasants—and people like Fenin—viewed those peasants who managed to acquire substantial property.

81. *Muzhik* is the diminutive form of the word *muzh*, or "man." It was used to describe a peasant in tsarist Russia and, when used by the peasants' social superiors, has a tone that is at least patronizing, if not derogatory, although both peasants and members of the intelligentsia who sympathized with them used this term.

82. It is true that there was little direct or indirect state investment in agriculture after the Emancipation, but Fenin's picture of a neglected landowning class is a bit distorted. Besides considerable social advantages, the state had advanced the landowners significant amounts of cash for the land that serfs received, settling mortgages on land and

serfs at the same time. There was also considerable government support for railroad building in the 1870s, which benefitted agriculture. A less pessimistic assessment of gentry agriculture after the Emancipation appears in Seymour Becker, *Nobility and Privilege in Late Imperial Russia* (DeKalb, Ill., 1985).

83. V. P. Riabushinskii was a second-generation Moscow textile entrepreneur, as well as a banker and editor. His family, as well as the interesting milieu of old-fashioned, religiously dissident Moscow entrepreneurs, is discussed by Alfred Rieber in *Merchants and Entrepreneurs in Imperial Russia* (Chapel Hill, N.C., 1982), Chapter 7.

84. See Jo Ann Ruckman, *The Moscow Business Elite: A Social and Cultural Portrait of Two Generations, 1840–1905* (DeKalb, Ill., 1984) for a description of the Moscow merchants, particularly of the Riabushinskii clan.

Chapter Two.
My Early Career in the Donets Basin of Yesteryear

1. The Rutchenko brothers had mined on their own land, but in 1906 their operation was incorporated as the Rutchenko Coal Company, with mostly French and some Belgian capital. After a slow start it became quite profitable, producing high quality coal. It was bought by the great Briansk Ironworks Company in 1912.

2. E. A. Shteding later directed the Voznesensk Mine of P. A. Karpov's coal mines, served on the council of the Association of Southern Coal and Steel Producers and as president of the association's Fund for Injured Miners.

3. "Your lordship [*vashe blagorodie*]" was the standard form of address between a peasant and nobleman or between a soldier and an officer.

4. Iuzovka was the mining settlement founded by pioneering Welsh entrepreneur John Hughes and seat of his large, successful firm, the New Russian Company, founded in 1869. This was the first foreign firm to produce coal in the Donbass, and it later produced iron and steel products as well.

5. P. A. Karpov, a local landowner and coal proprietor, was a member of both the Ekaterinoslav provincial zemstvo and the governing council of the Association of Southern Coal and Steel Producers. Fenin probably followed Shteding here. In 1911 this operation would be incorporated as the Voznesensk (Ascension) Coal Company of d.s.s. P. A. Karpov.

6. *Artels* were work gangs, usually organized by workers themselves either in villages where a group of peasants planned together to go off for seasonal work or after arriving at the mines. The *artel* often ate and slept together in addition to working together, and the mine authorities dealt directly only with the *artel* boss, who delivered the agreed upon

number of men and who received all the wages owed to his gang. Because most of the miners in the nineteenth century were seasonal, *artels* tended not to be long lasting, but they probably provided more security and solidarity for migrant workers than Fenin suggests here. Russian workers won the right to unionize and strike only in the wake of the Revolution of 1905, but there were unsanctioned unions and strikes in many places, including the Donbass, as early as the 1880s.

7. Although Chekhov wrote often about peasants in his scores of stories, particularly in the tale "The Peasants," we have not been able to locate this passage.

8. A *barin* was a noble landowner. As Fenin notes later, peasants viewed the nobles' ownership of land as essentially unfair, although apparently inevitable. In the peasants' minds, "the land belongs to him who tills it," so it had never been fair for nobles to receive rents, crops, or labor in exchange for the peasants' use of arable land. Even after the Emancipation of 1861 peasants felt that it was unjust that they had received so little land and that they had had to pay for it. Although the average size of a Russian family's allotment compared favorably with the size of such farms in Western Europe, the notoriously low productivity of Russian farming led most peasants to believe that they suffered from a land shortage, and the peasants above all blamed the noble landowner for this.

9. Ivan Grigor'evich Ilovaiskii was a landowner and coal producer in Ekaterinoslav Province, one of the old breed who exploited the coal on their own estates without technical training. He was a co-founder of the Aleksei Coal Company in 1879.

10. *Pokrova* was a semiofficial Orthodox feast celebrating an apparition of the Holy Virgin in Constantinople in the twelfth century. It was celebrated on 1 October, according to the Julian calendar in use in Russia before the Revolution (twelve days behind the Western calendar in the nineteenth century).

11. The Emanciapation legislation of 1861 freed former serfs to move about the country in pursuit of a livelihood, but the great majority of freed peasants were required to take on large debts for the land they received in settlement from their former masters. The government acted as mortgage holder for the peasants, paying off the landowners and requiring peasants to repay the Treasury, over a forty year period at 6 percent interest. Consequently, many peasant men went away for wage work to factories or mines for part of the year, though most went away during the winter months, returning for agricultural work on their land in the spring. It was virtually impossible for peasants to pay off their large debts, especially as they also were obliged to pay hefty taxes. The redemption payments were cancelled after the Revolution of 1905, but until then most peasants who worked in industry retained some connection and obligation to the land. Fenin may refer to Tula and Orel miners

as "itinerants" because peasants in these provinces typically received inadequate land settlements after 1861 and were among the poorest people in the country, presumably many of them having virtually no allotment at all by the 1880s.

12. In Russian, *sezonnaia igra*—"*zabastovka.*" Trinity is a Christian holyday that occurs fifty days after Easter. Orthodox peasants celebrated it by bringing branches into their houses in honor of the start of spring.

13. Lazar' Grigor'evich Rabinovich was one of the most remarkable and famous of Fenin's colleagues. Although Fenin narrates many details of this remarkable man's life below, here it should be noted that Rabinovich managed, successively, the mines of P. A. Karpov, the Maksimov Coal Company, the Irmino Coal Company, and then served as president of the Donets-Grushevka Coal Company. He was a founder of the latter two. He also held numerous responsible positions in the Association of Southern Coal and Steel Producers, including a post on the council and leadership of the Fund for Disabled Miners.

14. As Fenin casually admits here, it was illegal for managers not to conform to contract conditions, which usually stipulated more frequent paydays. Not surprisingly, many of the earliest strikes were over issues of contract compliance. Workers often "won" such strikes, but only temporarily. Managers generally took the same view as Fenin; that is , that withholding pay was a justifiable tactic in the fight against drunkenness.

15. Social distinctions were so pronounced in Old Russia that different terms for "person" were used for people of different status. *Liudi* the plural of *chelovek*, was used for persons of at least middling status, such as master craftsmen, townsmen, and the gentry. Peasants and most factory workers would be called, as Fenin usually calls them, *muzhik*, literally "little man." In this phrase, Fenin's language suggests much about the aspirations of some workers to ascend to a higher rank and about the qualities managers looked for as qualification for such movement.

16. Fenin probably is exaggerating the ease of renting private quarters. By some reports, in most of the mining areas of the Donbass independent housing was quite scarce and consequently very expensive, perhaps as much as 10 to 12 rubles per month (the average miner's wages were about 19–27R per month by 1900). A Soviet historian concludes that only about 13 percent of Donbass coalminers lived in private housing by 1913, although 75 percent of Donbass factory and furnace workers did so. Of those in firm-provided housing by 1913 only about 40 percent of miners had family quarters, whereas the great majority of factory workers had such quarters. Clearly the key to renting private quarters was money. Many of these issues are discussed thoroughly in Theodore H. Friedgut, *Iuzovka and Revolution: Society and Politics in the Donbass, 1869–1924* vol. 1 (Princeton, N. J., 1989).

Fenin seems about right in his reference to wages. There was great distinction among miners' wages, depending upon skill level, but one account suggests that the average annual income of Donbass coalminers was 266R by 1901. This represented only a slight increase over the 1886 average of 264; by 1905, however, after several strikes in the region the average had risen to 272R annually, and by 1906, after a year of revolutionary protest, the "average" miner's wage was 328R. See K. A. Pazhitnov, *Polozhenie rabochego klassa v Rossii*, vol. 3 (Moscow-Leningrad, 1924), p. 51.

17. S. P. Pod"iachev (1866–1934), "From the Life of the Muzhiks." Pod"iachev wrote primarily about peasant life, and joined the Communist Party in 1918.

18. A *baba* was a married peasant woman.

19. Both before and after the Emancipation of 1861 the self-generated peasant commune, or *mir*, supervised the details of day-to-day life on the estates of European Russia. The village elders who ran the *mir* periodically repartitioned the arable land, alloting more to families that had grown since the last repartition and less to those that had shrunk. Over the years this primitive welfare system of periodic repartition had resulted in a situation where a typical peasant family farmed very narrow strips of land, scattered randomly over two or three different fields. So individual peasant families generally did not "own" particular plots of land permanently, and most important farming decisions were made by the village elders, not by individuals.

20. Fenin is correct that many contemporary observers found the mine barracks appalling. L. A. Liberman wrote in 1905 that in one barrack he visited "the windows are [two feet] from the ground. The glass is broken . . . and through it blows a cold wind. . . . It is hard to tell the wall and ceiling from the floor. . . . Each worker has a one-board bunk . . . and when both shifts are in the barracks (on holidays) one shift sleeps on the bunks and the other on the dirt floor."

21. P. I. Fomin, *Gornaia i gornozavodskaia promyshlennost' iuga Rossii* (Kharkov, 1924). Fenin is probably correct that in general the public perception exaggerated the level of profits in the Donbass coal industry, although generally profits for steel producing firms were a good bit higher than those of purely coal producing firms. Still, this 1911 figure probably reflects the battering that these firms had taken in the recession of 1899 and the Revolution of 1905. According to a study by the Association of Southern Coal and Steel Producers itself, in 1895 southern coal companies as a group had earned profits representing over 12 percent of their basic capital and steel firms had paid dividends amounting to 17.5 percent of theirs. These averages do obscure considerable diversity, however. See S"ezd Gornopromyshlennikov Iuga Rossi, *Trudy 37 s"ezda* (Kharkov, 1912), 1:2a, p. 9.

22. V. G. Korolenko (1853–1921), was a half-Polish, half-Ukrainian poet and story writer who wrote in Russian.

Chapter Three.
Russian Heavy Industry in the Old Days

1. The Makeevka Mine belonged to the Ilovaiskii family and was managed by D. I. Ilovaiskii, son of the well-known I. G. Ilovaiskii whom Fenin described earlier. In 1895 D. I. Ilovaiskii formed the Donets Coal and Metal Company, known throughout this memoir by its place name, Makeevka. This corporation was formed with Russian, French, and Belgian capital. It was located at the easternmost edge of Ekaterinoslav Province. According to documents compiled by the Belgian consulate, the firm's output increased from 317,000 tons to 435,000 tons between 1895 and 1901, but the company paid no dividends to stockholders between 1896 and 1903. Fenin is describing the operation before the foreign investors took it over.

2. A troika was a typical Russian carriage drawn by three horses harnessed abreast.

3. Here Fenin mistakenly identifies as "K. M. Skal'kovskii," Konstantin Apollonovich Skal'kovskii about whom he speaks further later.

4. Fenin used the derogatory "*zhid,*" in quotation marks, for "Jew."

5. What Fenin means here is that Ilovaiskii was extremely wealthy and moved in the social circle of the richest landowners—a strata foreign even to young gentlemen like Fenin.

6. Vint was a card game.

7. Vasili Shuiskii was the famous "boyar tsar" during the Time of Troubles (1606–1610).

8. Zemstvo doctors had the reputation of being quite liberal; that is, of defending the interests of peasants and workers over those of landowners and businessmen. In Ekaterinoslav Province there eventually would be rival doctors' associations, one for zemstvo physicians and another for factory and mine physicians, these two groups generally seeing themselves as representing different interests. Factory and mine doctors, however, always denied that they served the firm before their patients.

9. This phrase may be an allusion to the fact that Russians were not supposed to show any sign of being drunk when they were drinking, and it was admiringly said of such accomplished drinkers that they "didn't even look drunk in one eye." Datskov was urging people to drink without restraint, to drink until they were drunk enough for "forty eighths," that is five eyes.

10. N. A. Nekrasov (1821–1877) was a poet and journalist devoted to social problems, whose main theme was compassion for the suffering peasants; he edited *Sovremennik* and later headed *Otechstvennye zapiski* with Shchedrin.

11. *Kisia* would mean "kitten," but, says Fenin, the poor man gave the word a ludicrous mispronounciation. Montenegro was a Balkan nation, today part of Yugoslavia.

12. It is interesting how often Fenin refers to marriages within the "mining community." The young woman Fenin married was Karlotta Feodorovna Wagner, descended from Germans who had settled in Russia in the eighteenth century. Her uncle was O. F. Wagner (Vegner), who presided over the sizeable medical establishment at Iuzovka for over thirty years. Earlier Fenin told us that he enjoyed visiting in this family of "cultured" people in his early, lonely days in the south. Later he refers to a marriage between one Mining Institute professor and the daughter of another.

13. *Totochka* is an endearing nickname for Karlotta (Charlotte); *ty* is the familiar (singular) form of "you," used only for family and very close friends.

14. Sakhalin Island is off the Pacific Coast of Russia.

15. This firm was founded in 1895 as a Russian corporation, by the great Société Générale de Belgique, the Russian Foreign Commerce Bank, and two Belgian metallurgical companies. It was a highly diversified firm that eventually produced coal, steel, rails, and hydraulics. It owned mines and factories in several locations throughout Ekaterinoslav Province. It was one of the most favored of the southern metallurgical firms, receiving substantial government orders, earning considerable profits, and paying dividends by 1903 of from 8 to 12 percent.

Chapter Four.
The Constructive Revival of the Basin

1. Both Ekaterinoslav Province and the Catherine [*Ekaterininskii*] Railroad bear the name of the empress who finally was able to wrest southern Russia from the Turks in the eighteenth century, Catherine [Ekaterina] the Great (1762–1796).

2. A. F. Mevius was an early leader of the Association of Southern Coal and Steel Producers and served as president of the association's council in the 1890s. He represented the mines of Count Orlov.

3. The Geological Committee (1882–1939) was the first organization in Russia to study the geological structure of the country systematically, making a general geological map of the whole country and then surveying individual mining areas.

4. There are several figures whose names would fit this abbreviation: I. V. Kamennov, P. A. Karpov, A. A. Kiriiakov, M. K. Kozlov, S. A. Kozlov, A. E. Kosenkov, or N. N. Kurmakov, although Fenin did note above that P. A. Karpov, for whom he worked briefly, had a difficult personality. Without more information, this rude person will have to remain, as Fenin intended, unidentified.

5. The insult in the remark lies in the fact that usually only men of the peasant estate wore long beards. Men of the upper estates were either clean shaven or wore very short beards.

6. Here Fenin does not specify which kind of power, but horsepower is likely.

7. In some parts of the world it is believed that gardens bring bad luck to mines, and they are quickly eliminated, but this obviously was not the case in the Donbass.

8. Nicholas II (r. 1894–1917), Russia's last tsar, disappointed liberals by demonstrating that he was no less reactionary than his father. He made this point in January 1895 at a reception for zemstvo leaders, where he labeled their ideas for expanding the zemstvo role "senseless dreams."

9. M. M. Kovalevskii (1851–1916) was a politically moderate, but critical, historian, jurist, sociologist, and ethnologist, as well as a member of the the the St. Petersburg Academy of Sciences from 1914 on. He was banned from teaching for his views in 1887, and his works were highly regarded by the Marxists, although Kovalevskii was not himself a Marxist. He was a member of the First Duma and later the State Council, elected from the academics' curia. After 1909 he was owner and editor of the famous journal *Vestnik Evropy.*

10. These memoirs are available in English as Witte, S. Iu., *The Memoirs of Count Witte*, ed., A. Yarmolinsky (Garden City, N.Y., 1921) and in Russian as *Vospominaniia*, 3 vols. (Moscow, 1960).

11. Dmitrii Ivanovich Mendeleev (1834–1907) was a famous chemist who discovered the periodic classification of the elements. He also took an active interest in social reform and the development of domestically owned industry, particularly the oil industry. For his outspokeness he was snubbed by the academic establishment and the government at the end of his life.

12. P. B. Struve (1870–1944), embraced Marx's theory of historical progression but did not accept the inevitability of revolution as the means of moving history from one stage to the next. Eventually he became associated with the "legal Marxists," who believed that capitalism would develop naturally and eventually would be replaced by socialism. In 1902 he started to edit *Osvobozhdenie [Liberation]*, around which outspoken liberal groups gathered. He was the author of numerous books and articles. Struve's life and thought are described in two works by Richard Pipes: *Struve: Liberal on the Left, 1870–1905* (Cambridge, Mass., 1970) and *Struve: Liberal on the Right, 1905–1944* (Cambridge, Mass., 1980).

13. The central disagreement between populists and Marxists concerned the inevitability of the development of capitalism in Russia. Populists, since the 1860s, had argued that Russia was unique, due to the communal nature of the peasantry and to the institution of the *mir*, the repartitional peasant commune. Marxists placed Russia in the universal pattern of history described by Marx, citing statistics to demonstrate that capitalism already was blossoming in Russia, which was a necessary

precursor to the eventual overthrow of the capitalist order by class-conscious workers heralding the dawn of socialism.

14. The Free Economic Society was a well-known, essentially liberal discussion society dating from 1765, which originally had promoted the modernization of Russian agriculture.

15. Author's note: See P. B. Struve, "To My Critics."

16. Author's note: A. A. Kizevetter, "At the Juncture of Two Centuries," pp. 212–213. The Russian title of Kizevetter's (1886–1933) book is *Na rubezhe dvukh stoleti* (Prague, 1929).

17. A. I. Chuprov (1842–1908) was a populist professor of political economy and statistics at Moscow University. He was active in the zemstvo movement and wrote widely on agrarian and railroad questions. We have not been able to identify Iarotskii.

18. The Briansk Ironworks Company was a large Russian firm that opened a rail rolling mill, steel mill, and mechanical factory in the city of Ekaterinoslav in 1887. The company acquired coal and iron mines throughout the Donbass, including, in 1912, the Rutchenko Coal Company. It was one of the biggest concerns in the region, the mills employing 6000 workers by 1907. Its stock was sold in Paris, Brussels, and Lyons, with the Bank Parisienne becoming the largest bondholder early in the twentieth century. A. M. Goriainov served on the council of the Association of Southern Coal and Steel Producers.

19. The profession of factory-doctor apparently ran in the Wagner family (Fenin's wife's family). The reader will recall that Fenin described his wife as the "niece of Iuzovka's factory doctor." After the Revolution Mrs. Fenin's brother emigrated with his family to Germany, where his German citizenship was restored. After the Nazi seizure of power he emigrated to Switzerland, where he became a lecturer in a medical school. He died during World War II.

20. The Duma was a limited parliament granted by Tsar Nicholas II after the Revolution of 1905. See note 21, Chapter 8.

The Constitutional Democrats, known as the K.D.'s or Kadets for short, were liberals who advocated civil liberties, property rights, a "responsible ministry," and other modifications of the Fundamental Law, or Constitution, of 1906. They and their most famous leader, the historian Pavel Miliukov, dominated the First Duma. Fenin was clearly in sympathy with the Kadets, as were many of the liberal industrialists of the South, although he tells us elsewhere that he cannot remember whether he ever officially joined the party.

21. The Provisional Government took over after the abdication of Nicholas II in March 1917, sharing power with the workers' and soldiers' soviets, or councils, until the Bolshevik Revolution of November 1917.

Fenin used the term "Volunteer Army" to describe those who took up arms against the Bolshevik-led government during the Civil War (1918–1921), under the leadership of General A. I. Denikin (1872–1947).

This was the self-descriptive term generally used by those others would call the *Whites*.

22. By *staff* Fenin means only the most senior employees. The term *cultured* [*intelligentnyi*] attests to the strong differences in social position— so strong that Fenin's family could not mix socially with people from lower estates.

23. Reading aloud was a common entertainment. Usually someone with a pleasant voice was asked to read a chapter or two at the end of an evening, while his audience sipped tea. In later years his grandchildren recall their delight at hearing Fenin read Jules Verne.

Chapter Five.
Directing an Industrial Enterprise, 1899–1906

1. Fenin refers here to marketing syndicates that were formally organized with government sanction, first for southern coal, in 1901 under the name *Produgol*, and later, in 1903, for iron and steel products, known as *Prodameta*. Some of the leaders of the Association of Southern Coal and Steel Producers clearly had a hand in establishing these organizations, with the blessing of Finance Ministry officials, although it is not clear how unequivocal was the support for the syndicates among engineer-managers.

2. The companies to which these mines belonged were, respectively: the Golubovka Berestov-Bogodukhovka Mining Company, the Irmino Coal Company (French and Belgian), the Briansk Iron Works (Russian, French, and Belgian), the Krivoi Rog Iron Company (French), the Alekseev Mining Company (Russian), and the Russian Coal Mining Company (English).

3. The Kadievka Mine was owned by South Russian Dnepr Metallurgical Company, a Belgian firm.

4. Apparently the Russo-Turkish War of 1877–1878.

5. The word *communal* [obshchestvennyi] carries a special meaning in the context of the old Russian village and suggests among other things that individual peasants did not consider these earnings their personal property. On the other hand, after the Emancipation individual peasants could enter into private rental agreements to procure additional land for family farming. In Russian land-use law underground rights were held by the owners of the surface land, and frequently, as in this case, a mine found itself in possession of considerable acreage of surface land for which it had no use—which it then often leased to agriculturalists.

6. At Easter and the days just following, whenever a Russian Orthodox meets a relative or friend, he greets him saying, "Christ is risen!" to which the response is "He is risen indeed!" Then the two,

regardless of sex, exchange three kisses on the cheeks, the number three symbolizing the trinity. Sometimes a painted egg is offered as well.

7. The position of land captain [*zemskii nachal'nik*] was established in 1889 as part of Alexander III's conservative counterreforms. The persons who held these positions usually were hereditary noblemen who were to oversee peasant activities, exercise the administrative functions of the central government including judicial functions and empowered to rescind decisions made by the peasant village assemblies. The point of the position was to place peasants solidly under the control of the nobility.

8. Author's note: Cleaning up and building fences was the peasants' responsibility.

9. *Kurkul* does not mean anything precise, but evokes the clucking of a rooster. Like *kulak*, from the word for "fist" used to describe rich peasants, *kurkul* is a peasant term, not one invented by noblemen.

10. The war referred to here is the Russo-Japanese War of 1904–1905.

11. State councillor was an honorary rank in the tsarist civil service.

12. Vladimir Ivanovich Bauman (1867–1923) was a liberal professor at the Mining Institute from 1899 on and author of the basic text, *Course in the Art of Surveying (1905–1908)*.

13. The *third element* refers to liberal or radical zemstvo employees who were doctors, teachers, and the like. Conservatives often considered it the hotbed of radicalism (even Fenin makes such a suggestion elsewhere in this memoir), whereas the Bolsheviks disdained them as naive "do gooders."

14. The merchantry was one of several *sosloviia* (singular, *soslovie*), or, roughly "estates," into which all Russian subjects were divided by law and custom. Merchants had certain rights and obligations; and although they could own land, such ownership did not automatically confer upon them noble status. After the Emancipation, the *soslovie* categories grew increasingly archaic, bearing ever less connection to a person's actual profession or work. Hence, while Fenin and Iakovenko did roughly the same kind of work, they belonged to different *sosloviia*. For an interesting discussion of this phenomenon, see Leopold H. Haimson, "The Problem of Social Identities in Early Twentieth Century Russia," *Slavic Review* 47, no.1 (Spring 1988): 1–20.

15. In 1918 and 1919 Civil War raged in southern Russia and throughout the Ukraine, as various White armies resisted the establishment of Bolshevik power. In the bewildering confusion that reigned during this period, various groups established governments in the area, including Ukrainian nationalists and White General Denikin, whose army Fenin supported. It may be that the "hetman," or chief, referred to here was Hetman Skoropadski, considered by many a puppet of the Germans, who controlled the Ukraine under the terms of the Brest-Litovsk Treaty between February and November 1918.

16. Author's note: I received this manuscript from the agronomist

V. E. Brunst, a great admirer and collaborator of Kolokol'tsov, now also deceased.

17. A serious recession began around 1899 that adversely affected the Donbass coal and steel industry, including the prices of stock. Recovery was slow until about 1910.

18. We use *estate* here for Fenin's *ekonomiia,* a word that suggests a modern-type of private farm in the Ukraine, one that used hired laborers and agricultural machinery.

19. This was the popular name of the South Russian Dnepr Metallurgical Company.

20. This scant regard for the "white collar" worker was typical of aristocrats and apparently even of the rather open-minded Fenin, who displays a much higher regard for the *muzhik,* the "real man" who works with his hands. Apparently, by the turn of the century the pervasive "antibourgeois" attitude, which gripped people from virtually every caste in Russian society, extended in some degree even to so committed a technocrat and proponent of private enterprise as Fenin. This distaste for the accounting and clerical side of business on the part of some of the country's keenest business advocates is but one of the complexities of Fenin's and his associates' position.

21. This is the famous author, better known in the West as Leo Tolstoy.

Chapter Six.
My Neighbors and Colleagues

1. All of these mines were introduced in the previous chapter except the Mar'evka Mine. This mine belonged to the Russian Petro-Mar'evka Coal Company, which merged with the Belgian Varvaropol Coal Company in 1912.

2. Baldness was considered a bit ridiculous in old Russia. To avoid jokes some people used to shave off their remaining hair, as can often be seen in portraits. Of course, this was also the fashion among the military, for hygenic reasons.

3. This syndicate, the Donets Basin Coal Supply Company, was actually hammered out in 1903 and chartered by the government on 5 May 1904. Fenin may remember 1907 as the year by which a substantial portion of the South's coal production was sold by Produgol. This marketing organization, unlike its counterpart in metal products, Prodameta, was always far from airtight. This organization and others described in Russian by the word *sindikat* functioned most like what is called in English a *cartel.*

4. Actually, the sugar producers formed a cartel earlier, in 1886. Produgol certainly was the first great coal cartel in Russia, however.

5. The Russian government sanctioned Produgol as it had sanctioned Prodameta a few years earlier, but these marketing cartels, organized

as joint stock companies, consistently attracted hostile public opinion. A formidable array of agriculturalists, manufacturers outside the coal and steel industry, and the antiforeign press complained frequently about the artifically high prices that resulted from the cartel arrangement. The government warned against overly high prices, although it continued to place orders with syndicated firms. It yielded to antitrust pressure in 1908, however, in prohibiting the consolidation of coal and iron marketing by a proposed giant trust.

It is interesting that Fenin asserts here that the cartels were the creation of foreign capitalists, as this was one of the chief complaints against them at the time by forces outside the coal and steel industry. His statement appears to support the interpretation that although the cartels were promoted at meetings of the Southern Association, the native engineer-managers who dominated that organization may have been less enthusiastic and unanimous about the marketing arrangements than were foreign investors and directors, such as the giant Belgian investment bank Société Générale de Belgique.

6. A. M. Bezobrazov was a former guards officer who promoted what usually is viewed as a recklessly expansionist policy in the Far East, luring Tsar Nicholas II away from Count Witte's more cautious position on the eve of the Russo-Japanese War of 1904–1905. Bezobrazov, acting as a private businessman, secured timber concessions that foreshadowed a Russian annexation of Korea, which the Japanese considered within their sphere of influence. In 1903 Bezobrazov became secretary of state for Far Eastern affairs.

7. Fenin certainly means Admiral Evgenii Ivanovich Alekseev (1843–1918), commander of the Pacific Ocean Squadron (1895–1897), imperial viceroy over the region east of Lake Baikal in 1903–1904, where he advocated an expansionist policy toward China, Korea, and Japan, and member of the State Council in 1905.

8. The Putilov Works was the great steel and machine firm in St. Petersburg, whose workers were among the first to go over to revolution in 1917. Fenin may credit the well-known Bolshevik leader Grigorii Zinov'ev (1883–1936) with Krzyzanowski's arrest, as Zinov'ev was chairman of the Petrograd Soviet.

9. Fenin means the Russo-Polish War of 1920, which took place in the midst of the Civil War.

10. This is a possible translation of the Polish town Fenin calls, in Russian, Khodakov. Chorzow is in southern present-day Poland, about 100 miles south of Lodz.

11. NEP stands for the New Economic Policy, instituted by the Bolsheviks at their Tenth Party Congress in 1921. It called for a mixed economy, permitting private grain marketing and private trade outside the "commanding heights" of the economy. Major industries were nationalized. During NEP the Soviet leaders were eager to employ experts such as Rabinovich, regardless of their class background. NEP

effectively ended in 1928 as Stalin launched what became known as the First Five Year Plan.

12. In the Shakhty trial of 1928 many engineers and technical experts in the South who had gone to work for the new Bolshevik enterprises were identified and convicted as "wreckers"; that is, as people who had conspired to undermine the very plants and mines they were building and supervising. The affair is perhaps best understood as a reaction against the "capitalist" elements of NEP and as part of a "cultural revolution" that would see the expulsion of most people from "suspect" class backgrounds and their replacement by younger people from humbler origins. A good source on this phenomenon is Sheila Fitzpatrick, *The Russian Revolution, 1917–1932* (Oxford, England, 1984).

13. N. V. Krylenko (1885–1938) was a prominent party member, jurist, and prosecutor. He was the head prosecutor at the Shakhty trials. He became People's Commissar (i.e., minister) of justice in 1936, in the midst of the great show trials and was himself arrested the following year.

A fascinating account of this trial and of Rabinovich's role in it is in Eugene Lyons, *Assignment in Utopia* (New York, 1937). He supports Fenin's assertion that Rabinovich stood out from the other accused as a calm and dignified man. Says Lyons, "We had become familiar with the seventy-year-old Rabinovich in the weeks before his turn came. Again and again he had been yanked into the recitals of other men. The rest were small fry compared to this stocky, gray-haired, earnest old man. In 1920 Lenin himself had summoned Rabinovich and invited his cooperation, as the foremost coal-mining engineer in Russia. In the following seven years, until the day of his arrest, he was virtual coal dictator. . . . His presence among the accused engineers was the most fantastic touch of all." Lyons notes that Rabinovich was sentenced to six years in prison, not ten years as Fenin recalled (see pp. 127–128). I am grateful to Ted Friedgut for pointing out this passage.

14. This was a Russian emigré paper published in Germany.

15. The Orlov-Elenov Mine belonged to the French-owned Krivoi Rog Iron Ore Company.

16. In fact Sokolov was young enough to continue his professional career abroad, and his grandsons are both successful French professionals.

17. The Commercial, Industrial and Financial Union was the most famous of the associations of Russian industrialists in emigration. The CIFU was based in France and, like the other organizations, was modeled on prerevolutionary regional, sectoral business organizations. Most of them seem to have faded away after the Five Year Plans began.

18. Sokolov became a member of the association's governing council in 1914.

19. General Mikhail Vasil'evich Alekseev (1857–1918) was an infantry general in World War I and thereafter a founder of the anti-Bolshevik

Volunteer Army, holding the title of supreme commander of the Volunteer Army in 1918. In his role as chief of staff of the general headquarters from 1915–1917, he convinced Tsar Nicholas II to abdicate on 15 March 1917.

20. General A. P. Kutepov (1882–1930) was a World War I colonel who became a general in both the Volunteer Army and another White army led by Baron Wrangel. General Mai-Maevskii also was a commander of the Volunteer Army, who fought against the Reds in the coalfields of the Donbass. He had a reputation as a debaucherer, an alcoholic, and a commander whose troops abused civilians. Removing him from command became a preoccupation of other officers of the Volunteer Army.

21. Mironov worked as the assistant manager of the Irmino Mine and later as manager of the salt mines of the Bakhmut Salt Company.

22. Baron Peter Wrangel succeeded Denikin in command of the Whites in South Russia and was able to consolidate his hold on considerable territory, including the Crimea. After the Polish War ended in October 1920, the Red Army was able to defeat Wrangel, forcing about 150,000 troops from the Crimea to Constantinople.

23. Nikolai Stepanovich Avdakov (1847–1915) was a towering figure in southern industry and achieved considerable fame in national industrial affairs. Besides presiding over the council of the Southern Association from 1900 to 1905, he was a founder and chairman of the board of the coal cartel, Produgol, a member of the board of the steel products cartel, Prodameta, and a chairman of the St. Petersburg-based Association of Industry and Trade in 1907 to 1915. On that organization see Ruth A. Roosa, "The Association of Industry and Trade, 1906–1914" (Ph.D. dissertation, Columbia University, 1967).

24. See Fenin's Introduction, note 5, for a description of the state council. As gentry-based organizations were far better represented on this council than industrial associations, von Ditmar's modern industrial notions indeed must have seemed "heretical."

25. In the years just before the 1905 Revolution several political parties were coming into existence, none of them legally. In 1901 the populist Socialist Revolutionary Party (SRs) was organized. Its agrarian program would be most attractive to peasants and its often terroristic tactics led the police to consider it the most dangerous of the parties. The first meeting of the nascent Russian Social Democratic Labor Party, the Marxists (SDs), had taken place in 1898. By 1903 that small group would split over tactical and other questions, into the Mensheviks and the Bolsheviks. Besides the socialists, liberals were organizing, too. Their base had long been the zemstvos, in which various strands of liberalism had mingled since the 1870s. In 1902 a group of zemstvo officials met semilegally to organize a zemstvo union. By the next year a group calling itself the Union of Liberation came into existence, which secretly advocated the replacement of autocracy by a constitutional monarchy

based upon universal, direct, secret, and equal suffrage. This is the *liberation movement* to which Fenin refers. Despite his assessment, a number of impressive men did head this group, among them the noted economist and writer Petr Struve and the historian and future Kadet leader Pavel Miliukov.

26. Author's note: The presidium of the association's council was under arrest; that is, Ditmar, myself, and Sokolov, the manager of the council's affairs.

27. M. N. Bazkevich, a technical engineer, was a member of the council of the Southern Association. Skoruta was the unfortunate engineer described earlier who fainted while giving false testimony.

28. Maxim Gorki (1869–1936) was the pen name of A. M. Peshkov, a well-known writer of plays and novels, who opposed tsarism and who continued writing in the Soviet period. He is highly regarded by the Soviets.

29. A shelf or a wall hung with holy pictures, reminiscent of the front wall of an Orthodox church.

30. This idiom does not have an exact English equivalent. A bear's den [*medvezhii ugol*], to a Russian, suggests an out-of-the-way, lost rural place.

Chapter Seven.
Echoes of Political Struggles at the Mines

1. Because the majority of miners in the Donbass originally came without their wives and children for seasonal work, they sent most of their pay back to their families. Managers strove to create a permanent, settled work force, however; and after 1900 more and more workers did forsake their meager farms entirely for the mining life, settling their families in the Donbass. Ironically, however, the arrival of thousands of dependents for whom there was little remunerative work further strained the already inadequate social amenities, such as housing and health care.

2. *Novoe vremia* was published from 1868 to 1917; *Grazhdanin*, 1872 to 1914; *Moskovskie vedomosti* 1756 to 1917; and *Russkii vestnik*, 1856 to 1906.

3. The Union of the Russian People was an extreme-nationalist political group that opposed the limited constitutional system created by the tsar in late 1905. The union stood for election to the First Duma in 1906, but in fact was antiparliamentary, and its delegates advocated a return to unlimited autocracy.

4. January 9, 1905, became known as "Bloody Sunday" after a group of St. Petersburg factory workers and their families, led by a priest named Father Gapon, marched peacefully toward the Winter Palace seeking better living conditions and were fired on by the tsar's troops. As many as 1000 people may have been killed, and the country-wide

protests against the shootings accelerated into the Revolution of 1905.

Prince P. D. Sviatopolk-Mirskii (1857–1914) served as governor or governor-general of several provinces besides Ekaterinoslav before becoming minister of the interior in August 1904. In that post he was relatively liberal, weakening censorship, allowing a meeting of zemstvo delegates in November 1904, and proposing that zemstvo and city government delegates be placed in the State Council. He was fired about one week after Bloody Sunday.

5. The idea of the "golden warrant," as it is called here, was very old: the tsar was kind and wished the best for his people, but the scheming noblemen repeatedly distorted or circumvented his instructions. Whenever the tsar learned of such doings he ordered the peasants to burn and plunder the wicked landowners. In fact, such a thing never happened, of course, but the peasant faith in a "good tsar" and deep resentment against the noble landowners played a role in most peasant rebellions. Fenin is here referring to peasant rebellions in the Ukraine in the summer of 1902.

Chapter Eight.
The Revolution Approaches

1. Fenin is describing the revolution of 1905, which did not topple the tsarist regime but did force Nicholas II to grant a constitutional government of sorts. The revolutionary events lasted throughout 1905 and into 1906.

2. The *Zemskii sobor* was an estate-based consultative assembly in old Muscovy, not unlike the Estates General in France. It had moments of considerable power in the early seventeenth century, but by the early eighteenth it had withered away entirely.

3. Assemblies of the Nobility existed in each province following legislation of Catherine the Great in the 1760s–1780s, which effectively incorporated the provincial gentry as a legal body that could petition the monarch on matters that concerned them. Nothing compelled the tsar to listen to these petitions, but the right to address the throne was one denied to other social groups. It is interesting that Fenin attended this meeting. As a member of an Ekaterinoslav gentry family he was eligible, but this was a very different circle from the one he describes in this memoir, the world of engineers and managers, and by the twentieth century contact between those two worlds was rather limited.

4. M. V. Rodzianko was a local zemstvo leader in Ekaterinoslav, his home province, but is better known as the later president of the State Duma, the legislative body created by Tsar Nicholas II in response to the Revolution of 1905. Rodzianko was a member of the conservative Octobrist party, dedicated to maintaining the constitutional monarchy proclaimed in October 1905. However, as popular discontent mounted in the streets of Petrograd in early 1917, Rodzianko warned the tsar that

more sweeping concessions would be needed to ward off radical revolution, and finally declared the creation of a Provisional Government on 12 March 1917.

5. N. I. Pirogov (1810–1881) was a mid-nineteenth century surgeon and reformer who promoted medical reform and other progressive causes, such as the education of women.

6. The question of whether terrorism was an acceptable or necessary tactic for achieving the ultimate socialist peasant revolution had divided populists since the 1870s. Many, but by no means all, Socialist Revolutionaries [SRs] embraced terrorism against the state as an essential precursor to popular revolution. Those who were devoted to terrorism concentrated in the more or less autonomous combat section of the party. Indeed, in these years the tsarist police considered the SRs much more dangerous than the Marxist SDs, or Social Democrats, who did not endorse terrorism.

7. N. P. Bogolepov was the minister of education from 1898 to 1901 who cracked down on students, especially at Kiev University in 1900; he was killed in 1901. D. S. Sipiagin was the minister of the interior, killed in 1902. V. K. Pleve (1846–1904) became the minister of the interior in 1902. He took action against ethnic minorities, especially Armenians, Finns, and Jews, as well as striking workers; and when these measures failed to restore social calm, he advocated a short, victorious war as a guarantee of political unity. In this way he was largely responsible for the Russo-Japanese War of 1904–1905, which, of course, did not prove to be a victorious one for the Russians. He was killed in 1904.

8. Grand Duke Sergei Aleksandrovich was the tsar's uncle, the much-hated governor-general of Moscow, killed by Kaliaev in February, 1905.

9. Admiral F. V. Dubasov was governor-general of Moscow from November 1905 to July 1906. The SRs made two attempts on his life in 1906, both of which failed. He then served in the State Council. P. N. Durnovo headed the department of police from 1884 to 1893 and became minister of the interior in October 1905, serving there until April 1906. He was "sentenced" by the SRs in 1906, but not killed. P. A. Stolypin (1862–1911) was a famous statesman, governor of the provinces of Grodno and Saratov before becoming minister of the interior and finally prime minister in 1906. In these posts Stolypin is most famous for closing down the First Duma, altering the electoral rules in an effort to achieve a more conservative body, executing accused terrorists under martial law, introducing sweeping proposals for agrarian reform, and operating in complete disregard of the Fundamental Law after June 1907. Although an earlier attempt on his life failed, Stolypin was assassinated in 1911 by a revolutionary and police agent, Dmitrii Bogrov.

10. The Pirogov Memorial Society of Russian Physicians was founded in memory of scientist and surgeon N. I. Pirogov. The congresses met every two years and were known for promoting public health movements.

11. This government decree is dated 12 December 1904 [O.S.], as

Fenin accurately notes later. It was a response by Nicholas II to the urging of his interior minister Sviatopolk-Mirskii to make some positive response to the swelling liberal movement. It promised some religious toleration, some relaxation of censorship, and some zemstvo reform. It did not address Mirskii's proposal that zemstvo officials be invited to participate in the purely consultative state council. Generally, by this time, most liberals would have considered such a consultative body insufficient in any event.

12. The meeting of zemstvo representatives Fenin refers to here took place in November 1904, at which a majority called for a freely elected and binding assembly as well as a constitution. The Union of Unions was an unprecedented and illegal grouping of professional unions assembled by the Kadet Pavel Miliukov. Fenin's memory is probably a bit sketchy here, as by most accounts the Union of Unions came together in the spring of 1905. About the Union of Engineers, formed in late 1904, see more later.

13. The Russo-Japanese War, which began in January 1904, went badly for the Russians almost from the first. After a long siege Port Arthur fell in December, followed by the terrible battle of Mukden in February 1905 and the destruction of the Baltic fleet at Tsushima in May 1905. Generally the Russians were not able to supply troops and equipment to the front in sufficient quantity, as the capacity of the newly constructed Trans-Siberian Railroad was quite limited until the very end. The war ended in defeat for the Russians, the treaty being negotiated by President Theodore Roosevelt in Portsmouth, New Hampshire, in September 1905. The unpopular war, fought as it was for obscure imperial reasons, cost each side nearly half a million men in killed and wounded and cost the Russians about 1 billion dollars. Defeat at the hands of an Asian power humiliated the Russian government, and the war played a role in the popular unrest that erupted in early 1905.

14. January 9, 1905 (O.S.), was "Bloody Sunday" (see Chapter 7, note 4). News of this shooting sped throughout the empire, unleashing a series of local strikes and rebellions. Peasants rebelled in the summer, and the government was very hard pressed to quiet all of these disturbances with so many of its troops still in the Far East. In June the great, new Battleship Potemkin mutinied at Odessa. These events have become known to history as the Revolution of 1905.

15. Nicholas II received a fourteen-member delegation from the more moderate zemstvo men in June 1905. In his book *The Shadow of the Winter Palace* (New York, 1976), Edward Crankshaw makes the point that, "It was in fact the first time that Nicholas had ever met these intelligent, responsible, deeply troubled and patriotic men. But he was unable to recognize them for what they were, received them politely but without lively interest, and sent them away empty. It was the last chance he was to have of winning the more sober elements of 'society' to his side" (p. 344).

Prince S. N. Trubetskoi (1862–1905) was a philosopher, brother of the famous religious philosopher E. N. Trubetskoi, and a Kadet.

16. S. N. Trubetskoi died unexpectedly in September 1905, shortly after becoming rector of Moscow University in the midst of unprecedented student rebellion. He had just delivered a speech declaring the university no place for political rallies.

17. The Union of Engineers and Technicians grew out of a meeting in St. Petersburg in December 1904. Led by Professor V. I. Kirpichev, the union took a very active role in the Union of Unions and adopted a progressive platform linking personal freedom, economic development, and technical proficiency. Alfred Rieber describes this St. Petersburg branch of the organization as basically opposed to factory owners of that city, who established a separate organization. He describes the southwest as a region that strongly supported these declarations of engineers in the capital, although he detects important differences between academic engineers, factory specialists, and managers of southern mining and metallurgical concerns. Regarding the last group, Rieber finds that "close identification with the interests of the owners converted engineer-managers into defenders of the existing order." See his *Merchants and Entrepreneurs in Imperial Russia* (Chapel Hill, N.C., 1982), pp. 354–357.

18. The electoral law for the First Duma was profoundly undemocratic. It was neither universal, direct, secret, nor equal. Most Duma deputies were to be chosen by electors, who were chosen in turn by voters according to their social standing. There were 151 electors from the industrial workers, 1955 from the landowners, 1352 from the townsmen, and 2532 from the peasants. The system satisfied no one with the exception of conservative landowners. Fenin must have been elected from the landowners' curia, because later he tells us that he represented Slavianoserbsk, not the big city of Kharkov where he was then living. The Kadet Party is described in Chapter 4, note 20.

19. The Party of Peaceful Renovation *(Mirnoobnovlentsy)* was a constitutional monarchist party of the big businessmen and noble landowners. It was formed in January 1906 by Left Octobrists and Right Kadets such as Prince N. N. L'vov and Prince E. N. Trubetskoi. It differed from these two parties mainly in tactics, but never attracted a large following. The Party for Democratic Reforms was also formed in January 1906 by Kadets who thought the Kadet leadership too leftist. M. M. Kovalevskii, the historian and editor about whom Fenin speaks in Chapter 4 (see note 9) and in the Appendix, was a leader of this party and member of the First Duma. *Vestnik Evropy*, the journal he edited, was this party's paper. Together these two parties formed the "progressist faction" in the Third Duma in 1907, a precursor to the Progressist Party.

20. Members of the Labor Party *(Trudovaia Partiia)* Fenin refers to were commonly known as the Trudoviki. They were a nonterrorist

offshoot of the populist Socialist Revolutionary Party. The main body
of the SRs would not stand for election to the First Duma, but the
Trudoviki did. In an election that was weighted against peasants, the
Trudoviki garnered about one-fifth of the seats in that assembly.

21. After granting the October Manifesto in the midst of social chaos
in 1905, promising a constitutional monarchy and creating the Duma,
Nicholas II began retreating as early as February 1906. He stipulated
that the Duma would serve only as the lower house of the parliament,
with the upper house remaining entirely appointive. Constitutionally
the Duma was to be very weak, as the Fundamental Law, issued in
April 1906, made clear. It was to have only limited power of the purse,
no power to approve or remove ministers, and no role in foreign policy.
The tsar retained the power of absolute veto, the right to prorogue the
Duma at any time and the right to make laws in the Duma's absence
as long as they were subsequently approved. The government's idea of
the proper scope of Duma activities was seen in its original legislative
agenda, which included improving laundry facilities at Dorpat University (among other things.) The Kadet leaders, buoyed by their plurality
in the First Duma, staked everything on fundamentally altering this
constitutional arrangement before undertaking any other business. This
stance resulted in an immediate stalemate between the tsar and the
Duma. When Nicholas closed down the Duma, the Kadets reassembled
illegally in Finland and issued a manifesto urging Russians to neither
pay taxes nor answer the draft until a new Duma was convened. Many
Kadet leaders were subsequently arrested and briefly imprisoned, and
the party lost much of its influence. Thereafter the Kadets gradually
would adopt a less confrontational posture, settling for gradual change.

22. There were numerous strikes in the big cities of Ekaterinoslav
province in 1905, particularly in Ekaterinoslav itself and its suburban
steel and ironworks. Toward the end of that revolutionary year, when
civil order had effectively evaporated and pitched battles were being
fought between peasants, disloyal soldiers, and sympathetic office workers on the one hand, against loyal troops on the other, several coal
mines did send delegates to a meeting of the Ekaterinoslav Soviet (council of workers.) Generally, however, although 1905 saw considerable
disruption and violence in Ekaterinoslav, Fenin seems to be correct that
not much of it was centered in the distinctly coal mining regions, except
for those regions that adjoined a railroad station, where a fight occurred
in conjunction with the railroad workers' strike at the end of 1905 and
early 1906.

23. V. G. Bogoraz (1865–1936) was a writer known by the pseudonym
N. A. Tan. He was a populist and member of the People's Will exiled
to Siberia from 1889 to 1898. He wrote novels and stories about revolutionaries.

24. Fenin is referring to December 1905, when the anarchy in the
province reached its apex. In addition to a general strike coordinated

by railroad workers who seemed to be more or less in charge, there were peasant riots. The countryside, especially the railroad stations, were the scenes of many pitched battles.

25. Pugachev's Rebellion was a great peasant uprising along the Ural (Yaitsk) River in 1774.

26. Railroad workers at Gorlovka station struck when they got news of the general railroad strike around December 8/21. Miners at the nearby Gorlovka Mine of the French-owned South Russian Coal Company joined the strike. Soldiers were sent to confront the strikes four days later. Fenin therefore had happened upon a meeting about the most serious confrontation to occur in the Donbass coalfields in 1905.

27. *Pan* is a Polish and Ukrainian word for nobleman or master, roughly the equivalent of *barin* in Russian—in either language, a word not warmly used by peasants, especially not in 1905. This woman was speaking Ukrainian. By old tradition, peasants blamed noble landowners for their troubles and not the tsar. This was changing by 1905, however.

28. Most likely this is a reference to Khlestakov, the infamous scoundrel in Gogol's play *The Inspector General*.

29. Mscychowski's company was the Seleznevka Coal and Limestone Company, founded in 1900.

30. Sergei Muromtsev was a Kadet who had been elected Speaker of the Duma at its original opening and who reconvened the assemblage in Vyborg.

31. The Second Duma, elected under conditions that encouraged the harassment of all leftist parties, turned out to include even more socialists than had the First. It was closed down in short order by the tsar and Stolypin. After this the election laws were changed to enhance the voice of conservative landowners. Consequently the Third (1907–1912) and Fourth (1912–1917) Dumas each survived their whole five-year terms.

32. Here Fenin reiterates the epigraph from Turgenev's *Faust*, with which he began chapter 2:

Life is not a trifle, not a joke
Life is not even a delight . . .
Life is hard toil . . .
Fulfilling one's duty is the thing one should care about.

Appendix:
A Brief Survey of Russia's Economic Situation
at the Turn of the Century and of Alexander III's Reforms

1. M. I. Tugan-Baranovskii was a Russian economist whose most famous work is *The Russian Factory in the Nineteenth Century*, trans. A. Levin and C. Levin (Homewood, Ill., 1970).

2. We have not been able to identify this author or work.

3. V. I. Grinevetskii (1871–1919) was a thermal engineer, professor, director of the Moscow Technical High School, and an expert on steam engines, boilers, and the internal combustion engine.

4. On Witte's campaign to convince Alexander III of the virtues of industrialization, see T. H. von Laue, "A Secret Memorandum of Sergei Witte on the Industrialization of Imperial Russia," *Journal of Modern History* no. 26 (1954): 60–74.

5. Fenin refers here to the first two Five Year Plans launched under Stalin, which were to increase industrial production across the board by substantial amounts. The first ran from 1928 to 1933, the second 1933 to 1938. Although it is hard to compare figures, Fenin probably is correct here. The figures show that Soviet output of steel (not cast iron), for example, rose from 5.9 million tons in 1928 to 12.1 million tons in 1933; the Soviet figures for hard coal in the same period are 35.4 million tons and 64.3 million tons, respectively. See Alec Nove, *The Soviet Economy* (New York, 1967), pp. 191 and 225. There were other sectors, however, in which growth between 1928 and 1940 were remarkable. For example, the output of electrical power increased in that period by 964 percent, and of ferrous metals, 433 percent, according to Stanley H. Cohn, *Economic Development in the Soviet Union* (Lexington, Mass., 1970), p. 39.

6. Foreign capitalists introduced important technical improvements in the steel and iron producing industry of the South, where both Bessemer and Martins methods of smelting were used. On the other hand, as Gatrell notes, "Technological change in coal mining could hardly have been more limited. As in oil extraction, the initial gains in productivity derived from the fact that deposits were easily accessible, and output per person increased sharply between 1885 and 1900. This increase was not sustained. Where mechanization took place in coal mining, it was confined to bringing coal to the surface; coal was hewn from the face and carried to the shaft manually." See Gatrell, *The Tsarist Economy 1850–1917*, pp. 158–160.

7. Basic studies of the very thorny question of the amount of foreign investment in Russian industry before 1914 include P. V. Ol', *Inostrannye kapitaly v Rossii* (Petrograd, 1922); I. F. Gindin, *Russkie kommercheskie banki* (Moscow, 1948); John P. McKay, *Pioneers for Profit: Foreign Entrepreneurship and Russian Industrialization, 1885–1913* (Chicago 1970); Olga Crisp, "French Investment and Influence in Russian Industry 1894–1914," *Studies in the Russian Economy before 1914* (New York, 1976); and Rene Girault, *Emprunts russes et investissements français en Russie, 1887–1914* (Paris, 1973).

8. N. K. Bunge was finance minister from 1881 to 1886; I. A. Vyshnegradskii followed him in that post from 1886 to 1892. The gold standard was introduced by finance minister Witte between 1894 and 1897.

9. P. P. Migulin (1870–?) was a liberal economist, Octobrist, and professor at Kharkov University. He served in the Finance Ministry in 1914;

wrote several books on credit, banking, industry, and agriculture; and published and edited the journal *Ekonomist Rossii* from 1909 to 1917.

10. L. K. Martens (1875–1948), born in Bakhmut, was a scientist, member of the precursor to the Communist party of the Soviet Union from 1893 on, organizer of the Society of Technical Assistance to Soviet Russia in the United States, and member of the all-important Presidium of the Supreme Council of the National Economy [VSNKh] from 1921 on. Between 1926 and 1936 he headed an institute for research on diesel engines.

11. See chapter 4, note 9.

12. Almost surely the work to which Fenin refers here is Mendeleev's mammoth study *The Tariff* (St. Petersburg, 1892).

13. A. I. Del'vig (1813–1887) was an engineer, promoter of railroad schools, and organizer of the Russian Engineering Society. His memoirs are *Polveka russkoi zhizni: vospominaniia, 1820–1870*, 2 vols. (Moscow-Leningrad, 1930).

John Hughes (1814–1889), was the famous Welshman who founded the New Russian Company at Iuzovka, the first foreign coal and steel firm in the Donbass.

14. The Peasant Bank, created by the government in 1883, lent peasants money to purchase almost 15 million acres of land between 1897 and 1903. See G. T. Robinson, *Rural Russia Under the Old Regime* (New York, 1932), p. 101.

INDEX